The beauty of holiness

Plan of the tabernacle

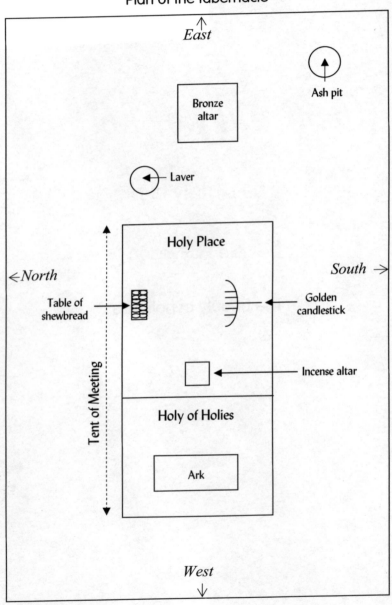

The beauty of holiness

Leviticus simply explained

Philip H. Eveson

 EVANGELICAL PRESS

EVANGELICAL PRESS
Faverdale North, Darlington, DL3 0PH, England

e-mail: sales@evangelicalpress.org

Evangelical Press USA
P. O. Box 825, Webster, New York 14580, USA

e-mail: usa.sales@evangelicalpress.org

web: http://www.evangelicalpress.org

First published 2007

British Library Cataloguing in Publication Data available

ISBN-13 978-0-85234-640-2   ISBN 0-85234-640-9

Printed and bound in Great Britain by Biddles Ltd, King's Lynn,
Norfolk

To past and present students
of the
London Theological Seminary

Contents

Part 4. Obeying the holy God: rules concerning moral purity (17:1 – 27:34)

Illustrations

Preface

When I first gave Bible Studies on Leviticus there were few commentaries to hand. All that has changed in recent years and I have benefited from some very detailed and informative exegetical and theological works.

My sincere thanks to all who have played some part in the production of this book, especially to Pauline Spence and my dear wife Jennifer, who have read through the manuscript and made helpful comments.

I am grateful to David Clark of Evangelical Press for setting me the task of writing the commentary. Working through the text of Leviticus has been a most humbling and uplifting experience. I trust that the contents of the book will be of help in making others wise about salvation through faith in Jesus Christ and in encouraging them to live a God-honouring life.

Philip H. Eveson

Introduction

Leviticus is among the least read and understood books of the Bible. The contents seem boring and uninviting. Why should we study a book that begins and ends with animal sacrifices and presents detailed laws concerning ritual purity and priestly practices? Living in a part of London where there are more synagogues than church buildings does have the advantage of bringing certain chapters to life, especially those dealing with festivals and holy days. But not even the Jews are able to observe many of the rituals laid down in the book because they no longer have a holy place and a priesthood to carry out the stipulated practices. Why, then, should Christians be bothered with it? Do we read the book merely out of historical interest, or to understand Jewish culture better?

Understanding Leviticus

Leviticus is part of God's Word. It tells us what is true and of eternal benefit for our lives. Here is a book to make us wise about salvation (2 Tim. 3:15-17). As the third book of the

Law it occupies the central position among the five books of Moses. In order, therefore, to appreciate Leviticus, we need to remember what is recorded in Genesis and Exodus. In the beginning God created human beings in his image for fellowship with himself and for them to be his royal representatives on earth. The devil's opposition and human rebellion have spoiled all this, but these things did not take God by surprise. Without in any way condoning sin or compromising his holy character, he used the rebellion to display the glory of his justice and grace. As soon as Adam fell into sin, God made a promise that would involve a great struggle on earth which would finally result in victory and salvation for humanity through a remarkable man, 'the seed of the woman', who would crush the old serpent, the devil (Gen. 3:15). The 'seed' or 'descendant' theme dominates the book of Genesis. In furthering his plan God entered into a special agreement (a covenant) with Abraham and made him some amazing promises that included blessing for all nations. God showed Abraham and his descendants, through all that happened to them in their individual lives and as a group, something of what that remarkable person would do.

Abraham's descendants through Isaac and Jacob eventually came to live in Egypt and became a supposed threat to the Egyptians. They were redeemed from Egyptian slavery and, under the leadership of Moses, came to Mount Sinai, where God met them and entered into a special arrangement with them. In the desert they were formed into a unique nation to be to the praise of God. A mobile earthly home (the tabernacle) was erected in the centre of the camp where God chose to meet with his people in preparation for their journey to Canaan. It is at this point that the contents of Leviticus are given.

In all this, God was beginning to fulfil his promises to Abraham that he would make his descendants into a great nation, would be their God and would bless them in such a way that all other nations would find blessing (Gen. 12:2-3). Thus we see that it was to be through Israel (later called the Jews) that the world's Saviour would come (see John 4:22,42). If you belong to this Saviour, Jesus Christ, then you have found the blessing promised to Abraham (Gal. 3:14,29).

Old Testament symbols

The things that happened to Israel in God's providence are symbolic pointers to the wonderful salvation we have begun to enjoy in Christ. All who look to the promised Redeemer have been delivered from slavery to sin and Satan. We have been brought, through Christ's death, into a special relationship with God (the new covenant) to be his very own people, the Israel of God (1 Peter 2:9). God by his Spirit not only makes his home within us individually, but chooses to be present with his people wherever they meet together in the name of his Son, Jesus Christ. Like Israel of old, we are an army — only our weapons are not worldly. We are also, like Israel, a pilgrim people on a journey. This present world order is not our home. With Abraham, we seek a better country. We belong to the heavenly Jerusalem and look forward to the new creation, when we shall inherit a renewed earth and see the King face to face, and where he will make his home among us for ever.

Purpose

Until that time comes, we need to be constantly reminded of who God is, how he is to be approached and worshipped and how we should live our lives as God's people in a hostile environment. Leviticus served this purpose for God's ancient people and in the light of the New Testament we can see

how it continues to do this for Christians today. It indicates
the kind of people God's covenant community ought to be in
the light of God's grace. At the same time and in its own
special way, Leviticus points us forward to the one who
came to save his people from their sins and bring them to
God. Without this book we cannot begin to understand the
death of Christ and his priestly work on our behalf, as the
author of Hebrews constantly indicates. Neither can we
appreciate the many references to cleansing, purity, wholeness, separation and holiness that we find in the New Testament. It is also from this book that Jesus quoted the second
great commandment: 'You shall love your neighbour as
yourself' (19:18; see Mark 12:31; cf. Rom. 13:9; Gal. 5:14).

The theme

The great theme and demand of the book is summed up in
the words: 'You shall be holy, for I the LORD your God am
holy' (19:2). It stresses separation from all uncleanness and
sin in order to live wholesome, God-honouring lives. At the
same time, it recognizes Israel's proneness to sin and shows
the need for atonement and cleansing in order to maintain
their relationship with the holy God. It is with this background in mind that the New Testament calls Christians to
holiness (1 Peter 1:14-16; Matt. 5:48) and urges them to be
clean and separate (2 Cor. 6:14 – 7:1). When they fall, if they
confess their sins, there is forgiveness and cleansing through
the blood of Jesus (1 John 1:7 – 2:2).

The author

Moses received this revelation while the Israelite people
were at Mount Sinai. On almost every page of Leviticus God

speaks directly to Moses, and Moses is commanded to pass on what he hears to the people. That he is responsible for putting this divine communication into book form is made clear in other parts of the Bible. The priests in the days of Joash, the King of Judah, offered burnt offerings to the Lord 'as it is written in the Law of Moses' (2 Chr. 23:18). When Jesus cleansed the leper he told him to go and offer to the priest 'those things which Moses commanded' (Mark 1:44; cf. Lev. 14). Paul introduces a quotation from Leviticus 18:5 with the words: 'For Moses writes about the righteousness which is of the law' (Rom. 10:5). Not only is Leviticus quoted in the New Testament (18:5 in Rom. 10:5 and Gal. 3:12; 19:18 in Matt. 22:39 and Rom. 13:9), but Ezekiel also refers to the book in his prophecies (see particularly 10:10 and Ezek. 22:26; 18:5 and Ezek. 20:11).

This book, it must be emphasized, is not only a true record of all that Moses received from God but, as with the rest of the Bible, it is itself God's revealed Word. As we read Leviticus, God is speaking to us and we do well to listen and take God's Word to heart.

The title

The English title comes to us via the Latin Vulgate from the title in the Septuagint, the ancient Greek translation of the Old Testament. 'Leviticus' suggests that the book was originally written for the Levitical priesthood, but the text indicates that much of the material was also for the people's ears. What the title does convey is that, in addition to the very detailed instructions for the priests in their service at the sanctuary, there are also rules and regulations that the priests are to teach the people concerning ritual and moral purity. The name of the book in the Hebrew Bible is 'And he called', which follows an old custom of naming a book by its

opening word. It focuses attention on God's summoning of
Moses.

The structure of the book

The central position of Leviticus within the Law of Moses
witnesses to its importance. It is, as we have seen, the sequel
to the book of Exodus and prepares us for all that is to follow
in Israel's life as a worshipping community. While it is part
of the whole Law, it is a distinct and complete work in itself.
It has its own introduction (1:1-2) and the final chapters
(25 – 27) bring the work to a satisfying conclusion. The book
falls into two major parts (chapters 1 – 16 and 17 – 27) with
the regulations concerning the Day of Atonement lying in
central position (Lev. 16). Three subjects dominate the first
part — sacrifice, priestly ministry and ritual purity — while
the second part is predominantly about living the godly life.

Part 1.
Communion with the holy God: rules concerning sacrifices (1:1 – 7:38)

Give to the LORD the glory due his name;
Bring an offering, and come into his courts.
Oh, worship the LORD in the beauty of holiness!
Tremble before him, all the earth

(Ps. 96:8-9).

1.
God and his spokesman

Please read Leviticus 1:1-2

On the night I was ordained a minister of the gospel, the presiding minister presented me with a copy of the *Presbyterian Service Book*. In it were orders of service for Sunday morning and evening worship and special occasions, complete with prayers and Bible passages to read, and suitable hymns to sing. It was not compulsory to follow the forms outlined, but for a new minister it was helpful to have a guide, especially when conducting marriages and funerals. Leviticus is a bit like a service book for priests in their duties as ministers of the old-covenant worship. Unlike church manuals, this book is God's Word and contains mandatory instructions that are often very detailed.

An introduction

The opening words serve as the heading for the whole book as well as introducing the first major section, which takes us up to the end of chapter 7. These chapters present regulations for the five main sacrifices. There are instructions for the people (1:3 – 6:7) and for the priests (6:8 – 7:38). We must see these rules within the context of the covenant that God made with Israel at Mount Sinai. They are for the maintaining

of fellowship with the holy God. At the same time the introductory verses provide a link with the closing chapters of the
previous book of Moses. Exodus concluded with the setting
up of the tabernacle in the wilderness of Sinai and the glory
of the Lord filling the place. Leviticus begins with God
speaking to Moses from the tabernacle. It is important that
we remember the context. The many laws that we find in this
book were not given in a timeless setting, but against the
background of God's deliverance of his people from Egypt
to bring them, first to Mount Sinai, and then to the land of
promise.[1]

God's voice

Leviticus opens with a very solemn introduction. God is the
subject of the first sentence and he is referred to as **'the
LORD'** (Jehovah or Yahweh). This is God's personal name
and it became very precious to Israel as a result of the
Exodus and redemption from Egypt. Normally, we read of
God speaking to Moses (see 4:1; 5:14; 6:1; etc.) but here he
'called to Moses' as well as **'spoke to him'** (1:1). This call
is not in the sense of naming Moses, or calling him to dis-
cipleship or service. It is a summons that introduces special
revelation. The combination of **'called'** and **'spoke'** emphasizes the importance of the communication.

The living creator God who first spoke to Moses at the
burning bush is the same God who made promises to Adam
and Eve, to Noah and to Abraham and his family. He acted
to further those promises by delivering the people of Israel
from Egyptian slavery and bringing them to the foot of
Mount Sinai. It was there they heard his thunderous voice
proclaiming the Ten Commandments and there they formally
accepted the special relationship that God graciously entered

into with them. It was this God who now summoned Moses and spoke further words of revelation to him.

The New Testament reminds us that this same God, 'who at various times and in different ways spoke in time past to the fathers by the prophets, has in these last days spoken to us by his Son' (Heb. 1:1-2). Jesus Christ is the ultimate revelation. He not only passes on God's Word, but he *is* God's Word, the one who displays the perfection of God's character and in whom all God's saving promises are realized.

God's presence

God had already summoned Moses three times. He called out to him from the bush (Exod. 3:4), from the mountain (Exod. 19:3) and from the cloud (Exod. 24:16). Here God called **'from the tabernacle of meeting'**.

There are two words used for the tabernacle: one emphasizes that it was the place where God chose to live and meet with his people or with their representative (*mishkan* = 'dwelling place'; see 8:10; 26:11);[2] whereas the word used here reminds us that it was a portable structure (*'ohel* = 'tent'). When Israel moved from one place to another then the tabernacle was taken down and transported to the new site.

Before this tabernacle, with its furniture, was constructed according to the plans revealed to Moses (see Exod. 25:1 – 31:11), a temporary 'tent of meeting' was pitched outside the camp as a result of the golden-calf incident (Exod. 33:7-10). This was the place where God ordained that he would meet with Moses until the proper 'tent' or 'tabernacle of meeting' was built. Some think it is this temporary structure that is being referred to here. This is unlikely. When the official tabernacle was set up in the middle of the camp (Exod.

40:17-33; Num. 1:53; 2:2,17), the other tent was no longer
needed. Furthermore, the opening of Leviticus continues the
narrative from the closing verses of Exodus.

The 'glory cloud', the evidence of the Lord's presence,
had settled first on Mount Sinai (Exod. 19:11,16-20; 20:21;
24:15-18). This same cloud now covered the recently erected
tabernacle and God's glory filled the place (see Exod.
40:34-38). Moses could no longer enter at will because of the
Lord's presence. He needed to await the divine summons as
he had done previously (Exod. 24:16). Leviticus begins with
that call and thus Moses continued to meet with God and to
receive further revelation, only now it was from within the
tabernacle (see Exod. 25:22; Num. 7:89).

God is everywhere (see Ps. 139:7), yet he has freely
chosen to associate himself with one place more than another. Although the heaven of heavens cannot contain God
(1 Kings 8:27), he is described as being 'in heaven' (Eccles.
5:2) and Jesus taught his disciples to pray, 'Our Father in
heaven' (Matt. 6:9). Heaven is spoken of as God's home
(John 14:2). This would suggest that God's presence and
glory are experienced in heaven more than anywhere else in
all creation. Home for God is in that place where he has
ordained to display his stunning importance as nowhere else.

Solomon asks a profound question in his prayer at the
dedication of the temple: 'But will God indeed dwell on the
earth?' (1 Kings 8:27). Can God have a second home? Is it
possible for God to live in this sinful world? This is one of
the great themes of the Bible. God was specially present in
paradise (Gen. 3:8). The tabernacle and later the temple in
Jerusalem were reminders of the garden in Eden and also a
reflection of God's heavenly home. In Jesus Christ God did
dwell on the earth in the person of his Son: 'And the Word
became flesh and dwelt [literally, "tabernacled"] among us,
and we beheld his glory...' (John 1:14). Those who belong
to Jesus Christ are individually temples of the Holy Spirit

(1 Cor. 6:19) and, corporately, the people of God are a living temple where God ordains that he will reside in a special way (1 Cor. 3:17; 2 Cor. 6:16). To anyone who loves the Lord and obeys his word, Jesus promises that he and his Father 'will come to him and make our home [literally, "dwelling"] with him' (John 14:23; cf. 14:2). In the new creation, heaven and earth are one and it will be loudly proclaimed: 'Behold, the tabernacle of God is with men, and he will dwell with them…' (Rev. 21:3). What privileged people Christians are! Do you know something of the felt presence of God in your life and when you meet together with other Christians for worship?

God's prophet

Leviticus opens and concludes with a reference to Moses: **'the LORD called to Moses'** (1:1) and 'the LORD commanded Moses' (27:34). In fact, the name of Moses is mentioned whenever a new section of material is introduced. He is the mediator of the covenant that God made with Israel. The book of Exodus has emphasized the place of Moses as the great prophet of the Lord. He was God's spokesman. The Israelites did not wish to hear the direct voice of God again after the Ten Commandments had been given and pleaded that Moses should act as their intermediary (Exod. 20:19). Thus Moses declared God's will to the people. He is the Old Testament prophet *par excellence* and all true prophets of the Lord were to speak and act in line with what God had revealed to Moses.

There is only one prophet greater than Moses and he is Jesus the Christ. He is a prophet like Moses whom the Lord knew face to face, but he is worthy 'of more glory than Moses' for he is the unique Son of the Father (Heb. 3:3; John 1:1,14). On the mountain where Jesus was transfigured, God the Father's voice was heard from the cloud: 'This is my beloved Son. Hear him!' (Mark 9:7). Instead of a substitute voice, in Jesus we have the voice of God in the flesh.

The voice of Jesus spoke and taught as someone with authority, and not like the scribes. His disciples were dumbfounded. The people were astonished and glorified God, who had given such authority to men. This selfsame Jesus said, 'All authority has been given to me in heaven and on earth. Go therefore and make disciples of all the nations...' (Matt. 28:18-19).

From the dissonant, confusing voices of this world, have you heard the commanding voice of Jesus: 'Follow me!' Have you come under his authority?

Have you heard the Saviour calling
All to leave and follow him?
Have you felt his person drawing
With compulsion lives to win?[3]

God's people

God communicated through Moses to **'the children** [literally, "sons"] **of Israel'**. Exodus has shown how the descendants of Jacob have become a very large body of people. It was this enormous company that God redeemed out of Egypt. He adopted them to be his 'firstborn' son and selected them to be his unique people, joining them together to form a nation set apart for himself. They were to be God's personal treasure on earth, a nation ruled by God and having a priestly role in the world (Exod. 19:5-6). The formal covenant confirmation and consecration ceremony setting them apart for this worldwide mission is described in Exodus 24:3-8. Leviticus shows how Israel's unique status was to be worked out in daily life, where in every detail they were to express their position as God's people, serving him in a right and honourable way.

All this was in fulfilment of promises that God had originally made to Abraham with a view to the coming of Christ and his rule. Israel is a pale shadow in the Old Testament period of the true Israel of God. In the first place, Jesus himself is the fulfilment of all that the nation of Israel failed to be. He was the real servant of the Lord and a light to the nations (Isa. 42:1-7). Simeon had this in mind as he held the baby Jesus and spoke of him as 'a light to bring revelation to the Gentiles, and the glory of your people Israel' (Luke 2:32).

We are also taught that all who put their faith in Jesus Christ fulfil Israel's destiny. Those who are the new creation in Christ belong to Abraham and are the Israel of God (Gal. 3:26-29; 6:15-16). Christians are the elect people of God (1 Peter 1:2), who can be described in the same language that was originally used of the Israelites: 'You are a chosen generation, a royal priesthood, a holy nation, his own special people, that you may proclaim the praises of him who called you out of darkness into his marvellous light; who once were not a people but are now the people of God...' (1 Peter 2:9-10). God's rule on earth at present is to be seen in the obedient lives of those who belong to Jesus Christ. Christians are to exercise their priestly calling by being light and salt, showing to the world a better way and that the gospel does work.

God's directives

It was to this newly formed nation that God gave further directives. Before the detailed rules concerning sacrifice are set out, the Lord through Moses presented Israel with a general case: **'When any one of you brings an offering to** the **LORD…**' The word translated **'anyone'** is 'human being' (*adam*) and therefore refers to male and female (see Gen. 1:27; 5:2). As we shall see later, women as well as men were required to offer sacrifice, so it is fitting for inclusive language to be used.[4] The phrase also reminds us that the law at this point is dealing with voluntary sacrifices made by individual Israelites. They are personal in nature. National mandatory public sacrifices, such as the daily and festival offerings, are treated separately (see Num. 28 – 29; Lev. 16; 23).

This reminds us that, although the Lord's people are to recognize that they belong together as a nation, each individual is not lost in the group. There are personal sacrifices to be made. Each person is significant in God's sight and each is to worship God in a way that is agreeable to him. We cannot do what we like and expect God to accept whatever we might feel appropriate. There is a right and wrong way to worship. Cain thought he could do what he liked, but God was not pleased with him and what he brought. Here God directs his people that they might offer to God what is acceptable.

God's sacrifices

Costly giving

In this introductory ruling the main point is that animal sacrifices were normally to be made from **'the livestock'**. Those creatures living in the wild were therefore excluded. More specifically we are told that blood offerings were to be taken from the herds of cattle and the flocks of sheep and goats. This would suggest the costly nature of the offerings. It would not do to present to the Lord some offering that a person happened to find and kill in the open countryside. It must come from the offerer's 'own pocket'. The people would experience some loss as they deliberately gave up what belonged to them. When we think of sacrifices today this is generally what we have in mind. Something valuable is given up for the benefit of others. In our worship, whether publicly or privately, do we offer to God what costs us little? David was insistent, in his negotiations over the site where he was to rear an altar, that he would not offer to the Lord that which had cost him nothing (2 Sam. 24:24).

An act of worship

But sacrifice in the Bible means more than giving away something valuable. It is a religious activity, where someone offers something **'to the LORD'**. The Hebrew word for **'offering'** (*qorban*) is the general term for gifts and offerings made to God. It is related to the verb 'to bring near, to approach'. These gifts are to be 'brought near' to the Lord.[5] Jesus referred to this technical word for gift, 'Corban', in his condemnation of the Pharisees (see Mark 7:11).

In the pagan world around them, sacrifices were being made to all kinds of gods, but the Israelites were instructed to bring their offerings **'to the LORD'**. They were to sacrifice to no other God but Jehovah (Yahweh). Our worship as Christians is directed to this same God who has saved us through his Son, Jesus Christ: 'Worship God!' (Rev. 19:10).

Sacrifice often involved the death of a victim. The following chapters consider the main sacrifices ordained by God, their significance at the time and what we can learn from them for today. In general, the sacrificial system was set up to maintain the special relationship which God had with Israel and to heal breaches in that covenant bond. It was not to be used in a mechanical way. The people were not to behave like pagans, thinking that God thrived on such offerings, or that outward devotion could be substituted for heart religion (e.g. 1 Sam. 15:22; Amos 5:21-24).

Fellowship with God

Sacrifice was ordained to provide access to God and to remove defilement so that fellowship with God could be maintained. Our English word 'sacrifice' is associated with the words 'sacred' and 'sanctify'. In a book the main theme of which is holiness, or sacredness, it is a most appropriate term in drawing attention to this important element concerning the offerings. The holy God had ordained that he would live among them in the tent of meeting and therefore it was essential for the tabernacle, the priests and the people to be clean from every defilement. The principle is the same in the New Testament. In order for us to have fellowship with God and one another, the sacrificial blood of Jesus Christ God's Son is necessary to cleanse us from all sin (1 John 1:5-9).

It was God who ordained these sacrifices and ultimately he is the one who provided them. The blood and grain offerings were from his creation. He instructed the people which items to offer. They were not to think that they were offering God something he needed in order to exist. In David's great prayer at the time when the people offered so willingly all the gifts for the building of the temple in Jerusalem, he acknowledged God's greatness, that all in heaven and in earth was God's: 'For all things come from you, and of your own we have given you' (1 Chr. 29:14). The ultimate sacrifice is God's, who gave his very heart in the person of his Son so that we might live with him. We cannot give anything to God to ransom our souls (Ps. 49:7-8). We are to embrace the Saviour whom God has given to bring us to himself.

2.
The burnt offering

Please read Leviticus 1:3-17

Overcooked food is sometimes jocularly described as 'a burnt offering'. This is an indication of the way in which English has been influenced by the language of the Bible. In context, however, the offering was no joke; it was a holocaust. It was a sacrifice that was wholly consumed by fire. When the foot-and-mouth epidemic struck the United Kingdom in 2001 it was a gruesome and sad sight to see all those burning pyres of animal carcasses. Thousands of sheep and cattle had to be wholly destroyed by fire, and their smoke ascended into the sky and could be seen for miles around.

Similarly, the directive concerning burnt offerings meant that everything went up in smoke, as the Hebrew word implies.[1] No part of the sacrifice was allowed to be eaten by the priests or the people. It is described later as 'a whole burnt offering' (1 Sam. 7:9). Only the skin of the animal, or the crop with its feathers in the case of a bird, was not burned. The skin was given to the priests (7:8) and the crop and feathers were thrown into the ash pit (1:16).

Of all the sacrifices, the burnt offering is the most common and one of the most ancient. Noah brought this offering to the Lord, and so did Abraham (Gen. 8:20; 22:13). It is possible that this is the offering that Abel brought to the Lord (see Gen. 4:4). Besides the voluntary, spontaneous offerings (the context here),[2] the law demanded that this sacrifice should be made every morning and evening. It was also the most important sacrifice required on the feast days (see Num. 28 – 29).

Much of what we read in Leviticus concerning the slaughter of animals is so alien to those of us who invariably buy our meat from the supermarket all neatly cut and packed. In addition, the Christian influence on Western societies has removed the need for ritual slaughter. The purpose of working through these chapters is to see the way they all throw light on the one real effective blood sacrifice that Jesus Christ offered to end all such offerings.

The ritual

The victim

The rules concerning burnt offerings are divided into three sections according to the victim to be sacrificed. From the herd of cattle the required sacrifice was a bull without blemish (1:3-9); from the flock of sheep or goats, a male without blemish (1:10-13); and from among the clean birds, a turtle dove or young pigeon (1:14-17). This latter provision should be considered an exception to the rule. As we gather from other parts of Leviticus, it enabled the poor to have an equal part in the worship of God (see 12:8; 14:30-31). According to the Jewish rabbis, 'It matters not whether one gives much or little, so long as he directs his heart to heaven.'[3] The worship that God demands from his people is not based on how big our bank balance is, or how influential we are in society. A humble spirit and an obedient heart constitute the service that God requires.

The animal was to be **'without blemish'** (literally, 'perfect'). There was to be no obvious defect in the male animal. Only the best was to be good enough for God. To present poor-quality gifts would be an insult and indicate an attitude of disrespect and lack of gratitude. The prophet Malachi attacks priests who failed to honour God by offering unworthy sacrifices:

> And when you offer the lame and sick,
> Is it not evil?
> Offer it then to your governor!
> Would he be pleased with you?
> Would he accept you favourably?
>
> (Mal. 1:8).

Is our service in Christ's kingdom half-hearted and second-rate? In an effort to shun formalism in the church, we must also be careful to avoid the opposite extreme of either a slick, superficial approach, or a sloppy, disorganized attitude to the public meetings for worship.

The offerer

The offerer was to bring the victim to the courtyard near the tabernacle entrance where the priests gathered (1:3). Bringing the offering to the priest near the Holy Place helped to guard against pagan practices, such as sacrificing to demons (see 17:1-9). The hand of the offerer was placed firmly on the head of the creature and it was possibly at this point that the reason for presenting the sacrifice was declared. The psalmist describes how he went to God's house 'with burnt offerings' to pay his vows with a thankful spirit (Ps. 66:13-15). Confession of sin may have been included in

view of the atoning nature of the sacrifice (1:4; cf. 16:21).
Isaac Watts expresses the Christian's understanding of this
part of the ritual in the light of Christ's sacrifice on the cross:

> My faith would lay her hand
> On that dear head of thine,
> While like a penitent I stand,
> And there confess my sin.[4]

The slaughter

The offerer was responsible for the sacrificial slaughter of
the animal.[5] It involved draining the blood from the victim's
body. The activity was carried out on the north side of the
big bronze altar (see 1:11). Christ the sacrificial victim
offered himself for the world's salvation. He laid down his
life for his people. Having completed the work of redemption, he cried, 'It is finished!' and then, having committed
himself to his Father, he breathed his last and died.

The sprinkling of blood

It was the priest's duty to collect the blood in a basin and to
splash it all round the sides of the altar. In the case of birds,
the blood was drained out at the side of the altar. Blood was
the most sacred part of the sacrifice. The poured blood
indicated that the creature's life had been poured out to the
Lord. It spelt the death of the victim. The splashing of the
blood was the method of cleansing those items that were
polluted by human sinfulness and physical impurities. 'And
according to the law almost all things are purged with blood,
and without shedding of blood there is no remission' (Heb.
9:22). It is not the blood of beasts but the 'richer blood' of
Christ, the heavenly Lamb, that can alone deal with the
pollution that our sin causes.

The burning

The victim was then skinned and cut into pieces by the worshipper and given to the priest, its entrails and legs having been washed clean of any excrement (1:9,13). Birds were split at the wings but not completely severed (1:17).[6] It was the job of **'the sons of Aaron'**, the official priests, to **'put fire on the altar, and lay the wood in order on the fire'**, to lay the pieces of meat on the wood and to see to it that **'all'** was burned up (1:7,9,13). The division of the animals into pieces is reminiscent of the covenant-making activity which Abraham was instructed to arrange (Gen. 15:10). In addition, when Abraham was preparing to sacrifice his son as a burnt offering the text speaks of him as having the fire and setting the wood in order on the altar (Gen. 22:6,9). These references suggest a pattern stretching not only back into antiquity, but forward to the day when our Saviour was nailed to the wood of the cross in order to establish the new covenant (Acts 5:30; Gal. 3:13; 1 Peter 2:24). There the Lord's body was broken and the soldier's spear pierced his side. In body, mind and spirit he suffered. New Testament phrases such as 'he gave himself' or 'he gave his life' stress that the Son of God offered the whole of himself in sacrifice upon the cross.

The significance of the burnt offering

There are a number of indications in the passage to help us appreciate why this sacrifice was appointed.

The hand of the offerer was placed firmly on the head of the victim. This was to be no light touch. The force of the verb 'to rest heavily upon' is brought out in the words of the psalmist: 'Your wrath lies heavy upon me' (Ps. 88:7). The act of pressing the hand on the head of the animal indicated that the offerer was trusting himself to this provision of God. The life of the animal or bird was a substitute for the life of the offerer. When the life of the animal was poured out in death, this is what should have happened to the worshippers. It was just as if the persons bringing the sacrifices had died.

Only in association with such sacrifices was the hand-laying ceremony commanded. Non-bloody sacrifices did not require this ritual. The reason for blood sacrifices in the first place was due to human sinfulness. Leaning upon the creature in this way meant that the offerer was not only identifying himself or herself with the sacrificial victim, but indicating that the victim was to experience the curse that the offerer should have received. The sprinkled blood would have reminded worshippers that they deserved to have their own lives taken on account of their sins.

The gesture with the hand also made it impossible for someone else to make this offering on behalf of the worshipper. The worshippers themselves must come with their offerings and at the place of sacrifice identify themselves with the offerings.

The translation, **'of his own free will'** (1:3, see also AV), would be better rendered 'that he may be accepted'.[7] This is the meaning in the following verse: **'... and it will be accepted on his behalf'** (1:4). The sacrifice had been ordained by the Lord and, if everything was done properly, then God was willing to accept it as a substitute for the worshipper.

It is also described as a sacrifice **'to make atonement for him'** (1:4). Atonement is one of the key terms in Leviticus and it conveys the idea of being delivered from our sins and brought near to God through a substitute sacrifice. It suggests that God's righteous anger at human sinfulness needs to be appeased (propitiation) and that the pollution caused by human sin needs to be cleansed (expiation). All those items connected with God and his presence that had in any way come into contact with sinful human beings needed to be wiped clean, and almost all things were cleansed with blood.[8]

The burnt offering produced **'a sweet aroma to the LORD'** (1:9; cf. 2:2; 3:5) and this emphasizes the propitiatory nature of the sacrifice. Very graphic language is used here to convey the truth that God is pleased with the offering and the one who offers it. When human actions are applied to God we call such language 'anthropomorphic'. Just as God is said to see with his eyes and hear with his ears, so in this case he is said to have the sense of smell. Such an offering appeased God's holy wrath against human sin. Not only was there a need for cleansing, but God's anger needed to be pacified. The animal was a substitute for the offerer. As Jacob sought to pacify his brother Esau with his gifts, so the burnt offering appeased God's righteous indignation. In this way Israel's relationship with God could be maintained and a person could approach God with confidence.

The enduring value of this sacrifice

We are not left to our own devices when it comes to worshipping God. The people were to sacrifice what God commanded. They were called to trust God and offer what was acceptable to him. In the book of Genesis we have an early example of one who did not accept the way that God had appointed. Cain was angry that his brother's offering from the best of the flock was accepted and his vegetable sacrifice was rejected. We cannot come to God and hope to be accepted on our own terms or in the way we think appropriate. What we are told concerning the burnt offering directs us to Jesus Christ. There is only one way to God and that is through his Son, the Lord Jesus Christ. Our trust in coming to God must be in the offering he has accepted, that once-for-all atoning sacrifice that Jesus made on the cross.

Christ's propitiatory sacrifice

As the burnt offering was a pleasing aroma to God, so Christ became such a sacrifice for all who put their trust in him. 'Christ also has loved us and given himself for us, an offering and a sacrifice to God for a sweet-smelling aroma' (Eph. 5:2). Christ's whole person was offered up on the cross like a burnt offering. During his life he had lived in total obedience to the Father's will and he continued to do so as he surrendered himself to death on the cross. 'He was led as a lamb to the slaughter' (Isa. 53:7).

As the burnt offering, which represented the worshipper, was totally consumed by fire on the altar, so Christ experienced in totality the destruction that sinners deserve. On the cross he received the cup of God's wrath and in body, mind and spirit felt the horrors of hell. What we sinners deserved, he experienced. All who identify themselves with Christ and what he did are preserved alive.

We all deserve to be dedicated to the Lord for destruction, for we are all in rebellion against God by nature and by practice. This is what happened to apostate sinners in Israel and to the inhabitants of many cities in Canaan in the time of Joshua (Deut. 13:16; Josh. 6:17,24). The fire that destroyed those sinners presents us with a picture of the hell we all deserve. Those who trust in Christ, who is their substitute burnt offering, are free from the coming wrath of God in hell. They died in Christ's death and they live by faith in the Son of God who loved them and gave himself for them.

A personal interest

Just as the worshippers needed to come themselves and lay their hands on the sacrifice, rather than rely on any surrogate to make the offering on their behalf, so no one else can trust in the Saviour for you. Neither your parents nor your minister can stand in for you. You must yourself lean upon Christ, and Christ alone, in order to be accepted by God.

Total commitment

In so far as the substitute sacrifice was wholly dedicated to the Lord for destruction, it suggests that the offerer was to see himself or herself as preserved alive to be wholly for the Lord. The apostle Paul picks up on this as he encourages Christians to offer themselves to God in the light of his merciful kindness towards us in Christ. If you are a Christian you are called to offer 'your [body] a living sacrifice, holy, acceptable to God' (Rom. 12:1).

> My faith looks up to thee,
> Thou Lamb of Calvary,
> Saviour divine!
> Now hear me while I pray;
> Take all my guilt away;
> Oh, let me from this day
> Be wholly thine![9]

3.
The grain offering

Please read Leviticus 2:1-16

Today, when grain offerings are mentioned, we might imagine harvest festivals with sheaves of corn decorating the inside of church buildings. Instead we should think of such things as semolina, pancakes, fried bread and roasted grain. In many societies where the Christian message has had little permanent influence, it is customary to see tiny shrines on the roadside with food offerings to ancestral gods or spirits. The grain offering must be carefully distinguished from all forms of paganism. God revealed this offering through Moses for the people of Israel to teach them lasting lessons and to prepare them with further truth concerning Messiah's sacrifice, which would make this grain offering obsolete.

Meat, meal, cereal or grain?

The name for this offering (*minhah*) is the general word for a 'present' or 'gift', particularly one offered to someone in a superior position. Jacob sent such a 'gift' to his brother Esau to appease his anger (Gen. 32:13,18,20-21). Later, the word is used of the 'present' that Jacob sent through his sons to

Joseph in Egypt (Gen. 43:11,15,25-26). It also stands for the tribute that a weak or defeated nation owed to an enemy or superpower. Israel sent 'tribute' or 'tax money' to Eglon King of Moab (Judg. 3:15) and Hoshea paid tribute money to the King of Assyria for a number of years (2 Kings 17:3). It can also refer in a general way to any kind of sacrificial offering. The sacrifices that Cain and Abel offered are both called a 'gift' to the Lord (Gen. 4:3-5). It is only when the word is associated with grain that it is called the **'grain'** offering.

In the Authorized (or King James) Version of the Bible, first published in A.D. 1611, this offering is called the 'meat offering', because at that time the word 'meat' meant any kind of food, including cereal crops. But when we use the word 'meat' today, we immediately think of animal flesh, and that is exactly what this offering did *not* include. Of all the five main types of offering, this one is unique in not requiring the sacrifice of an animal or bird. Some translations prefer the word 'food offering', but this also is too general and we could still mistakenly think that meat was included, as well as vegetables. The context makes it clear that this is an offering of grain that has usually been ground to powder like meal. It is for this reason that the sacrifice is sometimes referred to as the 'meal offering', but 'grain offering' is a better description, for it incorporates those sacrifices where the grain was not crushed (see 2:14).

Relationship to the burnt offering

It is natural for this offering to be described second, after the burnt offering, because the two offerings are often mentioned together (see Num. 15:1-16; 28; Josh. 22:23; 1 Sam. 1:24; 1 Kings 8:64; 2 Kings 16:13,15). The grain offering could be sacrificed on its own only when it was presented as an offering of first fruits at harvest time (2:14).

Some of the rabbis have suggested that the grain offering was the poor person's substitute for the burnt offering, as in the case of the poor person's guilt offering (cf. 5:11-13). But the fact that this offering could be independent of the burnt offering, that there were various procedures for preparing the sacrifice, from cooked to uncooked forms[1] and that only part of the offering was burned suggests otherwise. The grain offering had a significance of its own and was offered by all classes of people. Samuel's mother, Hannah, offered a bull for a burnt offering, flour for a grain offering and wine for a drink offering (1 Sam. 1:24).

Types of grain offering

The chapter divides into three sections and describes three kinds of grain offerings: uncooked grain (2:1-3), cooked grain (2:4-10) and the first fruits of grain (2:14-16).

Uncooked grain (2:1-3)

The **'fine flour'** of the grain offering was the food of kings and guests of honour (see 1 Kings 4:22; Gen. 18:6; Ezek. 16:13). Olive oil and incense were put on it, symbols of joy and pleasure (see Isa. 61:3; S. of S. 3:6; 4:6), in contrast to the solemn grain offering associated with the sin offering (see 5:11).[2] Then a handful was to be taken by the priest and burned on the altar as a **'memorial'**. Like the burnt offering, it was **'an offering made by fire'** and its effect on God was the same: **'a sweet aroma to the LORD'** (2:2,9,12; see 1:9,17).

The **'memorial'** was a reminder that the whole offering belonged to the Lord. God does not actually need food, so only a token was offered on the altar. The rest was given to his specially set apart ministers, the priests, who acted on his behalf, and they, of course, did need food to live. The grain offering is classed as **'most holy'** (2:3). This meant that only the priests could eat it within the tabernacle. They were not allowed to take it home to their families.

The 'memorial' was also a means of seeking God's blessing. As God remembered his covenant with Noah and all creation when the rainbow appeared, so he would remember his covenant with Israel through this memorial offering. Such 'remembering' did not mean that God could somehow forget. Rather, it assured the people that God would act on the basis of his covenant promises to Israel.

Cooked grain (2:4-10)

At times the regulations sound like a cookery manual for preparing cakes. The offering could be cooked in three different ways. One method was for it to be oven-baked. This involved either mixing the choice flour with oil to make unleavened cakes, or making unleavened wafers covered (**'anointed'**) in oil (2:4). A second way was for the offering to be fried on a griddle to make unleavened cakes using the same ingredients (2:5). Before being offered, the flat cake was broken in pieces and oil poured on it (2:6). The other option was to cook the mixture of flour and oil in a pan with a lid (2:7). As with the uncooked grain, **'a memorial portion'** was taken by the priest to burn on the altar as **'a sweet aroma to the LORD'** (2:9) and the rest was eaten by the priests in the sanctuary (2:10).

The first fruits of grain (2:14-16)

While the other grain offerings could be offered at any time of the year, this type of grain offering belonged to the harvest

season. It must be considered as an additional offering to the
other grain offerings mentioned in the rules governing the
first fruits of barley at Passover or the first fruits of wheat
during the Feast of First Fruits or Harvest (23:9-14,15-22).

The grain is described as newly formed **'green heads'**,[3]
and as having **'full heads'**.[4] In other words, the best-quality
freshly formed grain is to be used. It must be crushed and
roasted on the fire with oil and incense. Again a **'memorial
portion'** was used **'as an offering made by fire to the
LORD'**.

By offering the first fruits of the grain the Israelite worshippers acknowledged the Lord as the landowner and that
they were his tenants. This is emphasized later with the
regulations concerning the sabbatical and jubilee years (see
Lev. 25). Presenting the first fruits of grain indicated that all
the harvest belonged to the Lord.

Important regulations (2:11-13)

Two general rules are presented, one negative and the other
positive.

The negative

Firstly, neither **'leaven'** nor **'honey'** must be added to these
grain offerings. It has already been stated that the cooked
grain offering was to be unleavened. Here it is underlined
and the reference to sweet substances such as honey also
included. This ruling only applied to grain offerings that
included a memorial portion that was burned on the altar.
Yeast/leaven and nectar/honey could cause fermentation
and this suggested decay and corruption. The holy God is
associated with life and wholeness and, as we shall see later
(Lev. 11 – 15), the law impressed upon Israel that nothing

suggesting corruption, uncleanness or death could come near God's tabernacle, and God's priests were to avoid all contact with decay and death. Both Jesus and Paul sometimes refer to leaven as a metaphor for what is morally unacceptable (Luke 12:1; 1 Cor. 5:8).

As for the first-fruit offerings presented at the Feast of Harvest, which consisted of two loaves of leavened bread waved or elevated before the Lord (see 23:17), these were an exception to the rule. They were *not* to be **'burned on the altar for a sweet aroma'** (2:12). This is the reason why 'honey' was acceptable in the first-fruits offering during the reign of Hezekiah (2 Chr. 31:5).

The positive

Secondly, **'salt'** was to be added to all these grain offerings. In contrast to the forbidden items, this product acted as a preservative. It is referred to as the **'salt of the covenant'** (2:13; see also the references to a 'covenant of salt' in Num. 18:19 and 2 Chr. 13:5). Thus salt in the grain offerings served as a reminder of the permanent, binding nature of that special relationship ('covenant') that existed between the Lord and his people and that was established through blood sacrifices at Mount Sinai (Exod. 24:3-8).

The worshipper

Literally, the beginning of verse 1 could be translated: 'When a soul offers an offering…' This means that **'anyone'** from the camp of Israel, male or female, who wished to make an offering could do so. While the worshipper is referred to in the third person singular in the opening verses, this changes to the second-person singular 'you' from verse 4. Preachers have good biblical warrant, then, for fluctuating in their sermons from the more general impersonal form to the personal! It helps to keep interest and to bring the message home to individuals.

The significance and continuing value of the grain offering

Apart from the special first-fruits kind, the grain offering always accompanied the burnt offering as part of the daily morning and evening sacrifices at the sanctuary (Num. 28:4-5,9,13). It was not a blood sacrifice and therefore no atonement language is used in connection with it. However, its close relationship with the burnt offering meant that the worshipper was constantly reminded of the need of sacrificial blood for forgiveness and was assured of God's favour, for the memorial part that was burned on the altar of burnt offering produced an aroma that was acceptable to God. As we come before God we need always to be conscious of the atoning sacrifice of Christ. It is because of that one, complete, end-time offering that we have forgiveness and are assured of acceptance at all times. Participating in the Lord's Supper is like the significance of the memorial portion. It is a reminder of the new-covenant blessings and obligations.

Jesus Christ is the ultimate grain offering. As the true Israel of God he offered himself, being 'crushed for our iniquities' (Isa. 53:5, ESV) and broken, so that, through the furnace of affliction and death, he might save his people from their sins and bring us to God. His was the perfect sacrifice and by it he has established for ever the new covenant. He is also 'the firstborn' or 'first fruits' from the dead, the guarantee of the Christian's bodily resurrection to a new creation.

The grain offering also suggests the idea of a gift or tribute from a thankful worshipper. In the light of God's mercies in removing the divine anger and justifying us, we are to present ourselves as 'a living sacrifice' (Rom. 12:1-2), offering continually with our lips a sacrifice of praise to God, doing good and sharing what we have with others, for such sacrifices are pleasing to God (Heb. 13:15-16). Paul could describe the gift that the Philippians had sent as 'a sweet-smelling aroma, an acceptable sacrifice, well pleasing to God' (Phil. 4:18).

As the grain offered by the worshipping community in Israel provided the priests with daily food, so the new-covenant community is to support those set apart for the Lord's service. Paul states that, just as those who minister at the altar partake of the offerings, 'so the Lord has commanded that those who preach the gospel should live from the gospel' (1 Cor. 9:13-14; cf. Luke 10:7). 'Let him who is taught the word share in all good things with him who teaches' (Gal. 6:6). How well are we fulfilling our obligations towards those who minister God's Word to us week by week?

4.
The peace offering

Please read Leviticus 3:1-17

When we think of peace offerings we often have in mind the kind of gifts that are presented as a way of restoring a broken or damaged relationship. When a husband comes home late and offers his wife a bouquet of flowers, having previously forgotten that it was their wedding anniversary, the gift is thought of as a peace offering. The present is offered in order to restore peaceful or friendly relationships. In the Old Testament, however, the peace offering was presented not so much as a way of restoring broken relationships, but as an expression of gratitude for God's favour, or in anticipation of God's blessing.

A 'sacrifice of peace'

The word for **'sacrifice'** (3:1) appears here for the first time in Leviticus and is related to the word for 'altar'. It is the general term for the slaughter of an animal for sacrifice and is sometimes found combined with other words to signify a particular type of sacrifice, such as 'the Passover sacrifice' (Exod. 12:27) and 'the yearly sacrifice' (1 Sam. 1:21). When it appears on its own, especially in phrases like 'burnt offerings and sacrifices', it is referring to the peace offering (see Exod. 18:12; 1 Sam. 6:15). In all instances the term seems to refer to sacrifices that could be eaten by the worshipper (see Exod. 24:5,11; Jer. 7:21).

The precise meaning of the word translated **'peace'** is the subject of much debate. Because the emphasis is on expressing the benefits of a peaceful relationship with God over a meal shared with others, rather than seeking to restore peace, some English versions speak of it as 'the fellowship offering'. But the word used to denote this offering is related to the well-known Hebrew noun *shalom*, meaning 'peace', 'wholeness' or 'well-being'.[1] In the context of God's special relationship with Israel, *shalom* is the condition that results from being right with God. The peace offering provided the worshipper with an opportunity to celebrate this state of divine well-being with family and friends. It was 'a kind of religious party, where priests and worshippers enjoyed a sumptuous meal in the presence of God'.[2]

The animals for slaughter

In this introduction to peace offerings all the emphasis falls on what the worshipper is to bring and the activity of the priests. There is much repetition, making it easier for priest and people to remember the ritual. Offerings can be brought from the herd of cattle (3:1-5) or from the flock of sheep or goats (3:6-16).

While animals used for the peace offerings, like the burnt offerings, must be **'without blemish'** (3:1,6), there were some significant differences. For one thing, female as well as male animals could be brought (3:1,6; cf. 4:23,28). It meant, for instance, that a cow was as acceptable as a bull. This did not mean that the sacrifice was less important, but it did offer

greater choice, especially as one of the main purposes of the
peace offering was not only to provide an altar sacrifice to
God but food for the priests and worshippers (see 7:15-21).
The sex of the animal is not significant when the meat is for
human consumption. Matthew Henry remarks, 'In our
spiritual offerings, it is not the sex, but the heart, that God
looks at' (Gal. 3:28).

A second difference has the same purpose in view: no
provision was made for the poor to present birds. Pigeons
and turtledoves would not have provided enough blood and
fat for sacrifice and little in the way of meat to share with
everyone. In any case, this was not a sacrifice that the
economically disadvantaged were expected to bring. It was
entirely optional and the worshipper was probably encouraged to invite the poor to the sacrificial meal (see 7:15; Deut.
12:12,18).

The reason for the unusual distinction between lambs
(3:6-11) and goats (3:12-16) and the emphasis on the fat of
the animals brings us to the ceremony at the entrance to the
tabernacle.

The ritual

Again, much of the procedure is the same as for the burnt
offering. The worshipper brings the animal to **'the door of
the tabernacle'** (3:2), also described as **'before the tabernacle of meeting'** (3:8,13). This can refer to the whole area
between the entrance and the altar. The phrase **'before the
LORD'** (3:1,7,12) not only indicates the same area, but gives
the reason why the ritual is being carried out there. It is done
in the presence of God.

It would be normal for the man, as head of the household,
to bring this sacrifice, and he was to lay his hand on the
animal's head and slaughter it. The hand-laying gesture

meant that he was formally identifying himself with the sacrificial victim and indicating that the animal was taking the place of the worshipper (cf. 1:4), just as the Levites in a similar ceremony were substituted for ('instead of') all the firstborn of the children of Israel (Num. 8:10-18). The gesture also indicated that the animal was now set apart for God's use. The priests, as we shall discover later, were the only ones who were permitted to approach the altar. It was they who collected the blood of the slaughtered animal and sprinkled it around about the altar (cf. 1:5,11,15). It is 'the blood that makes atonement for the soul' (17:11).

In all this ritual slaughter we see again Christ's atoning sacrifice for sinners. He is the priest who is also the sacrificial lamb with no moral blemish whose substitutionary atoning death is effective for all guilty sinners who identify themselves with him. Is he your substitute?

Fat

From this point on the ritual is quite different from the burnt offering. In the burnt offering the whole skinned animal was consumed on the altar fire, but in the peace offering only the **'fat'** is placed on the altar (3:3-5,9-11,14-16). It is the suet protecting the innards that is to be taken out and burned along with the kidneys. Like the blood, it is the inner parts associated with the animal's life that are removed and offered on the altar. The fat was also considered to be the choicest part of an animal (cf. Gen. 45:18).

An additional rule applied to lambs. It was because of a certain breed of sheep in the Middle East that special mention is made of the **'the whole fat tail'** (3:9). This did not apply to goats. Herodotus, the fourth-century B.C. Greek author of the first great history of the ancient world, comments on the unusually broad tails of the sheep in that region. The tails could be as much as eighteen inches (forty-five centimetres) across and weigh between fifteen and fifty pounds (between seven and twenty-two kilograms). There was another type where the tails were so long that the shepherds made 'little trucks for their sheep's tails', so that the tails did not trail along the floor and become bruised and sore. It is these fat tails that were to be included as an offering **'made by fire to the LORD'** (3:11).

Food

The burning of the fat is described as a **'food'** (literally, 'bread') offering (3:11,16; cf. 21:6). It was a common view among the pagan nations that the gods needed physical sustenance to survive. To find such language used in reference to the true and living God is therefore at first quite startling. It is made clear in the Bible that God is spirit and is not dependent on sacrifices to nourish him and keep him alive. God uses graphic imagery to make this point to his people when he says:

> I will not take a bull from your house,
> Nor goats out of your folds.
> For every beast of the forest is mine,
> And the cattle on a thousand hills...
> If I were hungry, I would not tell you;
> For the world is mine, and all its fulness.
> Will I eat the flesh of bulls
> Or drink the blood of goats?
>
> (Ps. 50:9-15).

The word 'food' is used to remind the people that their offering to God is taken from what they need to sustain life. This is the only sacrifice where the worshipper is allowed to eat what had been dedicated to God (see 7:15-21). In this sense the worshipper, as Mark Rooker puts it, 'shared a meal with the Lord, which means that he had fellowship with him'.[3]

The other distinctive feature of the peace offering is not actually mentioned here, but is implied by the negative comments (3:17). Nothing is said in this passage about what happens to the rest of the animal once its blood has been sprinkled and its fatty portions burned on the altar. Later, however, we are informed that after the breast and right shoulder had been given to the priests (7:28-34), the remainder was to be given back to the worshipper to be eaten with his family and other invited guests (7:15-21). This sacrificial meal became the occasion of great joy and thanksgiving in the presence of the Lord. It expressed the good relationship that existed between the worshipper and God, as well as a healthy communal spirit of friendship and fellowship.

The significance of the peace offering

Peace offerings were to be offered at the ordination of the priests (9:18,22), the completion of a Nazirite vow (Num. 6:17-20) and at the Feast of Harvest/Weeks (23:19-20). They were also presented, like the burnt offerings, at crucial moments in Israel's history, such as the establishing of God's covenant with Israel at Sinai (Exod. 24:5), entering the land of promise after crossing the Jordan (Deut. 27:7), the appointment of Saul as the first king (1 Sam. 11:15) and on the occasion of the dedication of Solomon's temple (1 Kings 8:63-64). In these cases the peace offerings are associated with times of joy and, as the three separate types of fellowship offering indicate (see 7:12-18), expressions of gratitude.

Fellowship with God

The peace offering is thought by many scholars to have no atoning significance. But this is to ignore a number of obvious indicators to the contrary. Like the two previous offerings, this offering had a God-ward emphasis. Everything in this chapter concerns what is for the Lord — which animals could be offered and the parts to be consumed on the altar. They are offerings **'made by fire to the LORD'** (3:5,9,11,14,16). The burning fat was to produce **'a sweet aroma to the LORD'** (3:5,16). Furthermore, the ritual is similar to the burnt offering, which certainly spoke of atonement. It included the hand-laying, the slaughter, the splashing of the blood against the altar and the burning of the animal suet to produce a pleasing smell to the Lord. The connection with the burnt offering is made even clearer by the directive to burn the specified animal parts **'on the altar upon the burnt sacrifice...'** (3:5). Before reference is made to the communal meal, all the emphasis in this passage is on acceptance before God. This offering taught Israel that peace with God could not be established or maintained without a price being paid. Animal sacrifice reminded the people of the costly nature of reconciliation with God.

Leviticus is part of a five-volume work that began with Genesis. In that 'book of origins' we are informed of the initial rebellion against God by Adam and Eve and its sad consequences for all their descendants. The setting apart of Israel as God's chosen nation had the aim of preparing for the coming of the Saviour who would put the world to rights again according to the promise made at the time of the great rebellion (Gen. 3:15). But Israel as a nation was no different from the rest of the world in terms of her sinful state, and God taught the people truths, through the offerings and sacrifices, concerning the coming Saviour of the world. Sin breaks the relationship with God and disrupts a spiritually healthy state. There can be no peace for the wicked. To bring about reconciliation and a condition of well-being, God's wrath on account of our sins must be appeased. The peace offering reminds us of this and points us to Jesus, 'the Prince of Peace', who experienced God's wrath on the cross for all those who put their trust in him.

At a time when the God-ward focus is being played down, ignored, or taken for granted in some evangelical circles, it is good to be reminded that, before we rightly consider our responsibilities to one another in the family of God, our relationship to God is to be our primary concern. 'Therefore, having been justified by faith, we have peace with God through our Lord Jesus Christ' (Rom. 5:1).

Feeding on the sacrifice

It was necessary to include the peace offering in the list because no one sacrifice can adequately convey the truth concerning the ultimate atoning sacrifice. In the burnt offering the whole animal was consumed on the altar to show that Christ would offer the whole of himself on the cross (see Heb. 7:27). The peace offering indicates the need for the worshipper to feed on the benefits of Christ's death. Just as the substitutionary sacrifice was handed back, after the fat and blood had been taken, to be eaten by the worshipper and his guests, so the Christ who died in our place is offered to us in the gospel. As the Israelites ate from the peace offerings, so Christians symbolically eat of Christ's peace offering when they trust him for salvation.

Jesus spoke of himself as the bread of life: 'If anyone eats of this bread, he will live for ever; and the bread that I shall give is my flesh, which I shall give for the life of the world' (John 6:47-51). The Lord's Supper is a symbolic expression of the Christian's continuing need to feed on the benefits of Christ's atoning death by faith.

5.
The sin offering

Please read Leviticus 4:1 – 5:13

Ecological concerns have brought the whole subject of pollution to our attention. We have also heard of decontamination procedures being put in place in the event of exposure to radiation or dangerous chemicals during a terrorist attack. The sin offering is especially concerned with pollution and decontamination due to sin and its effects.

The sin offering is closely associated with the trespass offering (see next chapter) and these are clearly distinguished from the first three offerings.[1] But the sin and trespass offerings must not be confused. Some translations make it difficult to decide whether Leviticus 5:1-13 belongs to the sin offering or to the trespass offering. For example, the Authorized Version and New King James Version introduce the words 'trespass offering' in Leviticus 5:6, while the following verses suggest that the subject matter is still the sin offering (see especially 5:7-9,12). But as we shall see, the section dealing with the trespass offering only begins at Leviticus 5:14.

The meaning of the offering

We might think that the sin offering would deal with every type of failure and rebellion, but that is not always the case. In the laws of Leviticus there are many examples where capital offences result in immediate judgement. On the other hand, sin offerings are sometimes required of people who had not actually committed any particular sin. For instance, a sin offering was required of every woman after giving birth to a child (see 12:6-8). It is also the case that the Hebrew word for the 'sin offering' can have the opposite meaning, that of 'the removal of sin' or 'decontamination'. In Numbers 8:7, for instance, the word is translated 'cleansing' or 'purification' ('the water of purification'). A special sin offering was required on the Day of Atonement, when animal blood was used to cleanse the tabernacle (16:19). For these reasons many scholars believe that instead of 'sin offering' we should speak of the 'purification offering'. It is an important biblical truth, as we shall find in making our way through Leviticus, that sin pollutes and brings uncleanness. What is more, decay, disease and death, all originally associated with sin, also cause pollution. It was on account of these defiling situations, as well as pollution caused by moral guilt, that God gave the sin offering. He showed the people the need not only for a sacrifice that would remove God's wrath (propitiation), but would also remove the polluting effects of sin (expiation).

In the present passage, sin, guilt and forgiveness come to our attention frequently (4:3,13-14,20,22-23,26,27-28,31,35; 5:1,5-6,10,13) and right from the beginning it is made clear that it is the Lord's commandments that are being violated (4:2). It is appropriate, then, in this context, to translate by using the traditional name 'sin offering', while remembering that it is not the only offering to deal with sin and its consequences.

The type of sin covered

While the technical Hebrew name for the **'sin offering'** (as in 4:3) presents problems of meaning, the related noun 'sin' (as in **'his sin'**, 4:3) and the verb 'to sin' (as in **'If a person sins'**, 4:2) are undisputed. They convey the idea of 'missing the mark' or 'failing'. In a non-religious setting the verb is used of left-handed men who could sling a stone at a single strand of hair and 'not miss'! (Judg. 20:16). Sin involves a failure to live up to God's standards as revealed in his holy law.

The word translated **'unintentionally'**, or 'through ignorance' (4:2), means sins committed 'in error' and is used in contrast to sins committed 'with a high hand', or 'presumptuously' (cf. Num. 15:30). In other words, the sins covered by this law are not sins associated with apostasy, where there are deliberate, defiant acts of rebellion, but those that are due to weaknesses arising from sinful human nature.

Have you ever driven along a road and then suddenly realized as you passed the derestriction sign that you had been breaking the speed limit without being aware of it? If a roadside speed camera had flashed, you would have been fined for speeding. It would be no use pleading that you did not intend to break the law, or that you were blissfully unaware that you were breaking the law. You would still be held accountable and guilty of an offence. On another occasion you may have accidentally gone over the speed limit, or even deliberately kept your foot on the accelerator, because you were late in getting to your destination. You did not do it because you were an anarchist and wanted to be rid of the government and all its laws, but still you did wrong. Supposing you received a speeding fine and were asked to pay by a certain day but then it slipped your memory and you failed to pay the fine on time. Even though you had every intention of paying, the fact that you did not pay up during the time allowed would mean that there was guilt through negligence.

Modern motoring offences are examples of the type of sin covered by this offering. But of course the sins of commission, of omission or of negligence mentioned in the text (4:2,13-14,22-23,27-28) are not failures to observe human regulations, but weaknesses due to the sinful human state that lead people to break **'the commandments of the LORD'** (4:2). So many of these commands are found in this book of Leviticus. All sin is serious in God's sight and needs to be dealt with properly.

Examples

Four specific examples of the kind of sins covered by the sin offering are mentioned in the closing part, and arranged in a memorable way (5:1-13).[2]

In the first case the sin is one of omission, where a person fails to testify in a court of law. We are all aware of cases that fail to come to court because people are afraid to testify for one reason or another. Failure to speak about an incident that one is fully aware of when publicly called to do so (**'the utterance of an oath'**) makes that person guilty of an offence and he must bear the punishment — **'he bears guilt'** (5:1; cf. 20:20). The temptation not to get involved when we have witnessed a crime or car accident because of the inconvenience it may cause us, or the possible repercussions concerning our own safety, is a real one. This law, however, reminds us that it is a sin and detrimental to the cause of truth and justice.

The middle two cases are examples of sins of negligence or ignorance. One concerns contact with unclean things like the carcass of an unclean animal (5:2), and the other contact with **'human uncleanness'** (5:3). People may become guilty only when they are informed afterwards that they had sat where an unclean person had just been sitting (see.15:6). In the final example we are back with a situation involving **'an oath'** (5:4). This time the person himself makes a thoughtless vow, whether good or bad, which he probably has no intention of keeping, and thinks nothing more about it, but his failure to keep it is drawn to his attention later. That person is still responsible for his rash words and worthy of the punishment they deserve.

These small peccadilloes, that we like to think are not important, are still sins in God's sight and God holds us responsible. Jesus said that we shall have to give an account of every idle word we have spoken. But the examples also remind us that forgiveness was available for all types of sin and foreshadow what is said concerning the great Sin-Bearer. The blood of Jesus deals with 'all sin' and 'all unrighteousness' (1 John 1:7,9). Only in the case of those who deceive themselves by saying they have no sin and make God a liar is there no forgiveness.

In all the cases cited, whether the sins are committed in ignorance or knowingly, it is assumed that the guilty, once they are aware of the gravity of what they have done or failed to do, have a repentant spirit and will want to confess their sin and offer the appropriate atoning sacrifice. Paul received such forgiveness even though he persecuted the church 'because I did it ignorantly in unbelief' (1 Tim. 1:13). Reflecting the same idea is the well-known prayer of Jesus from the cross: 'Father, forgive them, for they do not know what they do' (Luke 23:34). This is quite different from those sins committed 'with a high hand'. The latter are not only deliberate, but express a rebellious hatred of God and his rule. Unlike the sins to which the sin offering applies, presumptuous sins are those committed by people who are not repentant, who see no need of forgiveness. Such deliberate defiance is behind those solemn warnings in the letter to the Hebrews, where we read, 'For if we sin wilfully after we have received the knowledge of the truth, there no longer remains a sacrifice for sins...' (Heb. 10:26; see also 6:4-6).

Paul, in answering the problem of 'inadvertent' sin ('For the good that I will to do, I do not do; but the evil I will not to do, that I practise' — see Rom. 7:15-24), presents Christ as the one sent to deal with sin (Rom. 8:3). The phrase that Paul uses ('on account of sin') is exactly the one that the Greek translators of the Old Testament regularly employ when referring to the 'sin offering'.

The categories of sinners

In the previous animal offerings the instructions were set out according to the kind of animal offered, but what is said about the sin offering is arranged according to the status of those who were required to bring it. Four categories of sinners are highlighted.

Heading the list is **'the anointed priest'** (4:3,5). Since all the priests were anointed with oil (8:30; Exod. 28:41) the title could be a general reference to the priesthood (cf. 4:16; 6:22). On the other hand, most scholars consider the phrase to be a reference to the high priest, who received a special anointing as 'chief' and representative of the other priests, as well as of Israel as a whole (8:12; 21:10; Num. 35:25).

The second category concerns **'the whole congregation of Israel'** (4:13). This may refer to a large body representing the entire **'assembly'** of God's people, or to the whole covenant community itself, with the terms 'congregation' and 'assembly' used interchangeably (cf. Exod. 12:6). Either way, the whole nation is involved and they become aware of their guilt at a later date and confess it.

The third type of sinner is **'a ruler'**, meaning anyone other than the religious head who is in a position of leadership (4:22).

Finally, the law deals with any member of the covenant community who is not a leader of any kind (4:27).

Segregating different types of sinners is not for economic reasons but according to their status in society. In other words, this regulation is not concerned with how rich or poor the sinners are, and what animals they can afford to offer, but with the sinner's standing in society. The more important the person or group, the more serious the case, and hence the more expensive the required offering. Concern for the poor in the community who are required to present sin offerings is dealt with at the close of the section (5:7-13).

Proportional guilt

Identifying these different 'classes' of sinner presents us with an important principle running through the Bible. In God's sight the guilt of sin is 'proportional to the rank, office and responsibilities of the offender'.[3] Jesus clearly defined the principle in this way: 'For everyone to whom much is given, from him much will be required; and to whom much has been committed, of him they will ask the more' (Luke 12:48). For this reason Christians are warned, 'Let not many of you become teachers, knowing that we shall receive a stricter judgement' (James 3:1).

Collective guilt

This law also brings to our attention the need to recognize the place of collective sin and guilt. This is a notion foreign to those brought up in modern Western societies, who have been conditioned to think in purely individualistic terms. We cannot assume as individuals that, even though we belong to a particular nation, we are not implicated in the sins of that nation, or that we have no responsibility for doing something about the wrongs within it. Jeremiah and Daniel could have taken the high moral ground as individuals and distanced themselves from their people. Yet they identified themselves with them and confessed that they belonged to a nation that had rebelled against God and pleaded that God would show mercy. Jesus taught that God judges not only individuals but nations (see Matt. 25:31-32). The prophets also spoke out not only against the sins of Israel and Judah, but against such nations as Edom, Syria and Babylon (Isa. 13 – 23; Amos 1 – 2).

The ritual

Much of the ritual is similar to that for the burnt and peace offerings. The animal is brought to the tabernacle entrance and, after the hand of the offerer is laid on the animal's head, it is slaughtered (4:4,14-15,23-24,28-29). In each case the fat suet is removed, as in the peace offerings, and burned on the altar, with the smoke rising as **'a sweet aroma to the LORD'**, thus making atonement and bringing forgiveness (4:10,20,26,31,35). The type of animal to be brought depended on who the offerers were: the more serious the case, the more expensive the victim. In the case of the **'anointed priest'** or the **'whole congregation'** a **'young bull'** was required, the most expensive of the sacrificial animals (4:3,14). A ruler was to bring a **'male'** goat (4:23), less expensive than a member of the cattle herd, but of higher sacrificial value than a female member of the flock — a **'female'** kid goat (4:28) or a **'female'** lamb (4:32) — which was the usual offering for an ordinary member of society (see 5:6).

The blood of the sin offering

The distinctive feature that stands out in the sin-offering ceremony is what happened to the blood. It was not splashed around the altar as was done with the previous blood sacrifices. Where the blood was placed depended on the standing of those offering the sacrifice. When the sin involved the **'anointed priest'** (4:3-12) or the **'whole congregation'** (4:13-21), the blood was taken *inside* the Holy Place of the tabernacle. On the other hand, if the sin involved the **'ruler'** (4:22-26) or an ordinary Israelite (**'anyone of the common people'**, 4:27-35) then the blood was brought to the altar *outside* the Holy Place. As we shall see, there was a third area where the blood of the sin offering was taken, but that was special for the Day of Atonement alone, when it was brought into the holiest place of all where the ark of the covenant was kept (see Lev. 16). All this indicated that there were not only grades of holiness in the tabernacle, but that the impurity of the religious head of the community, who served in the very near presence of God, was more serious than that of the secular head, and that the impurity of the whole community was of greater significance than that of an individual member.

1. The secular leader and the ordinary Israelite

In the ritual for the ruler or for an ordinary person, there are two separate acts involving the blood: some of the blood was taken by the priest and put **'on the horns of the altar of burnt offering'** with his finger; the rest was then poured out **'at the base of the altar'** (4:25,30,34). Putting the blood on the four horns of the altar was like placing blood on the right ear, thumb and big toe in the ceremony setting apart the priests and in the ritual for the purification of the leper (8:23-24; 14:25). It was a cleansing ritual, and the blood placed at the extremities indicated that the whole was cleansed. As so often in the rituals, the blood of a sacrificial animal was used to purify the effects of sin and other defilements that had resulted from the original rebellion in the Garden of Eden (see Lev. 11 – 15). Pouring the rest of the blood at the base of the altar was not a way of disposing of unwanted blood, but an important part of the ceremony. It was not only part of the cleansing ritual, but indicated that the animal's life had been fully poured out in death.

2. The religious leader and the nation

The ritual for the **'anointed priest'** or the **'whole congregation'** was more elaborate. It involved three separate acts. First, the priest dipped his finger in the bull's blood and sprinkled some of it **'seven times before the LORD, in front of the veil'** separating the Holy Place from the Most Holy Place (4:6,17). Then some of the blood was applied to **'the horns of the altar of sweet incense'** and, finally, the remainder was poured out **'at the base of the altar of burnt offering'** (4:7,18). The blood, sprinkled or applied, again cleansed from the defilement arising from sin. Sprinkling the blood seven times denoted completeness. Because the sin offering was made by the religious leader who represented the whole nation and had access into the Holy Place, it was necessary for those items that were so closely associated with the high priest to be made clean. The same applied when the offering was on behalf of the whole congregation. In the special sin offerings on the Day of Atonement, the blood was sprinkled on and before the mercy seat in the holiest place of all (see Lev. 16).

3. Sin's polluting effects

In this particular part of the sin-offering ritual we are shown the defiling effects of sin in relation to God's sanctuary. This was why the blood was applied to the altars rather than to the sinner. Impurity is 'incompatible with holiness and holiness is a necessary requirement' if God is to dwell among his people.[4] Sin, as one writer puts it, 'creates impurity and it violates and disrupts the clean and holy space'.[5] We are also taught that there are degrees of impurity in the same way as there are degrees of holiness.

This ritual involving the blood gives us further pictures of Christ's sacrificial death. As it was the priest alone who could apply the blood of the sacrifices to the areas that needed cleansing, so Jesus Christ, as the ultimate High Priest and sin offering, entered the real holy place, heaven itself, there to purify the heavenly things with his own blood (Heb. 9:21-26). Were it not for Christ and his atoning blood, our sins would pollute heaven itself. But we are assured that we can come with our prayers right into God's holy presence and that when we pass from this world we shall be present with the Lord.

The fat of the sin offering

The same procedure applies as with the peace offerings. The fat on the entrails and liver and the kidneys, with the suet on them, were taken from the slaughtered animals and burned on the altar of burnt offering (4:8-10,19,26,31,35). Like all the other offerings, these parts of the animal that were burned were for **'a sweet aroma to the LORD'** (4:31). The sacrifice still had a God-ward direction, suggesting the removal of God's wrath and the acceptance by God of the offerer. Through the burning of the fat on the altar that had already received the animal's blood, the priest **'shall make**

atonement for them, and it shall be forgiven...'
(4:20,26,31,35). What was done to the sin offering of the
priest was also to be done to the bull presented by the elders
of the congregation (4:20). All the fat of every sin offering
that was burned was for this purpose, even though the
details are not always stated in every case. While the blood
ritual dealt with sin's polluting effects, the fat dealt with
sin's guilt. Again, it illustrates the work of Christ, who died
for guilty sinners, the righteous for the unrighteous, in order
to bring us to God.

The remains of the sin offering

More details are given about the animal remains at a later
point (see 6:24-30), but here it is made clear that if the blood
of the animal is brought inside the tabernacle and sprinkled
and daubed in the Holy Place, then the remains, including the
bull's hide, flesh, head, legs, entrails and offal, must be taken
outside the camp **'to a clean place, where the ashes are
poured out'** and there burned (4:11-12,21). This ruling
applies to the sin offerings made by the anointed priest, those
made by the elders on behalf of the whole covenant community and the ones made on the Day of Atonement for the high
priest and nation (see 16:27). Priests were not allowed to eat,
and so benefit from, their own sin offering nor the offerings
presented on behalf of the entire community.

The law directing the priests to burn the sacrificial animal
'outside the camp' is used by the writer of Hebrews to draw
attention to the circumstances surrounding the death of
Christ. He describes the cross of Jesus as the altar 'from
which those who serve the tabernacle have no right to eat'
and then refers to the burning of the animal's carcass outside
the camp (Heb. 13:10-11). Hebrews shows that Jesus fulfilled the type by dying 'outside the gate' of Jerusalem in
order to 'sanctify the people with his own blood' (Heb.

13:12; cf. John 19:17,20). He died as an outcast from the covenant community in order that the whole new-covenant community, the Israel of God, might be cleansed and sanctified by his precious blood.

On the other hand, if the blood is not brought inside the tabernacle but used only at the altar of burnt offering, as in the sin offerings of the ruler and individual members, then the priests were instructed to eat the meat as a sign to individual worshippers that the offering was accepted by God (see 6:26).

Grace for all

Provision is made for poorer people to make the required offering. While the regular sacrifice for an ordinary Israelite was to be a female kid of the goats or a female lamb (5:6; cf. 4:28,32), for many this would be beyond their means. As a concession, two doves or pigeons could be substituted (5:7; cf. 1:14). Because of their size one bird was killed and its blood used to carry out the special feature of the sin offering, namely, the daubing and pouring of the blood at the altar (5:8-9). The other bird acted like the fat of the sin offering that was burned on the altar, which is the reason why it is offered as **'a burnt offering'** (5:10). If a person was so poor that birds were a luxury, then a special 'grain offering' was allowed (5:11-13). It consisted of **'one-tenth of an ephah of fine flour'** — in other words, good-quality flour and enough for about a day's supply of bread for one. Unlike the regular grain offering, no oil or incense was to be added (cf. 2:1,15). Items associated with joy and gladness were inappropriate, for this grain offering was to be understood as a substitute for the sin offering.[6]

God was very gracious to the poor, but what amazing grace he has displayed towards poor, wretched sinners like ourselves! The blessing of God's forgiveness is absolutely free:

> Nothing in my hand I bring,
> Simply to thy cross I cling.[7]

The significance and continuing value of the sin offering

Sin or purification offerings were not only used where human guilt was involved, as in this chapter, but in situations involving ritual uncleanness, such as bodily discharges and childbirth (Lev. 11 – 15), consecration ceremonies like the ordination of Aaron (Lev. 8), and festivals such as the Feast of Weeks (23:19; Num. 28:15 – 29:38).

Purification

The offering cleansed the worshipper of moral and ritual uncleanness and dealt with the uncleanness that affected the tabernacle, where the people worshipped. The ritual impurity laws were meant to teach lessons concerning our unclean natural state in sin, and the sin offering showed the need for cleansing from that sinful condition as well as from the sins that so easily ensnare us. Sin defiles us all and affects everything in which we are involved. Because the tabernacle was set up within the camp of Israel, with sinful people officiating and worshipping there, human sinfulness affected God's sanctuary and defiled it. God indicated that he could not live with pollution of any kind.

Sin leaves stains that no human effort can remove. Only sacrificial blood can cleanse such impurity. But the blood of animals cannot purify the results of human sin, only the blood of Jesus to which the animal sacrifices point. Through that one offering for sin every Christian becomes both a

cleansed worshipper and a purified temple fit for the Holy
Spirit.

Confession and forgiveness

In the ruling that **'he shall confess that he has sinned'** (5:5),
we have the first occurrence of the word **'confess'** in the
Bible. This confession is made before the person actually
comes to the tabernacle with the sin offering. Acknowl-
edgement of sin and the awareness of guilt are the ingredients of a humble spirit and contrite heart. 'The sacrifices of
God are a broken spirit, a broken and a contrite heart' (Ps.
51:17; cf. 51:19). It is with self-despairing trust that we are to
look to Christ our sin offering: 'If we confess our sins, he is
faithful and just to forgive us our sins...' (1 John 1:9).

This passage also draws our attention to the need of
forgiveness: **'it shall be forgiven him'** (4:35; see also
4:20,26,31; 5:6,10,13). All sin is disobedience to God's
commandments and the regulations concerning the sin
offering demonstrate very forcefully the seriousness of sin.
But they also show God's readiness to restore broken relationships (see 1 John 1:6-7). God's forgiveness, however,
is not cheap. It comes at a price — the death of a substitute.
In Christ, 'through his blood', we have 'the forgiveness of
sins' (Col. 1:14).

6.
The trespass offering

Please read Leviticus 5:14 – 6:7

It is a serious matter when a person is in debt with no ability
to repay, and it can lead people to take desperate measures to
obtain the sums they owe. As I write, a school secretary has
been convicted of stealing the pupils' dinner money in order
to pay off her credit-card debts.

Sin as debt

When we think of debt we naturally think of owing money to
a bank or some other financial institution. But have we ever
considered that we are in debt to Almighty God our Creator?
The Bible uses various pictures to point out the seriousness
of our position before God and behind the **'trespass offering'** there lies the thought that we sinners are totally unable
to pay off what we owe. We are in debt to God because of
our failure to obey God and to give him the honour that he
deserves. Every day of our existence we are multiplying the
wrong and increasing the debt, and unless this debt is paid
there can be no forgiveness or acceptance.

Our Lord, in his teaching on prayer, encouraged his disciples to think of sin as a debt.[1] He gave them a pattern prayer in the Sermon on the Mount which included the request: 'Forgive us our debts, as we forgive our debtors' (Matt. 6:12). Jesus also told two parables in which he depicted sinners as debtors to God — the unmerciful servant (Matt. 18:21-35) and the moneylender (Luke 7:41-42). These stories were told to show, firstly, that, though we are in great debt and deserve the severest of punishments, God does forgive great debtors, and, secondly, that as Christ's followers we must also have a forgiving spirit towards others and be ever grateful to God for releasing us from our burden of debt.

Forgiving debts

But for God, the creditor, to free us from the mess in which we find ourselves is not as straightforward as it sounds. Some of the so-called developing countries are in great financial debt to the richer nations and there are calls for the latter simply to write off the debt without further ado. Without getting into politics, this is not as easy to accomplish as some well-meaning people think. In a far more profound way it is no light thing for God to free us poor sinners of our debts. But why is forgiveness so difficult and costly for God?

Many consider that the whole idea of God needing some kind of satisfaction before he can forgive us is crude and sub-Christian. But this is basic to our being accepted by God. The whole sacrificial system, culminating in Christ's once-for-all offering of himself at Calvary's cross, emphasizes that sin is not something that can be brushed aside in an offhand way. Anselm, the Archbishop of Canterbury soon after the Norman invasion of 1066, was correct when he stated that anyone who thinks that God can simply forgive us as we forgive others has not considered the seriousness of sin. John Stott has written, 'The crucial question ... is not why God finds it *difficult* to forgive, but how he finds it *possible* to do so at all.'[2] The bread and wine on the communion table remind us of the costly way our sins are forgiven. As Jesus instituted the memorial meal and took the cup he said, 'This cup is the new covenant in my blood shed for the remission of your sins.' This is the heart of the gospel — that 'Christ died for our sins' and that he did so just as the Scriptures said. The Old Testament Scriptures point to Messiah's death through prophecy and symbol. The trespass offering calls our attention to Christ, by his sacrificial death, enduring the penalty for the unpaid debt of human sin and at the same time making amends for the loss and wrong committed.

Features of the trespass offering

There has been considerable debate concerning the precise difference between the sin and trespass offerings. Though the two are often confused,[3] they must be carefully distinguished. Besides differences in the ritual there are some unique features about the trespass offering. The congregation as a whole through its representative never makes this offering. It is as individual members of the covenant community that they come with their trespass offerings. Only one animal is acceptable — an unblemished ram or male lamb, with no exceptions allowed for poorer members. This male sheep must be of a certain value, measured according to the sanctuary shekel. Furthermore, the trespass offering is associated with offences that called for compensation. For this reason many scholars prefer to call this fifth offering the 'compensation offering', or 'satisfaction offering'.

The offering is seen as a payment to compensate for wrong done. Just as in the previous offering the same Hebrew word is used for 'sin', the 'punishment of sin' and 'sin offering', so the Hebrew word for 'trespass offering' can often mean 'penalty' or 'guilt' (see 5:7,15) and in some contexts 'compensation' (see Num. 5:8). While the sin offering emphasizes the fact that sin pollutes and the need for purification, the trespass offering focuses on the truth that sin incurs a debt and on the need to make amends.

The structure of the section

The text gives some specific examples that call for the trespass offering to be made, and these are set within the context of the special relationship that God had with his people. The section is in two main parts and each part begins in the same way (5:14-15; 6:1-2). **'If a person (sins and) commits a trespass'** is how some translate the opening phrases of 5:15 and 6:2, but a better translation would be: 'If a person … commits a breach of faith …' The sin concerns violating one's obligations arising out of the covenant relationship with God. It is about being unfaithful to God, 'breaking faith' with the Lord. The phrase is also used for the most unfaithful act of all — turning away from the living God and following pagan deities (see 2 Chr. 36:14).[4]

The first part (5:14-19) considers offences related directly to the Lord, while the second part (6:1-7) concerns a breakdown of trust between people over property.[5] However, even these acts of unfaithfulness in relation to others are regarded as an expression of unfaithfulness **'against the LORD'** (6:2). To defraud the people of God is to defraud God himself. This indicates the close relationship that exists between the Lord and his people and is a principle emphasized throughout the Bible. Jesus said, 'Inasmuch as you did it to one of the least of these my brethren, you did it to me' (Matt. 25:40,45). When Saul faced the risen Lord as he was making his way to persecute Christians, he was told, 'I am Jesus, whom you are persecuting' (Acts 9:5).

Defrauding the Lord (5:14-19)

Two cases are brought to our attention.

Unintentional sins

The first is that of sinning **'unintentionally in regard to the holy things of the LORD'** (5:15). The **'holy things of the LORD'** refer to all the property in the tabernacle, such as the ark, the incense, the table and bread of the Presence (the shewbread) and the sacrifices to the Lord, as well as the portion of the offerings given to the priests and the tithes belonging to the tabernacle staff and their families (see 22:2-13; 27:9,23,28-33). What has been dedicated to the Lord is holy and is the exclusive property of the Lord and the priests who represent the Lord. For an Israelite like Achan to take for himself anything that belonged to the Lord, when it had been specifically stated that all the goods of Jericho were to be dedicated to the Lord for destruction, was a wilful act of defiant rebellion against God that demanded immediate punishment.

Cases could arise, however, where a person could defraud God **'unintentionally'**. With all the complicated rules concerning sacrifice, an Israelite might inadvertently eat what belonged to the priests, or even fail to offer a sacrifice to the Lord. Unintentional sins, as we saw under the sin offering, can cover sins not done with the deliberate intention of defying God and flouting his law. Defrauding God is seen as a breach of faith, unfaithfulness to the covenant relationship with God. When the Lord rebuked his people for robbing him, the question came back: 'In what way have we robbed you?' God replies, 'In tithes and offerings' (Mal. 3:8). In order to be forgiven it was necessary to bring a trespass offering.

God's standard of valuation

The trespass or guilt offering consisted in presenting a ram without defect and **'with your valuation in shekels of silver according to the shekel of the sanctuary'** (5:15).[6] There is some debate as to whether the technical term translated **'with your valuation'**, or 'proper value', means that the guilty person presented a ram that possessed a value calculated according to the holy weights and measures held by the priests in the sanctuary, or that, instead of bringing a ram, the guilty person could bring an equivalent sum of silver set by the sanctuary and the priest would then purchase a ram for the person's trespass offering. Either way, an unblemished male sheep, from a yearling lamb to a ram (see 14:12; Num. 6:12), of prescribed worth, was required as a blood sacrifice for the forgiveness of covenant unfaithfulness. Where the blood is sprinkled is not as important in this offering as in the sin offering. The details are therefore left for a later time (see 7:1-7).

Compensation

Along with the offering, the guilty person was required to return to the priest what had been wrongfully taken and to add to it one-fifth of its value, thus making up for the loss incurred (5:16). All this emphasized the need not only for a substitutionary sacrifice that was of a standard acceptable to God, but also to compensate God for what he had lost out on due to human sin.

Christians too can defraud God in all kinds of ways. The story is told of Dafydd Morgan, the preacher used by God in the 1859 revival in Wales, who was returning home with an old minister late at night from an evening service at Devil's Bridge, near Aberystwyth, where God's presence had greatly affected the people present. After walking in silence for a number of miles, the minister ventured to say, 'Didn't we have blessed meetings, Mr Morgan?' 'Yes', he replied, and after a pause, added, 'The Lord would give us great things, if he could only trust us.' 'What do you mean?' asked the minister. 'If he could trust us not to steal the glory for ourselves.' Then at the top of his voice Morgan cried out in the midnight air, 'Not unto us, O Lord, not unto us, but unto *thy* name give glory.'[7]

Sins committed in ignorance

The second case is that of sinning **'in any of these things which are forbidden to be done by the commandments of the LORD, though he does not know it'** (5:17). Whether breaking one of the commandments of the Lord refers to the Mosaic law in general (see 4:2,13,22,27) or, as some think, to the Lord's sacred property mentioned in the previous verses, is difficult to decide, but the main difference between this and the previous case is that the sin is done in ignorance ('without knowing it') rather than 'unintentionally'. It is not that the offender is ignorant of God's commands. Rather, there may be times when a person does not know whether he or she has actually sinned; nevertheless the conscience troubles the individual. It is possible to lose sleep not knowing whether one has actually broken God's law or not.

Because the exact offence is not known, only surmised, the law directs that the trespass offering itself, consisting of the required value, is sufficient. No compensation with the added 20% penalty needs to be given to the priest. Fear of having committed an offence against God's law, or of having defrauded God in some way, without realizing it is thus dealt with by means of sacrifice alone. Anxious people with tender consciences were thus able to find peace through the trespass offering. It provides another illustration of the Christian message. Christ's death gives the guilty conscience peace.

Defrauding a covenant member (6:1-7)

In all the cases mentioned where a person is involved in defrauding his neighbour the sin is made worse by swearing falsely (6:3). This would suggest that God's name was being used wrongly, because oaths were sworn in the name of the Lord. Swearing falsely in the name of Lord meant breaking the Third Commandment and incurring guilt (see Exod. 20:7). Various ways of deceiving a member of the covenant community are presented. They include failing to return property entrusted to one for safekeeping, unlawfully seizing pledges, confiscating goods by deception, extortion, finding property that another person has lost and denying that one has done so (6:2-4), or other such deceptive practices (6:5). These are serious offences in themselves that are then compounded by swearing falsely. They are blatant sins and yet there is atonement and forgiveness **'for any one of these things'** that a person may do to incur guilt (6:7). This is so because the law envisages a change of heart on the part of the wrongdoer.

The law, in fact, encourages the wrongdoer to confess his guilt and gain forgiveness, for only in this way would the victim recover his lost property. The victim would have no way of proving in a court of law that the culprit actually possessed his goods. It would be the victim's word against that of the suspect who lied on oath. A further stimulus is provided for the guilty person to confess, in that the compensation to be paid to the victim is considerably less than that required of an unrepentant offender who might eventually be convicted in a court of law.[8]

It has been commonly thought that the law does not provide any means of atonement for intentional sins. This paragraph suggests otherwise. Atonement for deliberate sins, even sins that directly involved the Ten Commandments, was possible where a person voluntarily repented. Numbers 5:5-10 describes how the guilty come forward and confess their sin, restore in full what they have dishonestly taken plus adding a fifth (20%) as a penalty charge, and offer the ram of the trespass offering.[9]

God was gracious to members of the covenant community who repented and confessed their sins. Atonement and forgiveness were provided by means of the trespass offering for all confessed sin. It was highhanded rebellion against God and his law, where people brazenly and self-consciously defied God and remained unrepentant, that was unforgivable. Where a guilty person showed signs of genuine repentance, like David after the prophet Nathan pointed out to him his violation of God's law, there was mercy: 'According to the multitude of your tender mercies, blot out my transgressions' (Ps. 51:1). The hope of the true Israelite was in this God:

> If you, LORD, should mark iniquities,
> O Lord, who could stand?
> But there is forgiveness with you,
> That you may be feared...
>
> For with the LORD there is mercy,
> And with him is abundant redemption.
> And he shall redeem Israel
> From all his iniquities
>
> (Ps. 130:3-4,7-8).

The trespass offering finds its reality in the good news concerning Christ's atoning death and our response to him. It highlights three special items:

1. There is need for a substitute blood sacrifice. Only one animal is acceptable, a male sheep without blemish.

2. The male sheep must be of a certain value. The value is not to be calculated according to human estimates, but according to God's standard — the 'holy shekel'.

3. Compensation is required.

Isaiah's prophecy

Isaiah uses the trespass offering to direct us to the work of the Messiah. As he describes the sufferings of the Servant of the Lord on behalf of his people, he likens him to a sheep led to the slaughter. But he goes further, and this is not always conveyed in the English versions. The phrase often translated as 'offering for sin' (Isa. 53:10) is actually the word for trespass or guilt offering. Isaiah prophesies that the Servant will become like the ram of the trespass offering. Here is God's righteous Servant, his chosen one, without blemish, who meets God's standards, one 'in whom my soul delights!' (Isa. 42:1; 53:11). He is the substitute blood sacrifice on whom the Lord laid 'the iniquity of us all' (Isa. 53:6). In addition, the Servant makes full satisfaction, for he took the punishment that led to our peace (Isa. 53:5). The debt has been paid.

'Of whom does the prophet say this?' the Ethiopian eunuch asked Philip the evangelist, as he read from the Isaiah scroll on his way back home from Jerusalem. Immediately

Philip began telling him of Jesus the Messiah (see Acts 8:26-39).

The real trespass offering

Jesus is the true substitute sacrifice, who was holy, harmless and undefiled. He committed no sin, neither was there any deceit in his mouth (Heb. 7:26; 1 Peter 2:22). Yet it was he who bore the sins of his people. We are too heavily in debt to help ourselves, but Christ is our trespass offering, compensating over and above all the debts we owe. Our Saviour comes up to the right value according to the divine holy standard. Twice God the Father assessed Jesus, at his baptism and on the Mount of Transfiguration, in words reminiscent of the Lord's introduction of his Servant: 'This is my beloved Son, in whom I am well pleased' (Matt. 3:17; 17:5). Our Lord Jesus Christ has fully satisfied the demands of God's justice. The eternal God in the person of his Son, Christ Jesus, paid the price of sin. By his substitutionary sacrifice he has cleared in full the debt we owe. The equivalent of an eternity of suffering was undertaken by the Son of God for all his people when he experienced those three terrible hours of darkness and dereliction on the cross, resulting in a full and sufficient settlement.

> Sing, O sing, of my Redeemer!
> With his blood he purchased me,
> On the cross he sealed my pardon,
> Paid the debt and made me free.[10]

Sinners who recognize their guilt can find 'sweet relief' as they confess their sins and look to Jesus Christ. He is the priest and sacrifice who has made atonement for sin 'before

the LORD'. There is forgiveness 'for any one' of the things
that we do that incurs guilt (6:7).

Making amends

One other principle needs to be added. In the cases where it
was possible for repentant sinners to make amends to those
they had wronged, the law directed them to restore by 120%.
Christians too need to right wrongs by making amends to
those they have defrauded. This is evidence of a truly repentant spirit. We are duty bound to remedy known wrongs if we
would seek to know God's forgiveness.

There is a lovely account of this in the New Testament.
Zacchaeus, the lonely tax official despised by his own
people, opened his life and home to Jesus Christ. The evidence of his genuinely repentant spirit and changed life was
obvious in that he was prepared to repay not merely 120%
but 400% of what he had falsely taken from his fellow Jews.
Jesus was able to declare, 'Today salvation has come to this
house, because he also is a son of Abraham' (see Luke
19:1-10).

Post-baptismal sins

The story of Zacchaeus makes it clear that there is full and
free forgiveness for all who humble themselves to receive
the Saviour, even though they may feel they are hopeless
cases, or where others may think they are beyond redemption. But what about sins committed after a person becomes
a Christian? There were great debates after the New Testament era over post-baptismal sins. Some people were so
afraid that they might commit the unpardonable sin that they
held off being baptized until they were on their deathbeds.
All this led later to what is now official Roman Catholic
teaching concerning two kinds of sins: 'deadly sins' that put

a person back on the road to hell, and the not-so-deadly type, but sufficiently serious to make it necessary for people to pass through the fires of purgatory. But all this is contrary to the teaching of the Bible. Jesus Christ has made full satisfaction for our sins. On the divine side there is nothing more for us to pay. The debt has been wiped out completely and Jesus Christ has more than made up for the results of our defrauding God and our unfaithfulness. Through the obedience of the Son of God our Saviour, even to the death of the cross, an eternally sufficient compensation has been made.

Is there forgiveness for deliberate as well as unintentional sins after conversion to Christ? Of course there is! The New Testament presses home the truth that is taught through the trespass offering that, if we humble ourselves and confess our sins, God 'is faithful and just to forgive us our sins' (1 John 1:9). We are urged not to sin, but 'If anyone sins, we have an advocate with the Father, Jesus Christ the righteous. And he himself is the propitiation for our sins...' (1 John 2:1-2). It is defiant rebellion against God with no sign of a repentant spirit that is unforgivable.

When our Lord taught his disciples to pray it is clear that he saw it as an ongoing need to ask God's forgiveness. We are to keep short accounts with God. If anyone is worried whether they have committed the unpardonable sin this trespass offering reminds us that there is atonement and forgiveness for all repentant sinners who look to Jesus Christ the Lamb of God. Those who feel guilty, troubled over whether they have sinned without realizing it, can find relief in the finished work of Christ at Calvary.

> When Satan tempts me to despair
> And tells me of the guilt within,
> Upward I look, and see him there
> Who made an end of all my sin.[11]

7.
The offerings and the priests

Please read Leviticus 6:8 – 7:10

As if to assist our memories, all five offerings are mentioned again. This time, instead of the emphasis being on
what the people are to do, the priests are given practical
instructions for the administration of the offerings. The
latter are arranged in the same order as the previous list,
apart from the peace offering. This is reserved until last,
probably because the people as well as the priests are
allowed to eat part of the sacrifice and therefore more
detailed instructions are necessary.

The burnt offering (6:8-13)

The prominent position of the burnt offering in the list
proclaims its importance. It is the sacrifice most often
mentioned in the Old Testament, the one most frequently
offered and, as we find here, the one that is foundational to
all the other offerings made by fire.

The fire

Our attention is drawn to the fire on the bronze altar, which consumed the burnt offering and all the other offerings that involved burning, including the fatty parts of the peace offerings (6:12). It is forcefully emphasized in three verses that this fire must not be allowed to go out. It is put first in a simple, positive way: '**... the fire of the altar shall be kept burning on it**' (6:9). This is then repeated with an additional negative statement: '**... it shall not go out**' (6:12, ESV). Finally, all is repeated with the addition of the word '**continually**': '**Fire shall be kept burning on the altar continually; it shall not go out**' (6:13, ESV).

John Calvin suggested that it was because fire from heaven lit the first burnt offerings in both the tabernacle and later the temple that the law is so insistent on keeping the fire alight.[1] Divine fire miraculously devoured the first sacrifice (9:24; cf. 2 Chr. 7:1), and 'It is *this* fire', comments the Jewish scholar, Jacob Milgrom, 'which is not allowed to die out so that all subsequent sacrifices might claim divine acceptance.'[2] The implication is that when any future sacrifice was burned on the altar it was the Lord who consumed it with fire. From the beginning Israel was made aware of the fire of the divine presence in the cloudy pillar of fire and on Mount Sinai. That same fire of God's glory came near to the people and accepted them through the offerings that were burned.

Clearing the ashes

In days before central heating, it was a daily ritual, first thing in the morning, to clear away the dust and ash in the hearth after the previous day's coal and wood had been burned up. The ash would be placed in the bin that was emptied each week when the refuse collectors came round. Similarly, the first duty of the priests each morning was the removal of the enormous amount of ash that had accumulated at the altar hearth after the previous day's offerings had been burned up. The ash was initially removed to the side of the altar and afterwards taken **'outside the camp to a clean place'** (6:11). While holiness was compatible with a clean place even though the latter had not been set apart as holy, it was not compatible with a supposedly holy environment that had become polluted.

This menial task could not be undertaken by ordinary Israelites. Only the priests from Aaron's family could approach the altar to remove the ash (see Exod. 28:1; Lev. 8 – 9). They were not allowed to wear what they liked to do this. When functioning in their official capacity in the tabernacle or approaching the bronze altar, they were required to put on special priestly clothes — a **'linen garment'** and **'linen trousers'** (ESV, 'a linen undergarment', 6:10; see Exod. 28:39-42; 39:27-29). The holy underpants, rather like bloomers (Exod. 28:42), are specifically mentioned here and elsewhere to make a clear distinction between ancient Near-Eastern religious practices and the worship of Israel. Pagan priests would often sacrifice at the altars completely naked and it was common in Canaanite worship for all kinds of sexual acts to take place within the temple precincts. Such practices were not only forbidden in Israel, but precautions were taken so that there was no possibility of a priest's genitals being exposed while he served at the altar. No one was to think that human sexual powers influenced the God of Israel. Modesty in dress should be the concern of every Christian, and sexual misconduct and impurity have no place among God's people. Church leaders have a duty to see that communal acts of worship do not stimulate people's sexual drives.

When the priest on duty had collected the ash from the altar area he was required to change his clothes again before removing it from the tabernacle courtyard. His holy garments were reserved for use at the sanctuary, so he put on ordinary clothing when taking the ash to **'a clean place'** outside the camp (6:11; cf. 4:12). Ceremonially clean and unclean areas outside the camp were specified for the disposal of various types of waste (see 14:40-45; 16:27-28; Num. 19:9).[3]

The priests' holy garments were to be made of **'linen'** rather than wool to prevent the priests from sweating (cf. Ezek. 44:17-18). Bodily excretions and fluids, as today, were considered a source of uncleanness (see Lev. 15). Nothing unclean was to be associated with God's earthly home. Uncleanness was the very opposite of holiness. No unclean person could function in God's sanctuary.

The need for ceremonial purity impressed upon Israel the importance of moral purity. Human beings are in a state of moral uncleanness due to sin. Before we can live in God's holy city and come into the presence of the holy God we need to be washed and made clean. Against this background and that of the prophets (see Ezek. 36:25-27), we can understand Paul's reference to the 'washing of regeneration and renewing of the Holy Spirit' (Titus 3:5). This is why Jesus said to Nicodemus that he needed to be born again of water and the Spirit (John 3:5). There is a cleansing associated with water that points to the Spirit's work in the new birth, purifying us of our sinful state, and there is a cleansing associated with the blood sacrifices which point to Christ's work on the cross, cleansing us from our actual sins. Jesus mentioned this twofold cleansing when he took a towel to wash his disciples' feet. To Peter's request for other parts of his body to be washed after first being reluctant to allow Jesus to wash his feet, Jesus said, 'The one who has bathed does not need to wash, except for his feet, but is completely clean. And you are clean, but not every one of you' (John 13:10, ESV). While eleven of the disciples were clean in the sense that they had already known the Spirit's cleansing work in the new birth, they still needed daily cleansing from their sins through Christ's atoning blood.

The grain offering (6:14-23)

Unlike the burnt offering, which was wholly consumed by fire, portions of the other offerings could be eaten (see 6:16,26; 7:6,15,31). There were restrictions, however, on those allowed to eat them. The following three offerings — the grain, sin and trespass — belong together because they are described as **'most holy'** (see 6:17,25; 7:6). This means that only those who were closest to God, who represented God, could take for themselves the parts of the offering to be consumed and eat the food within the area specially associated with God. In other words, only the priests were allowed to eat from these offerings and they were to do so **'in a holy place'** which is further designated as the courtyard surrounding the tabernacle (see 6:16,25; 7:6). The less holy offerings, as we shall see with the peace offerings, could be eaten outside the tabernacle by the priest's family and by the Israelite worshipper together with his family and friends.

It must be remembered that under the old Sinai covenant ritual system, there were degrees of holiness just as there were degrees of uncleanness. The nearer the person or article was in relation to God, the greater the degree of holiness required. These three offerings partook of the highest degree of holiness and so only those separated to be nearest to God could eat that which God regarded as most holy: **'Everyone who touches them must be holy'** (6:18).[4] Christians are in the closest possible position in relation to God through God's Son, Jesus Christ. We are not only, like ancient Israel, called to be a holy nation, but individually our bodies are temples of the Holy Spirit (1 Cor. 6:19). Both corporately as the people of God meeting locally and as individuals, we are

God's holy sanctuaries. We partake of those items that are most holy (see Heb. 6:4-5). Those called to minister in the church are not necessarily any closer to God than individual members of the church. Nevertheless, they are specially set apart to engage in the holy occupation of prayer and the preaching of God's Word and therefore should set an example of holiness of life in their own private devotions and moral behaviour. 'My people's greatest need', said M'Cheyne, 'is my own personal holiness.' Three times in the Pastoral Epistles Paul directs that the overseer/elder must be 'blameless'. Another qualification is that he should be 'holy' or 'devout'.

The priest's portion (6:14-18)

We are reminded of what was taught earlier, that the 'memorial portion' of the grain offering — a handful of fine flour mixed with oil and frankincense — was to be burned on the altar of burnt offering as **'a sweet aroma'** to the Lord (6:15,21; cf. 2:2). So closely was it associated with the whole burnt offering that this bloodless sacrifice also appeased God's wrath and was accepted as pleasing in his sight. It points us forward to Jesus Christ, the living Bread, who offered himself as a sacrifice acceptable to God on behalf of sinners. Jesus said, 'The bread that I shall give is my flesh, which I shall give for the life of the world' (John 6:51).

The rest of the offering God gave to the priests: **'I have given it to them as their portion of my offerings made by fire'** (6:17). The priests were not to add yeast to it when they baked it to eat. As there was no leaven in what was burned, so they were to receive their portion as **'unleavened bread'** (6:16-17). Leaven is often associated with evil thoughts and corrupt actions, so that Christians are urged to live and worship together, 'not ... with the leaven of malice and wickedness, but with the unleavened bread of sincerity and truth' (1 Cor. 5:8).

It is emphasized that all the priests could eat from the sacrifices, not only the ones who were actually on duty: **'All the males among the children of Aaron may eat it'** (6:18; cf. 6:16). The New Testament draws out a principle from the benefit that the priests received from the people's grain offerings. Those who give themselves to proclaiming the gospel are entitled to receive material support from Christians. Ministers of the gospel are not sacerdotal priests, but a comparison is made between those set apart to officiate on behalf of the people in the tabernacle and those set apart to serve the good Word of God (see Matt. 10:10; 1 Cor. 9:7-14; 1 Tim. 5:18).

The priest's offering (6:19-23)

In Leviticus 2 the focus was on the voluntary grain offerings made by Israelite worshippers. Here the law covers the offerings made by the priests. There was a special grain offering sacrificed as part of the consecration of Aaron and his sons to the priesthood (8:26), but that is not the concern here. Instructions are given in these verses for the regular grain offerings that began on the day they were first set apart for the priesthood and which they were to continue to perform each day, morning and evening. This priestly offering may be associated with the daily burnt and grain offerings (see Exod. 29:38-41; Num. 28:3-6).

It was to be the particular concern of the high priest to offer this grain offering on behalf of himself and the other priests. Josephus refers to the high priest offering this sacrifice twice a day at his own expense.[5] It was to be prepared as if it were going to be eaten, but it was strictly forbidden for any part of this sacrifice to be consumed by the priests. They were not allowed to benefit from their own sacrifices. The ordinary worshipper's grain offering showed that the priests were separate from the people as God's representatives and able to partake of the offerings made to God. In the case of his own offering, the priest's position is seen to be distinct from God. In the priestly offering the whole was to be burned on the altar: **'It shall be wholly burned'** (6:22,23).[6]

These daily offerings **'for a sweet aroma to the LORD'** (6:21) indicated that the priests themselves were sinful and needed to make atonement for themselves. The writer to the Hebrews draws our attention to this as he shows the contrast between the ministry of Jesus and that of the Levitical priests. Our Lord did not need to offer up daily sacrifices for himself. He was the sinless one who offered himself as the one sufficient sacrifice for all time for the sins of others (Heb. 7:26-27).

The sin offering (6:24-30)

As we saw earlier (4:1 – 5:13), the sin offering teaches the polluting nature of sin and the need for cleansing. It points forward to the death of Christ, whose blood cleanses from all sin.

The sacrificial meal

The sin offering was to be killed on the north side of the altar, at the place where the burnt offering was killed (see 1:11). As with the grain offering, the priests alone were to eat the meat of the sin offering that was not burned, and they were to do so in the holy place of the tabernacle court (6:26,29). However, the priest who actually offered the sacrifice is the one first directed to eat at least some of the meat (6:26). In this way the officiating priest symbolically declared to the worshipper that God had accepted the sacrifice, that atonement had been made and the guilt had been taken away (see 10:17).[7] Our great High Priest, Jesus Christ, was himself the sacrifice that atoned for sin. He is the Lamb of God who takes away the sin of the world (John 1:29), 'who himself bore [took away] our sins in his own body on the tree' (1 Peter 2:24). The Lord was pleased with this sacrifice (Isa. 53:10).

If the blood of the sin offering was brought into the Holy Place within the tabernacle itself — as was the case when the anointed priest or the community brought sin offerings (see 4:3-21) — the priests were forbidden from eating the meat. All was to be burned (6:30). As with the grain offering, the priests were not allowed to profit from their own sin offerings, or the sin offering of the community of which they were a part. Hebrews 13:10-11 contrasts the priests, who were forbidden to eat their own sin offerings, and Christians who are encouraged to feed by faith on the benefits of Christ's great sin offering.

Respect for the purifying blood

Again, as with the grain offering, it is emphasized that anyone who touches the sacrifice once it has been dedicated to God must be holy (6:27; cf. 6:18). In this context we are to understand the reason why the purifying blood of the sin offering must be kept for its desired purpose. Any blood that was inadvertently splashed elsewhere, such as on the priest's clothes, or that would inevitably drop into the cooking pot, was to be washed and scrubbed clean. In the case of clay pots, where the blood might penetrate into the material more easily, these had to be destroyed (6:27-28). The blood was holy, kept apart for the purpose of cleansing the altar and other designated holy items, and was not allowed to remain anywhere else. It could not be treated in a thoughtless way as if it were for common use. Christ's sacrificial death also needs to be treated with the respect it deserves. Severe warnings are given to those in danger of denying the Christian faith, who spurn the Son of God and profane 'the blood of the covenant' (see Heb. 10:29-30).

The trespass offering (7:1-10)

The kinds of sins for which this trespass offering was appointed have already been described in 5:14 – 6:7. Here we are given a fuller description of the ritual.

'The trespass offering is like the sin offering' (7:7) in that the animal sacrifice was to be slaughtered in the same place (7:2; cf. 6:25), the fatty parts were to be burned on the altar (7:3-5; cf. 4:8-10), and the remainder regarded as **'most holy'** (7:1,6-7), which meant that it could only be eaten by male members of the priesthood within the tabernacle precinct (see 6:25-26,29).

The blood

The main difference between the ritual for the sin and trespass offerings lay in what happened to the blood. Whereas the blood of the sin offering was either sprinkled against the curtain in the Holy Place of the tabernacle or placed on the horns of the incense altar or the main bronze altar (4:6-7,17-18,25,34), the blood of the trespass offering was dashed all round the sides of the main altar (7:2).[8] The same procedure was carried out with the blood of the burnt offering (1:5) and the peace offering (3:2). Andrew Bonar, commenting on this sight of blood in the outer courts, refers to Psalm 84:1-4, in which the worshipper sang, 'How lovely is your tabernacle, O LORD of hosts!' He remarks, 'None but a deeply-convicted soul … could enter into the song.'[9] Likewise today, none but 'a sin-convinced soul' can appreciate the gospel preaching of a crucified Saviour and rejoice in that 'rich atoning blood'.

The skin

Mention of what the priests could eat from the trespass offering (7:6-7) enables further information to be given quite naturally concerning the priestly benefits from the burnt and grain offerings (7:8-10). The law stipulates that the priest who officiates at the burnt offering was given the privilege of receiving the animal's hide, or skin (7:8).[10] The animal skins remind us of the skins with which God clothed Adam and Eve (Gen. 3:21). There in the Garden of Eden God ordained the first animal sacrifices to be made after the couple's great rebellion against God. No doubt their son Abel first learned to offer an animal as a burnt offering from God's example in the garden (Gen. 4:4; cf. 8:20-21). The skins were used to cover the couple's nakedness in a way that was acceptable to God. Their own paltry efforts at covering their nakedness still left them feeling shame and guilt in God's presence. To the naked in the Laodicean church Jesus counsels, 'Buy from me ... white garments, that you may be clothed, that the shame of your nakedness may not be revealed' (Rev. 3:18).

The portions for the priests

The ruling concerning the portions of the grain offering that were for the priests takes us back to Leviticus 2. There we find that the grain offering was prepared in different ways — oven-baked, in a pan, on a griddle, or left uncooked. The cooked offerings, we are now informed, were to be for the officiating priest, but the uncooked type, whether mixed with oil or dry, could be distributed equally to all the priests.[11] The priests were entirely dependent on the people for their daily provisions. The Lord is careful to see that no one is left out. He is concerned that our physical needs are met, as well as our spiritual, and encourages us to pray for our daily bread.

8.
Peace-offering meals

Please read Leviticus 7:11-38

Most people in the Western world buy their meat from the butcher's shop or supermarket all neatly cut up and wrapped. For the ancient Israelites meat was a luxury and it was generally necessary to sacrifice peace offerings if they wished to enjoy roast beef or tasty slices of boiled lamb or goat. The peace offerings were the only sacrifices the ordinary worshippers were allowed to eat. A good portion of the meat was given back to the worshipper for him to cook and share with others. As the peace-offering ritual has already been given earlier (see 3:1-17), the main concern of this section is to regulate the consumption of the meat.

Types of peace offering (7:12-18)

We learn that there were three kinds of peace offering (cf. Deut. 12:17).

The offering of 'thanksgiving' or 'praise'

The **'thanksgiving'** type (7:12-15) would be better translated the 'praise' or 'confession' offering.[1] It was presented to glorify God in times of difficulty when there was need to confess sin (2 Sam. 24:25), or as an expression of love and gratitude for divine favours (Ps. 56:12-13; Jer. 33:11). With this offering in mind, the writer to the Hebrews shows the underlying principle, now that the law of blood sacrifices has ceased with the once-for-all sacrifice of Christ. He urges us to come through Jesus and 'continually offer the sacrifice of praise to God, that is, the fruit of our lips, giving thanks to his name' (Heb. 13:15; cf. Eph. 5:20; Phil. 4:6; Col. 4:2).

When the worshipper brought an animal from the herd or flock as a peace offering of the 'praise' type, a special grain offering was to be included. This consisted of three different types of unleavened pancakes mixed or smeared with oil (7:12) and leavened bread (7:13). A portion of each sort was to be given to the officiating priest as a **'heave offering to the LORD'**, or sacred contribution (7:14).[2]

Another unique feature of the peace offering of 'praise' was that the meat was to be eaten on the same day that it was presented. None of it was to be left for the next morning (7:15; 22:30). Some suggest that this ruling was to encourage the worshipper to share the sacrificial meat with others, especially the poor. In introducing his teaching on the Lord's Supper, the apostle Paul denounces the Christians at Corinth for disregarding the poorer members of the body of Christ (1 Cor. 11:17-22,29). The Christian fellowship meal is meant to express the unity of the people of God through the atoning death of Christ (see 1 Cor. 10:16-17).

Vows and voluntary offerings

The two other types of peace offering, the **'vow'** and **'voluntary'** offerings, are dealt with together (7:16-18; cf. 22:21).

'Vow' offerings were made to fulfil solemn promises to God. Hannah made a vow and when God answered her prayers, in the gift of Samuel, she offered peace offerings of the 'vow' type (1 Sam. 1:11,24).

The **'voluntary'**, or 'freewill', peace offering (7:16) was presented as a spontaneous expression of gratitude to God for his general kindness and generosity. Paul encourages spontaneous cheerful giving in support of poor Christians from a heart grateful to God for his generous, indescribable gift (2 Cor. 8 – 9). To encourage all to participate in giving freewill offerings minor blemishes were allowed in the animals sacrificed (22:23).

In these two peace offerings the meat could be eaten on the second day, but never on the third day. Any meat not eaten within two days was to be destroyed by fire (7:16-17). The meat was not allowed to putrefy. Any decay meant that it was ritually unclean. A warning is given to anyone considering eating meat that had become unholy (**'an abomination'**).[3] An Israelite who ate meat that was ritually unclean would lose the benefits of the offering — it would not **'be imputed to him'** (7:18). Furthermore, the person would **'bear guilt'**: in other words, he would bear the responsibility for the sinful action. This meant the offender would not escape divine punishment.

It is interesting that Christ, who is our peace offering, rose on the third day according to the Scriptures. Peter remarks in his Pentecost sermon that God did not allow 'his flesh [to] see corruption' (Acts 2:24-32; cf. Ps. 16:10).

Purity at the sacrificial meal (7:19-21)

The subject of uncleanness has already been introduced with regard to stale meat; now a short paragraph continues the theme. Because this was sacrificial meat that worshippers took to their own homes, the danger of its being eaten by unclean people, or contaminated through contact with something unclean, was greater. Thus we have the ruling that unclean sacrificial food from the Lord's peace offerings was not to be eaten but burned (7:19) and that only those who were in a clean state could partake of the meal. What constitutes an unclean state is only briefly described here (7:21; see Lev. 11 – 15; 22 for more detail).

Anyone violating this rule would be **'cut off from his people'** (7:20). This punishment, repeated for emphasis (7:21), is reserved for serious religious or sexual sins (see Lev. 20). It most probably meant direct divine intervention with no link to the future hope. God would see to it that the person would have no posterity and no inheritance among God's people (see Ps. 37:22). Premature death might also have occurred to underline the severity of the punishment.[4]

To die without belonging to God's people, through not belonging to Christ the promised deliverer, means being cut off for ever from all the future blessings of God's new creation. Our Saviour was 'cut off' on account of his people's sins in order that those who trust in him might never be eternally 'cut off', but live with God in the new creation.[5]

The memorial meal that our Lord instituted as a visual proclamation of his atoning death is similar in many respects to the peace-offering meal. God will hold any member of the Lord's community accountable if he or she partakes of this meal in a way that is not fitting. While Christ has paid the ultimate punishment, God does discipline his people through direct temporal judgements such as sickness and even death (1 Cor. 11:26-32).

No fat or blood to be consumed (7:22-27)

Both fat and blood belonged to the Lord and were specifically mentioned in the rituals. The fat of the sacrificial animals — ox, sheep and goat — was to be burned on the altar and not eaten. This meant not only that the priests or people could not eat the fat of the peace offerings, but also that priests could not eat the fat of the sin offerings. However, if a sacrificial animal died naturally or was killed by wild animals — thus making it unclean and unfit to be offered in sacrifice or for food — its fat could be used for domestic purposes (**'in any other way'**, 7:24), but not eaten. While there is a complete ban on consuming blood (7:26; 17:13), the ban on eating fat is only restricted to sacrificial animals. The prohibition on eating blood and fat is mentioned here in particular for the benefit of the people, because the peace-offering meals were open to all the Israelite worshippers. The penalty was the same as for eating meat in an unclean state: the offender would be **'cut off from his people'** (7:25,27).

While giving the fat to the Lord expresses the principle that God deserves our best (suggested by the reference in Genesis 45:18 to eating 'the fat of the land'), the prohibition on eating blood directs us to the importance of the sacrificial blood of Christ. The command to pour out the lifeblood of any animal to be eaten was a solemn reminder that life is a precious gift given by God and that killing such life for food and clothing had sacrificial overtones associated with human sin. It was through the gruesome act of pouring out the blood that God taught the people the costly nature of his acceptance of sinners. This action pointed forward to the self-giving love of God. God in Christ poured out his lifeblood in order that we sinners might be forgiven and brought near to God. The song for ever at the top of the heavenly charts concerns 'the blood of the Lamb'. Is Christ's sacrificial death precious to you?

Generous provisions for God's ministers (7:28-36)

The Israelite is now instructed that, after laying hands on the sacrificial animal and killing it at the entrance to the tabernacle court (see 3:2), the worshipper is then to separate the parts of the peace offering that belonged to the Lord and present them with his own hand. Thus the fat was first taken by the priest and burned on the altar (7:30-31) and the blood sprinkled all round it (cf. 3:2,8,13), while the breast and right thigh, which also belonged to the Lord, were given by God to the priests, as his representatives (7:30,33-35). Through the Authorized Version we have the expressions **'wave offering'** and **'heave offering'** (7:30,32,34). These translations are now disputed. It is possible that the 'wave offering' referred to the ceremonial lifting up of the breast in 'dedication' before God and that the 'heave offering' is to be understood as the donation of the right thigh as a 'gift' or 'contribution'.

This procedure, with the summary statement (7:35-36), prepares us for the next major section, when the newly ordained priests began to receive the **'consecrated portion'** (7:35). There was to be no dispute over what parts of the animal belonged to the priests, for the Lord had established it as **'a statute for ever throughout their generations'** (7:36). This did not stop Eli's greedy, godless sons grabbing what they wanted before the fat was offered to the Lord (1 Sam. 2:15-17).

These portions of the peace offerings made to the Lord that were for the priests to eat remind us of our Saviour, who was lifted up on the cross as the consecrated gift, provided and accepted by God to give the guilty conscience peace and to bring reconciliation between God and his people.

The priests had no income other than what the people gave them in tithes and offerings. These dedication gifts to the Lord from the peace offerings helped provide for their needs and gave the Israelite worshipping community an opportunity to share in God's work by supporting the priestly ministry. The principle still applies. Although Paul did not demand payment for his ministry as a servant of Christ, he defended his right to receive it and taught the church's responsibility to provide for the needs of God's servants (1 Cor. 9:7-14). As was the case in Israelite society, if the giving of Christians is poor towards the Lord's work, then the financial position of the Lord's ministers will suffer. Is it right that Christians on high salaries should keep their pastor and other servants of the Lord on minimum wages?

Concluding summary (7:37-38)

These verses provide a suitable close to the first major section of Leviticus. They remind us that the Israelite sacrificial system was not a human invention, but what God gave through Moses for the people to observe.

It should be no surprise that reference is made to the **'consecrations'** (7:37), or ordination offering, in the summary list of sacrifices. There have already been hints of the ordination (see 6:20; 7:35-36). Although this anticipates the contents of the next chapter, where rituals appropriate to the priestly ordination apply, the sacrifices presented include not only burnt and sin offerings, but special types of grain and peace offering called, respectively, 'consecration offerings' (8:28) and the 'ram of consecration' (8:22,29).

The sacrificial system emphasized God's provision for the maintenance of fellowship between sinful Israelites and the holy God. Without the blood offerings there could be no forgiveness of sins or acceptance by the Almighty. That whole system became outmoded and redundant with the coming of Jesus Christ, who, once and for all time, shed his own blood for the sins of all his people in order to bring them to God. In God's providence the temple, which had taken the place of the tabernacle, was brought to a sudden and permanent end with the destruction of Jerusalem in A.D. 70. However, the principle behind the sacrificial system remains — that there is only one legitimate approach to God. Our approach to God must be through the atoning death of the Messiah. That is why we end our prayers with such words as 'through Jesus Christ our Lord'.

The psalmist also reminds us of another important element that runs throughout the Bible when coming before God in worship. He urges us to 'Offer the sacrifices of righteousness, and put your trust in the LORD' (Ps. 4:5). While the outward form may be right, unless there is also sincerity of heart and a desire to live to please God, the sacrifices are unacceptable and worthless. A broken and contrite heart is necessary as we come in the name of Jesus into the presence of God (Ps. 51:17-19).

Part 2.
Serving the holy God:
rules concerning priesthood (8:1 – 10:20)

Let your priests be clothed with righteousness,
And let your saints shout for joy

(Ps. 132:9).

9.
The investiture of the priests

Please read Leviticus 8:1-36

When Charles, Queen Elizabeth II's eldest son, was proclaimed Prince of Wales, a special investiture ceremony took place at Caernarfon Castle in North Wales on 1 July 1969. This is just one example of the type of thing that often happens in different cultures when a person is set apart for some honoured position in the community. The solemnity of the occasion is impressed upon the favoured individual and all who witness the event through the special rituals that take place. In this chapter Aaron and his sons are formally invested with the honour of serving as priests. Such an important office demanded a ceremony that would fit them for this work and impress on everybody, including those who were being installed, their unique function in the life of the Israelite community.

This second main section of Leviticus reminds us that the Law of Moses is not a mere list of rules and regulations, but a narrative of the early stages in God's activity to fulfil promises he made to Adam and Eve and Abraham.

The need

If the whole nation had been called to serve as priests (see Exod. 19:6) why was it necessary to set apart a special class of priests? While Israel was to represent God to the world by being a light to nations who were ignorant of God and his purposes, they were still a sinful people. For a holy God to live among sinners, and to have fellowship with them, they had to be taught the need of a mediator. It was necessary for that mediator to offer sacrifices to appease God's anger on account of their sins, to cleanse from all the polluting effects of sin and, in this way, to proclaim forgiveness. The priests had this unique function of representing the people in the tabernacle where God chose to reveal his special presence on earth. At the same time their position would also require them to represent God to the people.

The need for such priests to act as mediators and to offer sacrifice for the people has ceased with the coming of the Messiah. The Lord Jesus Christ is the one mediator between God and humans who has offered himself as the sacrifice to end all sacrifices for sin.

Christians, like Israel of old, are called to be a holy nation and to serve as priests, mediating the gospel light. But the principle of a special priesthood still applies. The great difference is that it does not involve setting people apart in the church to a special priestly office, for God's Son, Jesus the Christ, is our representative High Priest who has fulfilled all the sacerdotal functions of the Old Testament priests. The risen and ascended Lord is there for us in the real tabernacle where God has ordained to be present in all his overwhelming radiance. Through him we have the right to come confidently to God.

Furthermore, all who belong to Jesus Christ are in a much closer position to God than the Israelites were. The Israelite worshippers could only come to the courtyard entrance of the old tabernacle. In fact, those united to Christ are in an even better situation than the Aaronic priests. We come by faith into the real sanctuary and into the most holy place, not just once a year like the high priest, but continually. This advantageous position in Christ involves a radical change that sets people apart for God. The priestly ordination rituals point us to spiritual realities that are necessary if we are to be found among the Lord's people.

The preparations (8:1-5)

While the whole tribe of Levi was set apart to assist in the tabernacle and to guard it from intruders (Num. 8:5-26; 3:11-51), only one family from this tribe was to serve as priests to offer sacrifices and to touch the most holy articles. God's command for Moses to **'Take Aaron and his sons'** alerts us to the fact that those who were about to be consecrated priests were men called by God for this special task: 'No man takes this honour to himself, but he who is called by God, just as Aaron was' (Heb. 5:4). There were priests in Egypt, Babylon and Canaan sacrificing animals at temple altars, but they did it to pagan deities. Aaron and his descendants were called to serve the living God who owns the whole earth. No reason is given in the Bible why Aaron's family was chosen for this high office. Maybe it was because he was the brother of the one whom God had ordained to be the leader of Israel and he had already been given a mediatorial position as Moses' spokesman before Pharaoh (see Exod. 4:14-16).

All Israel was to witness this important event. When Queen Elizabeth II was crowned in Westminster Abbey on 2 June 1953, television enabled the entire nation and every corner of the British Empire to witness the solemn ceremony for the first time. There were people the world over who thought of her as their queen and who wished to be witnesses to the occasion. So also the whole community of Israel assembled to witness and acknowledge God's choice of Aaron's family to be their representatives. Although only those nearest the entrance to the tabernacle could actually see what was going on, the whole assembly would have been caught up with the excitement and solemnity of the occasion and no doubt word would soon have passed from one to another of what was taking place. Interestingly, the ceremony took place at the door of the tabernacle, the very area where the priests were to receive the sacrifices from the people (8:3; cf. 1:3; 3:2).

As well as being God's spokesman (8:1) and leader of the people, Moses acted as a kind of high priest on this occasion. He was the one God appointed to prepare everything necessary for the ceremony (8:2; Exod. 29:1-9) and to officiate at the investiture.

The ceremony (8:6-13)

As if presenting a sacrificial offering, Moses **'brought'** Aaron and his sons to the Lord to be consecrated, or set apart, for this special priestly activity. The heart of the investiture consisted of four ceremonial acts: washing, clothing, anointing and sacrificing. We shall consider each one in turn.

Washing (8:6)

Moses **'washed them with water'**. Prior to robing and receiving their certificates at graduation ceremonies, most students would probably take a bath or shower. Moses washed Aaron and his sons not because they had forgotten to take a bath, but as the first part of this elaborate ritual. The ceremonial washing emphasized the important fact that only the clean could be set apart for God. Nothing unclean could become holy; it first needed to be cleansed before it could be sanctified. The same applied to people. We shall find later that, in order to restore Israelite people who had become unclean through various types of skin diseases or bodily emissions, water was used as part of the procedure (see 14:8-9; 15:1-27). The outward physical washing spoke of the need for inner spiritual cleansing from sin. Purity of heart is seen to be as important as the clean hands of outward con-formity to God's will (Ps. 24:4), and the constant message of the prophets is that the people wash themselves from their moral filth (Isa. 1:16).

Jesus, our great High Priest, had no need to be made clean. God the Father was thoroughly pleased with his Son. Though he is a sympathetic High Priest who feels for us in our weaknesses, being tempted as we are, yet he was 'without sin'. He is 'holy, harmless, undefiled, separate from sinners' (Heb. 4:15; 7:26). Nevertheless, in order to 'fulfil all righteousness', he submitted to a washing, or baptism, in the Jordan river by John the Baptist, identifying himself with his own unclean nation, and particularly with those in Israel who had a repentant spirit. It is significant that Christ's public ministry should begin with this cleansing ritual, marking him out as our representative and substitute (Matt. 3:13-15).

In order for us to be priests of the new covenant, possess-ing all the privileges of belonging to Christ, the washing of regeneration by the Holy Spirit and the gospel word is vital (James 1:18; 1 Peter 1:23; Eph. 5:26; Titus 3:5). This is what Jesus meant in his talk with Nicodemus when he spoke of the need to be born again of water and the Spirit (John 3:5). He was only stressing what Rabbi Nicodemus should have known. The prophets speak of God giving the people a new heart of flesh and sprinkling clean water upon them (Ezek.

36:25-27). The water of baptism is a symbolic pointer to this inner washing by the Holy Spirit and the Word of God.

Clothing (8:7-9,13)

Moses **'clothed'** Aaron and his sons. First, Aaron was dressed in the dazzling high-priestly robes described in Exodus 28 and 39. They are called 'holy garments ... for glory and for beauty' (Exod. 28:2). The **'tunic'** was a long embroidered short-sleeved shirt of linen worn next to the skin and fastened to the waist with a long **'sash'**. Over this Moses put on him **'the robe'** with a hem embroidered with pomegranates and golden bells. The brightly-coloured **'ephod'** came next, a kind of tight-fitting waistcoat with shoulder straps. On each of the shoulder straps was an onyx stone bearing the names of the tribes of Israel, six on one stone and six on the other. Tied to the ephod by gold chains and rings and made of similar material to it was **'the breast-plate'**, worn, as the name implies, across the chest. It was studded with twelve precious stones, each engraved with the name of one of the tribes. There was also a pocket for containing **'the Urim and the Thummim'** (probably meaning 'lights and perfections'). The latter seem to have been the divinely ordained way of casting lots to know God's will when making difficult decisions. To specific questions they could give a positive, negative or neutral reply (1 Sam. 14:41-42; 23:9-12; 28:6). Finally, a **'turban'** was placed on Aaron's head and on the front of it was attached **'the golden plate'**, known as **'the holy crown'**, bearing the inscription 'Holiness to the LORD' (see Exod. 28:36).

The other priests were clothed more simply. Their special dress of linen included the tunic and sash, and a 'hat' or headband 'for glory and beauty' (Exod. 28:40). Unique to the high priest were the robe, ephod, breastplate and turban. His clothes in shades of gold, blue, purple and crimson, all very expensive to produce, were similar to the colours of the materials used in the construction of the tabernacle curtains and veil (see Exod. 26:1,29,31-32,36-37). They emphasized that he was part and parcel of the sacred place that symbolized God's heavenly home and reflected something of the glory of the heavenly King himself. As Poythress expresses it, 'Thus he is not only a human being, sinful like ourselves, but a human being clothed with the majesty of heaven.'[1]

Aaron in his costly royal attire was at best only a poor copy of the genuine High Priest, Jesus the Messiah. The priesthood in Israel turned out to be a failure through moral as well as ritual imperfections, as we see in the case of Eli's two sons (see 1 Sam. 2:30-36). At a later period we are given a vision of Joshua the high priest, representing the state of the whole nation of Israel, dressed in filthy clothes with Satan accusing him. The Lord removes his sin and clothes him in rich robes that point to the work of Christ (Zech. 3:1-10). When our Lord commenced his public ministry he not only submitted to a washing ceremony, he had a special type of investiture. Jesus Christ possessed what Aaron could only symbolically represent. There were two occasions when God drew attention to his heavenly clothing. The first was at his baptism and the second was on the Mount of Transfiguration. After his baptismal washing we read that the heavens split open and God the Father acknowledged Jesus as his unique Son and drew attention to the purity of the Son's moral clothing. Of no one else could the Father say, 'I am well pleased.' Everything about his person spoke of cleanness and holiness (see Matt. 3:16-17; 17:5; Heb. 1:3; 2:9; 9:24).

As new-covenant priests, Christians must not only be spiritually washed by the Holy Spirit, they must also be clothed by the Son of God. As Aaron's sons were dressed in fine linen, so Christ's disciples must be arrayed in the pure white linen of Christ's righteousness. Echoing the words of Psalm 132:9,16 concerning God's priests, Isaiah 61:10 reads:

> I will greatly rejoice in the LORD...
> For he has clothed me with the garments of salvation,
> He has covered me with the robe of righteousness
> ... as a bride adorns herself with her jewels.

John then uses these words of Isaiah in his vision of the people of God, who are 'clothed with white robes', made white 'in the blood of the Lamb' (Rev. 7:9-14; cf. 3:18).

Anointing (8:10-12)

'Then Moses took the anointing oil.' A mixture of olive oil and aromatic spices (see Exod. 30:23-25) was used first to anoint the tabernacle and the furniture in it, then, in the courtyard, to anoint the laver, the bronze altar and the utensils associated with it, and in addition to sprinkle the altar seven times. Finally, the anointing oil was poured on Aaron's head. Again we notice how the high priest is closely associated with the place where he is to minister. This process sanctified the high priest and everything connected with the tabernacle; in other words, they were set apart or made special for the service of the Lord. Later, we find the kings being anointed with oil as a sign that they were chosen by God and ruled with his authority. From the Hebrew verb for 'to anoint' we get the word 'Messiah' ('Anointed One'). Some passages associate the anointing with the gift of God's Spirit to carry out other important tasks. For instance, when Samuel anointed David to be king, we read, 'The Spirit of the LORD came upon David from that day forward' (1 Sam. 16:13; cf. 1 Kings 19:16; Isa. 61:1; Zech. 4:6).

The high priest represented the people of Israel and the whole assembly gathered together to witness this sacred anointing. Sight, sound and smell all emphasized the solemnity of the occasion and impressed upon everyone the importance of this institution for the well-being of the nation. David used the symbolism of Aaron's anointing to describe the blessing of life that God graciously bestowed on his people as they worshipped together in unity (Ps. 133).

Symbols and shadows give way to the real and actual with the coming of Jesus the Messiah (the Greek equivalent is 'Christ'), the true Anointed One. He was anointed with the Spirit at the Jordan to be set apart for his prophetic, priestly and kingly ministry (Luke 3:21-22; 4:16-21; Acts 10:38). Jesus is the true Servant of the Lord who comes not only to govern the nations and proclaim God's good news, but to offer the ultimate sacrifice for the sins of his people and to 'make intercession for transgressors' (see Isa. 42:1-4; 52:13 – 53:12). It is Jesus Christ who unites the whole family of God. As our great High Priest, he has prayed for all his people through all generations and is himself our peace reconciling opposites, Jew and Gentile believers, in one body, putting to death the enmity that existed under the old covenant (John 17; Eph. 2:14-18). It is in association with Christ that God commands the blessing of life for evermore (Eph. 4:1-16).

As priests under the authority of Christ, Christians too 'have an anointing from the Holy One' (1 John 2:20,27). And by this anointing we are set apart for God's service. Paul describes the Corinthian believers, who were formerly unclean and immoral, in a way that reminds us of the priestly investiture (1 Cor. 6:11). Their status before God through Jesus Christ and the Spirit means that they have not only been washed, but sanctified (associated with the anointing) and justified (to which the metaphor of being clothed in special garments applies).

The offerings (8:14-29)

Unlike the real High Priest whose ministry they dimly foreshadowed, the old-covenant priests needed to have sacrifices offered for the cleansing and forgiveness of their sins and for their acceptance before God. The ritual involving the **'bull for the sin offering'** (8:14-17; Exod. 29:10-14) followed the rules laid down for the sin offering brought by the priest (see 4:3-12). To indicate the substitutionary nature of the sacrifice, Aaron and his sons were required to lay their hands on the head of the sacrificial victim. The ceremony differed from the norm in that Moses acted as the officiating priest and the blood was not taken into the Holy Place inside the tabernacle and smeared on the horns of the incense altar. This departure from the usual procedure was due to the fact that the priests had not yet taken up their duties in the Holy Place. Instead, the blood was smeared with the finger on the horns of the bronze altar, near to which they were all standing, and some was also poured out at the base of the altar in order to purify and sanctify it and **'to make atonement for it'**. The sin offering dealt with the polluting effects of sin. Any impurity connected with the altar had to be removed before other sacrifices could be offered.

Then Moses brought one of the rams **'as the burnt offering'** (8:18-21) and did with it as he had been directed, in accordance with the rules for burnt offerings (Exod. 29:15-18; Lev. 1:10-13). The sacrifice spoke of reconciliation with God and of his wrath being appeased.

The second ram was used for a special type of peace offering. It is spoken of as **'the ram of consecration'** or ordination (8:22-30; cf. Exod. 29:19-21). The word for 'consecration' is literally 'fillings' and is derived from the Hebrew idiom 'to fill the hand'. We can appreciate the significance of this in the present account (8:25-27), where portions of the sacrifice, along with three types of unleavened bread, were placed by Moses in the priests' hands to be presented as a **'wave offering'**. In this way their hands were filled. Because the offering was for their own consecration they were not allowed to eat from it, but were to burn it on the altar to produce a **'a sweet aroma'**. Moses was given the breast in his role as officiating priest, but whereas the priest would usually also receive the right thigh, this was added to the portions dedicated to God to be burned.[2]

An unusual feature in the ritual was the way in which the blood of the consecration offering was used. A similar ceremony took place during the cleansing of a healed leper (14:14). Besides being sprinkled round the altar (8:24; see 3:2,8,13), some of the blood was put on Aaron's right ear, the thumb of his right hand and the big toe of his right foot. What was done to Aaron was also done to his sons (see Exod. 29:20).[3] This was like putting the blood on the horns of the altar (see 8:15). These extremities of the body were like the extremities of the altar. It meant that the whole person, like the whole altar, was included. The parts stood for the whole, while the right-hand side was considered the more important and favoured side (cf. Gen. 35:18; 48:17-19). Applying the blood to the person as well as to the altar made everyone vividly aware of the close association of the priests with the altar. Thus, as Matthew Henry succinctly states, God 'did (as it were) marry them to the altar'. It also served as another sanctifying action indicating their total consecration to the service of God. Modern scholars have followed Andrew Bonar in commenting that the priest's ears were now dedicated to be ever attentive to the divine voice, his hands ever ready for immediate activity and his feet quick to move in the Lord's ways.[4]

Our Lord sanctified himself with his own blood in that he was obedient to the Father's will which involved his sacrificial death on the cross (see John 17:19; 6:38; Phil. 2:8).

Psalm 40:6-8 seems to have the consecrated life of the priest in mind for we read:

> Sacrifice and offering you did not desire;
> My ears you have opened;
> Burnt offering and sin offering you did not require.

The passage is quoted in Hebrews, but there the writer uses the Greek translation (the Septuagint), which, instead of 'My ears you have opened', has 'But a body you have prepared for me' (Heb. 10:5-7). The sense of the quotation is given in the Greek version, where we see that the bodily part (the ear) stands for the whole body, which is dedicated to God. Both the psalm and the letter to the Hebrews emphasize that the Messiah is dedicated to doing the will of God and that with his coming the old symbolic sacrifices give way to the true sacrifice and the true Priest. Our Saviour is the perfect consecration, or ordination, offering. Jesus has also consecrated a new and living way for us by his blood (Heb. 10:19-21). As the copies of the unseen heavenly realities needed purifying, so Christ has purified 'the heavenly things themselves with better sacrifices' (Heb. 9:23-24).

Why should the heavenly sanctuary need to be purified? Certainly there is nothing unclean about God's holy home. But for sinful people like ourselves to enter and not pollute the place, our High Priest has made it ready for our arrival. He has gone to prepare a place for us. We shall find that everything in heaven, like the blood in the earthly sanctuary, bears the marks of Christ's sacrifice on behalf of sinners. Not only that, but Christ's sacrifice brings about a cosmic reconciliation so that a new creation can come into being where heaven and earth are again one (Col. 1:20).

As members of the new covenant, Christians are called to be a holy priesthood. God the Father chose us, the Spirit sanctified us and Jesus Christ cleansed us by his blood and brought us near to God (1 Peter 1:2; 2:5; cf. 2 Tim. 2:21). Our Saviour died not only to redeem us but to 'purify for himself his own special people, zealous for good works' (Titus 2:14).

The final act (8:30)

Moses took some of the anointing oil plus some of the blood on the altar and sprinkled them upon Aaron and his sons and upon their priestly clothes. A similar ritual was required in the cleansing of healed lepers (see 14:10-20). This second action involving oil and blood reinforced their total sanctification to a life of service. The marks of their separation were not only on their persons but on their special garments as well. This priestly office brought them into close proximity to the God who is so pure that he cannot even look upon sin. Everything about the ceremony emphasized how separate the priests must be from all that is unclean and unholy.

Our Lord Jesus in his priestly office had the oil of the Spirit without measure but he did not need what the sacrificial blood symbolized. He was without sin and perfectly dedicated to the service of God. His people, however, need to be continually filled with the Spirit and cleansed by the blood of Christ to serve as priests under the new covenant.

The remaining procedures (8:31-35)

The concluding regulations called on Aaron and his sons to boil the portions of ram meat from the consecration peace offering and to eat it — not like ordinary worshippers sharing their peace offering with family and friends, but on their own at the entrance to the tabernacle. The sacrificial food was part of the investiture ceremony and had to be eaten within the tabernacle precincts and for all to see. As a side dish they also ate the remaining unleavened bread from the basket (8:31; see 8:2,26-28). Any meat and bread left over could not be kept for another day but had to be burned. The food was especially holy and must not be allowed to become unclean or to show any signs of decay (7:15-21). This special meal cemented the relationship between God and the newly ordained class of priests. It was like a covenant meal (see Exod. 24:6-11).

The final instruction to complete their consecration was the command to remain within the tabernacle compound **'for seven days, until the days of your consecration are ended'**. As Wenham pointedly shows, 'A man may defile himself in a moment, but sanctification and the removal of uncleanness is generally a slower process.'[5] It was common in the ancient world, in what sociologists call 'rites of passage', for a span of time to elapse between one state and another as part of the ceremony. Marriage rites could take several days, or in the case of funerals the ritual could even go on for several weeks. The change in their social status from ordinary Israelites to a special order of priests is impressed upon all by this seven-day period of confinement.

They were to be careful to **'keep the charge of the LORD'**; in other words, they were to carry out precisely everything that the Lord required of them during that seven-day period. The threat of death added weight to the solemnity of the occasion. It was an awesome task they were about to undertake, mediating between God and his people, and they needed to prepare themselves correctly. The complete week of segregation from ordinary, mundane life served to stress even more the importance of their new ministry. Though it is not stated here, a sin offering was brought on each of the seven days, as the law indicated and as the final verse implies: **'So Aaron and his sons did all the things**

that the LORD had commanded by the hand of Moses'
(8:36; cf. Exod. 29:36).

In preparation for his great priestly work, our Lord Jesus
Christ spent the first thirty years of his life away from
public gaze. During that time he grew in height and wisdom, and God and all those who knew him were very
impressed and pleased with him (Luke 2:52). After his
washing and anointing he spent a further forty days enduring a period of testing in the wilderness (Mark 1:9-15). In
all his experiences he learned obedience through the things
he suffered, 'And having been perfected, he became the
author of eternal salvation to all who obey him, called by
God as high priest "according to the order of Melchizedek"' (see Heb. 5:7-10).

All who follow Christ are priests of the new covenant,
dedicated to serving God 'acceptably with reverence and
godly fear. For our God is a consuming fire' (Heb.
12:28-29).

10.
Ministering for the first time

Please read Leviticus 9:1-24

When a newly ordained minister officiates for the first time, for instance at a marriage service, it can be a daunting experience. It is an important occasion and nothing must be allowed to go wrong. The bride and groom are very nervous and have forgotten all they practised the evening before. It is left to the presiding minister to see that the right procedure is followed, that the legal requirements are observed and, where necessary, to prompt the happy couple on what to say and do at the appropriate points in the ceremony. Imagine what it must have been like for Aaron, with the help of his sons, to commence the solemn task of offering the first sacrifices as the newly appointed ministers of the tabernacle. If anything went wrong and they did not carry out the correct procedures it would not be something to joke about later. These priests could be struck dead if they did not do as the Lord directed (see 8:35). That this was no idle threat is clear from the next chapter, where two of Aaron's sons are consumed by fire for their disobedience (10:1-2). However, on this first occasion, Aaron must have been glad to have had Moses, the super-priest, alongside him to guide and encourage him.

The eighth day (9:1)

After their week-long confinement at the tabernacle entrance as part of the ordination procedure, Moses now called upon Aaron and his sons to offer sacrifices to the Lord. Up to this point it had been Moses who had offered all the sacrifices, but now that duty was laid upon those newly qualified for the task. It is significant that their work began on **'the eighth day'**. The previous week's activities, when the tabernacle was consecrated and the priests separated for their task, were all in preparation for this climactic eighth day.

Following the pattern established by God at the initial creation, the formation of this new class of priests took seven days, after which they began their priestly task. On the first day of a new week, the tabernacle worship that was to be a copy of the true finally commenced (see John 4:21-24). It was a day when the people were blessed and experienced the overwhelming presence of God. Here we have the first of a number of pointers in Leviticus to the day of resurrection and new creation. The eighth day, the first day of a new week, is a reminder of Jesus the Christ, our great High Priest, who ever lives to make intercession for us. It was this same risen Lord who encouraged his disciples to meet for worship on this day and to experience together his powerful and gracious presence (see John 20:1,19,26-29). This indeed is the Lord's day *par excellence*; let us 'rejoice and be glad in it' (see Ps. 118:22-24; Acts 4:10-11; Rev. 1:10).

Preparing the offerings (9:1-7)

As on the Day of Atonement, the high priest was directed to make separate sin and burnt offerings, first on behalf of the priesthood and then on behalf of the people (see 16:6,11,15).

On this occasion, however, he was also to present grain and peace offerings on behalf of the people.

So we find that Aaron, following Moses' instructions, first brought for himself **'a young bull as a sin offering and a ram as a burnt offering'**, both animals, as was normal, to be without any obvious defect.[1] The phrase **'for yourself'** (9:2) is probably intended to include Aaron's sons. Aaron, the high priest, represented the priesthood.[2]

Even though Moses had offered sin and burnt offerings on behalf of the priests during their consecration, it was still necessary for Aaron to offer more. This emphasized the priests' own sinfulness as well as the inadequacy of the offerings they presented. Thank God for the holy, sinless Lord Jesus Christ, who had no need, 'as those high priests, to offer up sacrifices, first for his own sins and then for the people's'. Neither did he need to offer 'repeatedly the same sacrifices, which can never take away sins. But this man, after he had offered one sacrifice for sins for ever, sat down at the right hand of God' (Heb. 7:26-27; 10:11-12).

The people, presumably through the agency of the leadership elders (see 9:1; 4:15), were commanded to bring a male goat for a sin offering, a yearling calf and lamb as a burnt offering and a bull and a ram for a peace offering (with the breasts and right thighs being subject to the special wave-offering rite), together with an offering of grain mixed with oil. The peace offering suggests the festive nature of the occasion. By participating in the sacrificial meal, the whole congregation could celebrate the establishment of the divinely appointed means of fellowship with the Lord. This reminds us of the previous year when the covenant at Sinai was ratified and the same representatives of the people went up the mountain and saw God, and ate and drank in his presence (Exod. 24:9-11).

Thus Aaron had the task of offering each of the main types of sacrifice apart from the trespass offering. The reason why no trespass offering was required is that this was a special occasion, marking the inauguration of the regular public gatherings for worship, when it was not appropriate to draw attention to specific sins of individual people. There is a time and a place for everything. It would, generally speaking, be insensitive at some special meeting, where a number of people from other churches were present, to refer in prayer to a local pastoral issue that was causing concern.

Personal offerings (9:8-14)

Aaron quickly and precisely fulfilled the command of Moses to 'Go to the altar…' (9:7), for we read, **'Aaron therefore went to the altar…'** (9:8). The action of Aaron suggests more than merely stepping forward to the altar. It indicates that he was being given access where only those qualified to do so can go. Under the new covenant all true Christians have an 'altar' to which those priests who remained attached to the old tabernacle worship are not qualified to go (Heb. 13:10). By the blood of Jesus we are qualified to come to the heavenly sanctuary itself. Therefore, 'Let us draw near with a true heart in full assurance of faith' (Heb. 10:19-22).[3]

Aaron slaughtered the bull calf and his sons caught the blood so that their father could dip his finger in it and put it on the horns of the bronze altar. This ritual differs from the normal practice laid down in 4:3-7, where the blood is first taken into the tabernacle and sprinkled in front of the veil and put on the horns of the incense altar. The rest of the ritual conforms to the norm in that the remaining blood was poured out at the base of the bronze altar, the fat and kidneys were burned and the remaining parts, including the skin, were carried outside the camp and burned (9:8-11). The blood of the burnt offering was likewise caught by the priests and given to Aaron to sprinkle around the bronze altar (9:12⁻14)

By these offerings for the priesthood, Aaron acknowledged in a public way his own sinfulness and continuing need of God's forgiveness and acceptance, as well as expressing his devotion to God. Jesus, our great High Priest, was without any sin but offered himself as the perfect sacrifice on behalf of his people's sins in obedience to the Father's will.

Public offerings (9:15-21)

The procedures for the various offerings — **'according to the prescribed manner'** (9:16) — are not repeated in detail, for they have already been set out in Leviticus chapters 1 – 7. Everything was done according to the divine instructions mediated through Moses (9:21). The order of the offerings is of significance. As Aaron offered for the priesthood first a sin offering and then a burnt offering, so he did on behalf of the people. The goat of the sin offering was **'for sin'** (9:15) in the sense that it was for the cleansing of the altar due to the defilement that human sin produces.[4] The grain offering followed, with the memorial portion being burned in the prescribed way (9:17). A distinction is made between these offerings and the daily burnt offerings that had already begun during the ordination week (9:17). Only after sin had been dealt with and God's wrath appeased could the bull and the ram of the peace offerings be presented, with the communal meal expressing the joy and satisfaction of fellowship with God.

All the sacrifices point to Christ, whose atoning death brings about the real expiation, or purification, of our sins. His death is also the ultimate propitiatory sacrifice that God is pleased with, for it really does remove his wrath that hangs over us. It also indicates a life totally dedicated to God and one that brings us into the most intimate fellowship with God, so that all who identify themselves with that supreme sacrifice may 'rejoice with joy inexpressible and full of glory' (1 Peter 1:8).

The purpose of the offerings (9:4,6)

The reason for presenting these offerings on this special day is given: **'for today the LORD will appear to you'** (9:4).[5] This promised presence of the Lord is so central to the occasion that it is repeated: **'the glory of the LORD will appear to you'** (9:6). They are to carry out the rituals of this day for this very purpose — in order that God may appear among them.[6] When the phrase occurs the third time it is to announce the actual appearance of the Lord (9:23). 'The pagan nations around them,' as Warren Wiersbe comments, 'had priests and sacrifices, but they didn't have the glory of God.'[7] This supernatural revelation of God is what marks the uniqueness of Christianity, where the glory of God is seen in the Son of God, Jesus Christ, and in the Holy Spirit's activity from the Day of Pentecost onwards.

That God should disclose himself to people in a visible way was not something new or unique to this situation. We are told that 'The LORD appeared to Abram' (Gen. 17:1; 18:1) and to Moses at the burning bush (Exod. 3:4). Later, we read that 'The LORD came down upon Mount Sinai' in thick cloud and fire (see Exod. 19:9,16-20). When Moses asked to see God's glory, he was only allowed to see, as it were, the afterglow (Exod. 33:18-23).

Moses had the most intimate communion with God and was in such close proximity to God's visible presence that his own face shone with the reflected glory of God. Human language cannot begin to express the sight of God when he

appears in this way. When Moses and Aaron, Aaron's sons
and the elders of Israel 'saw God', the only description given
is what they saw under his feet (Exod. 24:9-11). Likewise,
Ezekiel is lost for words as he seeks to give some idea of
what the glory of God was like (Ezek. 1; 10). Experiencing
the indescribable God and knowing his felt presence is
something the Bible encourages us to seek, but that is bal-
anced with what God has revealed in the Bible about his
nature and character. We see this in the very passage where
the Lord revealed his glory to Moses. The Lord provided
Moses with words that expressed the glory of God's character. God proclaimed his name: 'The LORD, the LORD God,
merciful and gracious, long-suffering, and abounding in
goodness and truth ... forgiving iniquity and transgression
and sin, by no means clearing the guilty...' (see Exod.
34:5-8).

God's glory is the visible display of his stunning greatness. In Exodus it is associated with cloud and fire: 'The
glory of the LORD rested on Mount Sinai, and the cloud
covered it... And ... he called to Moses out of the midst of
the cloud. The sight of the glory of the LORD was like a
consuming fire on the top of the mountain in the eyes of the
children of Israel' (Exod. 24:16-17; cf. 13:21-22). It could be
said that the cloud revealed the divine presence for all to see
and hid the dazzling sight of the divine splendour so that all
who looked might not die.

It is interesting that at the first formal gathering of the
people for worship, with the newly ordained tabernacle
ministers officiating, they experienced the glory of God
among them. Do we, as Christians, gather for communal
worship with this end in view? Forms, rituals and ceremonies can easily become ends in themselves. We speak
rightly of 'the means of grace', but it is possible to be so
taken up with the means that we forget the grace of the

means. Do we expect to meet with God and to have God meet with us?

The priestly blessing (9:22-23)

Before the Lord's glory appeared, but after the sacrifices had been offered, the people were given priestly blessings. First, Aaron raised his hands towards the people and blessed them (9:22). We do not know whether the beautiful words of Numbers 6:24-26 were used, but certainly the essence of God's blessing has to do with his presence and his peace. Moses then took Aaron inside the tabernacle. We are not told what they did there, but this has been the subject of plenty of speculation, ranging from communing with God to handing over to Aaron's care all the tabernacle utensils, or instructing him how to burn incense, light the lamps and set the bread in place. The significant point is that Aaron, as the chief representative of the priestly office, was allowed into the holy sanctuary for the first time. It marked one of the climactic moments in Aaron's ordination as high priest. Prior to this Moses alone had this privilege and, as he had been overseeing the whole ordination ceremony, it was appropriate that he should go in with Aaron on this first occasion. Aaron went where he belonged. He had been set apart to carry out the sacred duties belonging to his office in that special holy area on behalf of the people. When Moses and Aaron came out again both of them **'blessed the people'** (9:23).

This action of the high priest reminds us of Jesus the Messiah. After completing his sacrificial work, he arose bodily from the grave to bless his people and to enter the heavenly sanctuary on our behalf. Our resurrected Lord greeted his bewildered disciples with words of peace, and before his final disappearance from earthly view 'lifted up his hands and blessed them' (John 20:19,21,26; Luke 24:50). At his ascension Jesus took his place where he belongs, now as the God-man and our great High Priest, ever living to be our mediator and to intercede for us. Not many days later, God's powerful presence, in form like tongues of fire, descended upon his people, the spiritual tabernacle or temple, as they were gathered together in one place. The disciples were all filled with the Holy Spirit and, through the ability of the Spirit, they began to tell out the wonderful works of God in the various languages known to the bewildered crowds (Acts 2:1-11).

The presence of God (9:23-24)

'Then the glory of the LORD appeared to all the people' (9:23) and fire from the divine presence devoured what remained of the smouldering sacrifices on the bronze altar. This demonstrated the Lord's acceptance of the offerings and caused the people to express vocally and by their posture their wholehearted worship of God. Some have supposed that this sight of God's glory is the same event as that de- scribed in Exodus 40:34. Most commentators believe, however, that the glory of God which descended on the tabernacle when it was first erected appeared again as a sign of God's approval of the sacrificial worship, to ratify the priestly ministry, and to give overwhelming evidence of the Lord's presence within the camp of Israel. Other occasions when God accepted people's offerings by sending fire included Gideon's call, the announcement of Samson's conception, the dedication of Solomon's temple and Elijah's contest on Carmel with the prophets of Baal (Judg. 6:19-24; 13:15-23; 2 Chr. 7:1-3; 1 Kings 18:38-39).

The high point of worship is to experience something of the presence of God among his people. The Day of Pentecost was a unique coming of the Holy Spirit in fulfilment of Old Testament prophecy and the promise of our Lord. But it also initiated the era of the Spirit, when similar experiences of God's powerful presence can be expected and prayed for. These experiences, when they occur on a large scale, we call 'revivals' or 'awakenings'.

To give a ringing cry of joyful praise and to bow in awesome wonder at the presence of God reminds us of the words of Psalm 2:11: 'Serve the LORD with fear, and rejoice with trembling.' In the assemblies of God's new-covenant people we should not suppose that because Jesus has promised to be with those who gather in his name, we should simply believe it to be so and not expect to experience that presence. Again, when Christians meet together, it is not only to build one another up in the faith — it is to worship God together and experience as a body the felt presence of God as his Word is proclaimed. In this way we anticipate the future glory when God's presence will be for ever experienced among his people. Unbelievers and the 'uninformed' should also be affected, as Paul describes in 1 Corinthians 14:23-25 when he states, '... and so, falling down on his face, he will worship God and report that God is truly among you.'

11.
Judgement and mercy

Please read Leviticus 10:1-20

In setting apart the priests for their special ministry and in their initial priestly activity everything was done exactly as God commanded through Moses. On numerous occasions it is stated that all was carried out 'as the LORD commanded' (8:4,5,9,13,17,21,29,34,35,36; 9:6,10,21). What a contrast to find in this chapter that the priests do what the Lord **'had not commanded them'** (10:1) and fail to do what God had commanded! (10:18).

Rebellion and punishment (10:1-5)

The scene dramatically changes. In place of shouts of joy at the fire of divine approval (9:24) the people are called to mourn and Aaron is reduced to silent worship at the holy fire of God's wrath that had killed his two oldest sons (10:2-3,6). Later, we find Moses angry with the remaining sons of Aaron for acting contrary to instructions (10:16). No sooner had this special priestly order been established than it was under threat of extinction.

It is clear from the reference to the priestly portions yet to be eaten (see 10:16-19; 9:15) that this tragic incident took place on the same day that the first offerings were presented by the priests and soon after God's glory had appeared and divine fire had consumed all on the altar. How could such a catastrophe occur within such a short space of time?

Unauthorized fire

While God commanded Moses to 'take' (8:1-2) and Moses instructed Aaron to 'take' (9:2), Aaron's two senior sons, Nadab and Abihu, **'took'** without any authorization (10:1). It would also appear that the censers or pans for holding ash or burning coal (see 16:12; Exod. 27:3) were their own — **'each took his censer'** — rather than any pans belonging to the sanctuary. Into these pans they placed **'fire'** and **'put incense on it, and offered profane** [literally, "strange"] **fire before the LORD, which he had not commanded them'**. For this rebellious act **'fire went out from the LORD'**. The same fire that came out from before the Lord and consumed the burnt offering (9:24) now **'devoured them'**. They were not burned to a cinder. It must have been like a bolt of lightning that struck them down so powerfully that **'they died before the LORD'** (10:2). Their priestly tunics, the sign of their office, became shrouds and Aaron's cousins, Mishael and Elzaphan, had the task of removing their bodies **'by their tunics'** from the tabernacle precincts and presumably burying them outside the camp (10:4-5).

What was so wrong about what these two newly ordained priests did that would justify such an instant, terrible punishment? It would seem that Nadab and Abihu's action was spontaneous and sincere with no ulterior motives suggested. They might have felt it appropriate to offer incense at this point. However, because of the glorious presence of God, they were probably afraid to come near the altar fire or enter

the Holy Place. So, using trays or censers of their own and
'strange' or 'unauthorized fire' (meaning fire that was not
from the altar),[1] they attempted to burn incense before the
Lord.

The point is that the two eldest sons of Aaron acted on
their own initiative. Up to that moment everything had been
done under the direction of Moses and as God intended. The
essence of their sin, as Kellogg observes, is 'will-worship'.[2]
Like King Saul they followed their own inclinations. We
have those memorable words of Samuel:

Has the LORD as great delight in burnt offerings and
    sacrifices,
As in obeying the voice of the LORD?
Behold, to obey is better than sacrifice,
And to heed than the fat of rams.
For rebellion is as the sin of witchcraft,
And stubbornness is as iniquity and idolatry
                                    (1 Sam. 15:22-23).

A solemn warning

We are warned in the New Testament about bringing alien
elements into the life of the church. A curse is pronounced
by Paul on anyone preaching another gospel which adds to
the finished work of Christ and the teaching of justification
by faith alone (Gal. 1:8-9; cf. 2 Cor. 11:4).

There are a number of parallels between this incident and
that of Korah's rebellion against the authority of Moses and
Aaron. Each of the 250 men associated with Korah 'took his
censer' with fire and incense in it, and fire came out from the
Lord and consumed these men who were offering incense
(Num. 16:18,35). Nadab and Abihu were the ones who had
the privilege of going up the mountain with Moses, Aaron
and the seventy elders to see God and to eat and drink in his

presence (Exod. 24:9-11). Yet they acted presumptuously and committed sacrilege and, despite their privileged position, or rather because of their amazing privileges, they were punished most severely.

The priests had been warned to 'keep the charge of the LORD, so that you may not die' (8:35), so they had no excuse for acting without authorization. Further warnings of death hung over the priestly family in their distraught state — **'lest you die'** (10:6,7).

Our God is still 'a consuming fire' and therefore we are called to worship him with reverence and godly fear (Heb. 12:29; Deut. 4:24). The New Testament parallel to this incident is the case of Ananias and his wife Sapphira who, when the Spirit of God was powerfully active in the early days of the New Testament church, lied to the Spirit and suddenly died. We are told that 'Great fear came upon all the church and upon all who heard these things' (see Acts 5:1-11).

Christian leaders, in particular, have a solemn duty to order their lives and minister among God's people in a way that is honouring and acceptable to the Lord. While all God's people are to live holy, self-controlled lives, those who are in leadership positions in the church are to be obvious examples of mature Christian living (1 Tim. 3:1-13; 1 Peter 5:1-3). Enthusiasm and the 'feel-good' factor are no substitute for doing what is decent and orderly. We cannot ride roughshod over God's revealed Word. More severe judgements await those who seek to become teachers of God's people (James 3:1; cf. Luke 12:48). Judgement begins at the household of God (1 Peter 4:17).

Approaching God

Moses calls to mind a most significant saying from God to
indicate clearly to Aaron the reason for this very terrible
judgement on his sons:

> **By those who come near me**
> **I must be regarded as holy;**
> **And before all the people**
> **I must be glorified**

(10:3).

The explanation for what happened satisfied Aaron — he
'held his peace' — and should be enough to satisfy all
believers in the true and righteous God who is holy. God acts
in ways that clearly demonstrate his nature and character. He
will not be treated in a casual manner. God will not be
mocked (Gal. 6:7). The priests who have the privilege of
approaching God and serving at the altar must take care that
they do so in a way that recognizes his uniqueness. God is
glorified before all his people when the priests live like that
and act according to God's instructions. Furthermore, God
glorified his name in this very public and dramatic act of
judgement, just as he had shown his glory to the Egyptians in
the defeat of Pharaoh and his army at the Red Sea (Exod.
14:4,17-18). The glory of God was seen in judgement on
Calvary's cross when Christ suffered the consequences of
human sin. It will one day be displayed again when the Lord
assigns all who do not know God or obey the gospel to
eternal destruction in the lake of fire (2 Thess. 1:8-9).

Special instructions for the occasion (10:6-7)

Interestingly, we find that, instead of the priests acting on behalf of the people, the people were called to mourn on behalf of the priests. Shouts of joy gave way to bewailing **'the burning which the LORD has kindled'** (10:6). Aaron and his remaining sons were directed not to show outward signs of mourning by letting their hair hang loose and unkempt or by tearing their clothes. They were not even allowed out of the tabernacle area to witness the burial of their close relatives. Although these restrictions were standard for the high priest they did not normally apply to the other priests (see 21:1-4,10-12). It was because Eleazar and Ithamar, as well as Aaron, had **'the anointing oil'** upon them and were about to eat the sacrificial food within the tabernacle precincts that this ban on displaying grief and attending the burial applied to them all. Presumption and disobedience gave way to submission and obedience, for Mishael and Elzaphan, the sons of Aaron's uncle Uzziel, did 'as Moses had said' and Aaron and his remaining sons **'did according to the word of Moses'** (10:5,7).

Death, the ultimate curse for human sin, is the very opposite of what God stands for. He is the very fountain of life and nothing savouring of death was allowed to be in his presence. Death was the most unclean state to be in and anyone touching a dead body became unclean (see Num. 19:11-22). The priests worked in the place that symbolized heaven and the special presence of God. Nothing unclean or associated with uncleanness was allowed to come near God or the place that represented God's presence. Being in a closer proximity to God than the people, the priests had to preserve a greater degree of holiness — something that their office demanded. It was for this reason that they were forbidden to handle the dead, express the cultural symbols of mourning or attend the funeral. Failure to comply would

mean their death as well as God's anger extending to all
Israel (10:6). Here is one of many examples where the
consequences of one person's sin, or the sin of a few, could
have a detrimental effect on all the people, even though they
had not personally done anything to provoke it.

This whole incident reminds us of the first rebellion in
God's holy garden, when the newly formed couple created to
serve as God's representatives allowed a stranger to stalk the
area and followed his cunning suggestions. Here the newly
ordained priests ordained to officiate in the holy area allowed
'strange', unauthorized practices to take precedence over
God's word. The punishment in both cases was death and
removal from the holy place of life. Nothing smelling of
death can live where God calls home. The future glory of
God's people is described in terms of the New Jerusalem on
a new earth where God 'tabernacles' among his people,
wipes away all their tears and where death is no more. God's
gracious invitation and promise is: 'I will give of the fountain of the water of life freely to him who thirsts' (see Rev.
21:1-6).

Distinguishing between holy and unholy (10:8-11)

The paragraph opens with a familiar formula except that in
this case it is not Moses who is being addressed by God but
Aaron. This is the only place in Leviticus where Aaron alone
receives direct instructions from the Lord[3] and it occurs right
at the heart of a chapter where disobedience by priests to
God's revealed order is the focus of attention. The regulations that the Lord is about to give are of fundamental
importance to Aaron and his sons in their position as specially ordained priests of the Lord. Three directives are
given.

An alcohol ban while on duty (10:9)

There is no absolute ban on fermented drink in the Bible. Indeed, there are texts which tell us that wine is given to cheer our spirits (Ps. 104:15). But we are certainly warned of the dangers of drinking to excess (Prov. 23:29-35; 31:4-7). The cases of Noah and Lot are brought to our attention in the book of Genesis. Jewish tradition believes that this ruling concerning the priests, coming as it does on the day that Aaron's sons died, suggests that their action was the result of being under the influence of too much alcohol. This may have been the case although the text does not actually spell it out.

Alcohol is a depressant and it can affect people's thinking and cause them to lose their inhibitions. As we shall observe from the other directives, this ban on drinking while the priest is on duty is an important precaution. They have witnessed what happens when rules are not kept. Their responsibilities are deadly serious. They need to have clear heads and be alert at all times while they function as priests in the tabernacle. The death penalty is attached to this ruling — **'lest you die'**.

The same principle applies under the new covenant, where church leaders are not to be given to much alcohol (1 Tim. 3:3,8; Titus 2:2-3). The same warnings concerning drunkenness are given to God's new-covenant people (Eph. 5:18; 1 Peter 4:3-4).

It is a sad sight and an indication of the poor spiritual state of the people of God when the leaders have 'erred through wine, and through intoxicating drink are out of the way' (Isa. 28:7-10). And what is true of alcohol can be said of any other drug that leads to loss of self-control.

Making accurate decisions (10:10)

The priests had the important task of keeping the God-appointed distinctions between what is **'holy and unholy'** and between **'unclean and clean'**. They were to function like health-and-safety inspectors, only their task was much more complicated than that. Though God created everything good, the laws take account of the fact that we now live in a world that is in rebellion against God and experiencing the consequences of that rebellion.

When God first created the world it involved a number of acts of separation. He divided the light from the darkness, the waters above the firmament from those below, and the sea from the dry land (Gen. 1:4,6,7,9,18). This is how God brought about an orderly world in which human beings and animals could live. Despite the rebellion which in turn led to the disaster of the great flood, and in order to accomplish his plans concerning the 'seed' of the woman, God has promised to maintain that order while the earth remains (Gen. 8:22). As part of his ongoing work to bring his saving plan to completion, God has been involved in other acts of separation. He separated Israel from the rest of the world to be a nation where God's rule and authority would, to some extent, be seen on earth. Within the camp of Israel, God made other separations. He separated the tabernacle area from the rest of the camp and separated the priests from the people. This meant that, although Israel was set apart to be a holy nation, within that nation there were degrees of holiness depending on how close a person or thing was to the place where God ordained to meet with his people. In comparison to the **'holy'** tabernacle, with its priests, utensils and furniture, the surrounding camp of Israel, with its people and things, was **'unholy'** or, more precisely, 'common'.[4] Such unholy or common people, animals and things could be either **'clean'** or **'unclean'** according to certain rules that will be set out later. Genesis has already informed us that Noah made a distinction between clean and unclean as he filled the ark with animals (Gen. 7:2; 8:20).

These divine acts and rules of separation and the instructions on purity and impurity helped to maintain order in a rebellious world among God's people and informed them of the gulf that existed between the holy God and his sinful people. Maintaining these distinctions was one of the great functions of the priests. No wonder they needed to be alert and in possession of their faculties!

Teaching God's laws to the people (10:11)

If the first directive helped towards the second one by reducing the risk of priests making hasty or wrong decisions, the second directive would encourage implementation of the third directive, in that the priests would be good role models for the nation. The priests had the task of teaching the people all the rules governing the sacrifices, the holy and the common, and clean and unclean foods and conditions. The people of Israel did not have personal copies of the Law to read in their own private devotions. They were dependent on the priests teaching them the right way to worship and to live as a community under the rule of God. At various places in the Old Testament we find the priests fulfilling this important duty. Jehoshaphat the king sent priests to all the cities of Judah to instruct the people (2 Chr. 17:7-8). Ezra was a priest 'expert in the words of the commandments of the LORD' and he made it his job to instruct the people in 'the Book of the Law of God' (Ezra 7:11; Neh. 8:1-18). Such a priest is described as 'the messenger of the LORD of hosts' (Mal. 2:7).

While there is no special class of priest in the church of Jesus Christ, ministers of the gospel function like these Old Testament priests in teaching the people of God and being examples to the flock. Such preachers, who are solemnly

charged with the duty of proclaiming the gospel, are told
they must answer to God their Judge (2 Tim. 4:1-2; James
3:1).

Eating the sacrificial offerings (10:12-20)

Moses makes sure that the priests and their families eat the
right portions of the people's offerings in the right place. The
distinction between holy and common, unclean and clean,
must be observed as they partake of the sacrificial meals.

The grain and peace offerings (10:12-15)

The offerings are those that have already been made (see
9:4,17-20). Moses reminds the priests concerning the law of
the grain offering (see 6:14-18). The priests were to eat the
bulk of it after a memorial portion had been burned along
with the burnt offering. They were to eat it within the **'holy
place'** (10:13), meaning the tabernacle precincts, because the
offering is **'most holy'** (10:12).

On the other hand, the breast and thigh of the peace
offerings, as the law indicated (see 7:28-36), could be shared
with the priests' families. These offerings are not described
as 'most holy' and therefore could be eaten in a **'clean
place'** outside the tabernacle (10:14).

The sin offering (10:16-20)

When Moses came to look for the portion of the people's sin
offering (see 9:3,15), which the priests were to eat, he found
that it had been burned. In the light of what had just happened to Nadab and Abihu, we can understand his anger with
Eleazar and Ithamar, the surviving brothers, that they had not
carried out the correct procedure (see 6:26,29). The priests

should have recognized that, as the blood of the bull calf had been smeared on the bronze altar of burnt offering and not taken inside the tabernacle (**'inside the holy place'**) to the incense altar, there was a priestly portion that should have been eaten by them in the tabernacle precincts (**'in a holy place'**).

In answer to Moses' question, **'Why have you not eaten the sin offering in a holy place...?'** (10:17), Aaron comes to the defence of his sons and himself. He argues that, on a day when God has judged his family so severely, eating the people's sin offering might not have been acceptable to the Lord. As Walter Kaiser puts it, 'Even though Aaron and his two youngest sons have not personally sinned, their con-sciences are so awakened to the holiness of God, and to their tendency to sinfulness, that they hesitate to venture into areas where they have no explicit directions.'[5]

Though it appeared that they had not obeyed God's commands concerning the sin offering, Aaron's explanation reveals a different spirit from the self-willed, presumptuous action of Nadab and Abihu. Moses accepted Aaron's rea-soned response and God did not further punish the family. This incident does indicate that divine regulations that seem unalterable can on occasions be overruled by a higher principle. A blatant violation of the law to gratify or promote human self-centredness receives the punishment it deserves. When, however, there are good reasons preventing the law being carried out to the letter, deviations are graciously accepted. There is a notable case in the days of Hezekiah when people from the northern parts of Israel had eaten the Passover contrary to the law. They had prepared their hearts but they had not had time to prepare themselves ceremoni-ally. The king prayed for them, 'And the LORD listened to Hezekiah and healed the people' (see 2 Chr. 30:18-20). Church leaders need wisdom and grace to discern between those who wilfully disobey God's commands and those

whose hearts are in the right direction but whose circumstances sometimes prevent them from doing what is required.

Another important principle is brought to our attention
from the reason why the priests should eat the people's sin
offering. For the first time the priests are told that they **'bear
the guilt of the congregation, to make atonement for
them before the LORD'** (10:17). This suggests that the
priests also functioned like the 'scapegoat' on the Day of
Atonement. They not only sacrificed the offering and daubed
the blood on the altar for the cleansing and forgiveness of the
people, but they ate the sacrificial portion to indicate that the
people's guilt had been taken away and the offering had been
accepted by the Lord. Jesus Christ is not only the ultimate sin
offering but the Priest who rose for our justification (Rom.
4:25; 1 Cor. 15:17).

Part 3.
Clean and whole for God:
rules concerning ritual purity (11:1 – 16:34)

Who may ascend into the hill of the LORD?
Or who may stand in his holy place?

(Ps. 24:3).

Cleansing and pollution

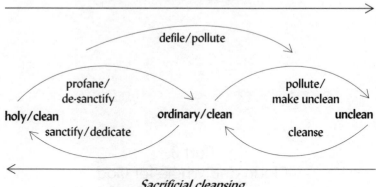

Sin and physical disorder

defile/pollute

profane/
de-sanctify

pollute/
make unclean

holy/clean   ordinary/clean   **unclean**

sanctify/dedicate   cleanse

Sacrificial cleansing

Sin's effects and Christ's power illustrated through the Levitical types, human disabilities and Christ's miracles

Increasing disorder and abnormality due to sin and its effects

Life	Death
Order	Total disorder and
Norm	abnormality
Wholeness	Unwholesomeness
Heaven	Hell
New creation	Outside / Outer darkness

Life, wholeness and new creations through Christ's atoning death

High priest	Priests	Israel	Gentiles	Corpse
Clean and whole		Clean	Unclean and unwholesome	
Most Holy Place	Holy Place	Israelite camp	Outside	Sheol
Sacrificial creatures		Edible creatures	Inedible	Dead creatures
Degrees of holiness			Degrees of uncleanness	

(I am indebted to Gordon Wenham for the ideas in these diagrams.)

12.
Uncleanness from creatures

Please read Leviticus 11:1-47

Much of the legislation in this section makes good public-health sense but that is not the main reason why it was given, else it would not be annulled in the New Testament. It has symbolic significance.

What could be cleaner than a cuddly cat licking its fur as it sits on the living-room carpet? What could be dirtier than to see a herd of cows waiting to be milked, trampling in their own dung and urine? But according to the regulations in this chapter, it is the cow that is clean and the cat that is unclean. What principle is operating to divide up creatures in this way? For what purpose is the list given, and why do we need to study it today?

Be careful what you eat! (11:1-23)

For the first time the Lord speaks to both Moses and Aaron. It is appropriate, in a section dealing with clean and unclean items, that the Lord should address Aaron as well as Moses, for Aaron and his sons had the specific task of distinguishing between the holy and the common and the unclean and clean (see 10:10).

In the first chapter of Genesis we have been told how God created the creatures of the water and the sky on the fifth day, and the creatures of the land on the sixth (Gen. 1:20-25). God's estimate of all these creatures was that they were good. By the time we come to Noah's day we find that the creatures were divided into clean and unclean. It was from the clean animals that Noah offered sacrifice when he emerged from the ark (Gen. 7:2-3; 8:20). Now we are told how he was able to decide what was clean and what was unclean.

Creatures of the land (11:1-8)

A basic guide is given for examining what can be counted clean and wholesome from the land animals. Israel could eat **'whatever divides the hoof, having cloven hooves and chewing the cud'** (11:3). Some animals are named as examples of ones that are not to be eaten. The **'camel'** (11:4), though it chews the cud and does technically have a split hoof, is treated as unclean because a pad of tissue on its heel hides the split. The **'hare'** (11:6) does not technically chew the cud but appears to do so by the movement of its jaw, nevertheless it is unclean because it does not have a cleft foot.[1] Other animals, like the **'pig'** (11:7, ESV), part the hoof but do not chew the cud.

This meant that from among the domesticated animals the people of Israel could eat the ox and the cow, and the sheep and the goat. They could also hunt for animals in the wild such as the deer and the gazelle (see Deut. 14:4-5).

Creatures of the water (11:9-12)

Creatures pronounced clean that are found in rivers and seas are restricted to those that have both **'fins and scales'** (11:9). Here again, guidance is based on what is obvious to the sight. Every **'living thing'**, including **'all that move'** swiftly (some versions have 'swarming'— see 11:10), great or small, whether in the shallow or the deep, in salt water or in fresh, that do not possess fins and scales are pronounced unclean. This meant that the Israelites would not be selling cockles and mussels on the seashore or enjoying prawn cocktails and shark-fin soup! All shellfish were out of bounds, as well as eels and all those scaleless creatures that swim around scavenging for food at the bottom of the sea or riverbed. Instead of the usual term 'unclean', the word **'abomination'** (or detestable) is used four times in this short section to describe these water creatures that must not be eaten. It suggests something that is disgusting and abhorrent (cf. Isa. 66:17). From the same word family comes the term used many times for idols and everything associated with idolatrous practices (cf. Deut. 29:17).

Creatures of the sky (11:13-23)

The same word 'abomination' is used for all unclean creatures that fly.

First, all the creatures that look like birds are considered. There are no special physical characteristics that can be given to distinguish the birds that are clean. Instead, twenty birds that **'shall not be eaten'** are listed. Scholars are not sure about the identification of many of these birds. They include birds of prey and those that feed on carrion, such as vultures, hawks and owls. The phrase **'after its kind'** (11:14,15,16,19), familiar from the creation account, means that many more birds of similar species and variety are

banned. Although **'the bat'** (11:19) is technically a mammal
it flies like a bird. Anything associated with killing or eating
flesh and blood is to be considered detestable and inedible.

As for flying insects, even if they can walk **'on all
fours'**,[2] they are off-limits. An exception to this rule is made
for those insects that **'have jointed legs above their feet
with which to leap on the earth'** (11:21). Four are named
as clean. We are uncertain about their modern equivalents
but they seem to be varieties of locust or grasshopper having
hind legs to hop like birds. John the Baptist lived on locusts
in the Judean wilderness (Matt. 3:4).

Be careful what you touch! (11:24-40)

Becoming unclean through touching unclean creatures was
first mentioned in connection with the sin offering (5:2).
Here the subject is treated in detail. What happens if a person
touches an unclean creature that is alive or dead, or if such a
creature touches anybody or anything else? The following
help is given.

Carcasses of unclean animals (11:24-28)

It was possible to domesticate unclean animals without
becoming unclean oneself. For instance, an Israelite could
keep a donkey or camel and ride on it without becoming
unclean. However, if such an animal died, then to come into
contact with it would render a person unclean. Touching the
carcass of an unclean animal, even in an effort to remove or
bury it, meant that the person became contaminated for a
time. Beside the distinguishing marks already given for
separating clean and unclean animals, an additional mark of
an unclean land animal was that it **'goes on its paws'**,

walking on all fours (11:27), like the lion and bear, which do not have hoofs (cf. 1 Sam. 17:37).

This uncleanness was clearly something that was considered to be contagious. What is more, the contamination varied depending on the degree of contact with the unclean animal carcass. For a simple accidental touch, a person was considered unclean until evening (11:24). Someone who deliberately picked up the carcass to remove it would incur a greater degree of contamination and would not only have to remain unclean for the rest of the day, but would have to have their clothing washed (11:25,28).

Carcasses of unclean creeping creatures (11:29-38)

More unclean land creatures are mentioned by name in this section. They are ones that move swiftly along the ground such as **'the mole'** (or better the 'mole-rat' or 'weasel'), **'the mouse'** (or any small rodent) and various types of **'lizard'** (11:29-30). Again, their dead bodies caused a person who touched them to be polluted for the rest of the day.

Because these creatures tended to find their way into homes a further situation is highlighted. If one of these little animals died while in contact with household articles the latter items became unclean. Objects made out of wood, cloth, hide or sackcloth remained polluted until they were washed. However, items made out of clay, which could be replaced more easily, such as ovens and cooking pots, were to be broken (11:33; cf. 6:28). If there was food in the pot when the dead creature fell into it, pollution of the contents would depend on whether the food was wet or dry. In the case of dry food it would remain clean, but if the food was prepared with water it would become unclean. The same applied to any drink in a pot that had become contaminated (11:34). Stagnant water or any dampness was a breeding ground for disease. Similar logic applied to seed. If the seed was dry it remained clean even though the carcass fell on it. But if the seed was wet it became polluted (11:37-38). Maybe the seed was wet because it was being prepared for food, which would be an added reason for counting it unclean, whereas the dry seed was ready for sowing and therefore would not be a hazard.

If, on the other hand, one of these dead creatures were to fall into a spring or cistern, the water would remain clean, possibly because the water was continually being renewed and acted as a constantly purifying agent. But anyone removing a dead creature from the water would become unclean (11:36).

Carcasses of clean animals (11:39-40)

Clean animals that had been killed for sacrifice and food were not considered unclean when their flesh was handled and eaten. But what if the clean animal died naturally or was killed by another animal? In this case the dead creature, even though it was of the clean type, was rendered unclean. Anyone touching it was to be classed as temporarily unclean until the close of that day. If the flesh was eaten or the carcass removed by hand then the person doing so would not only be unclean for that day but was directed to **'wash his clothes'** as if he had handled a creature of the unclean type. Washing the clothes may be shorthand for washing the body as well, as the fuller regulation indicates in Leviticus 17:15.

The law stated that in order to be consecrated to God no one was to eat meat that had died naturally or had been killed by a wild animal; it was to be thrown 'to the dogs' or sold to people of other nations (see Exod. 22:31; Deut. 14:21). Yet here the possibility existed of an Israelite eating unclean meat where the blood had not been drained. The Lord was understanding in cases of extreme need or inadvertent action and allowed for a quick and easy return to a clean state. We have also seen that the fat from clean animals that died a natural death or were killed by a wild animal, though it could not be eaten as food, was not considered unclean and could be put to further use (7:24).

Be holy! (11:41-47)

As this set of regulations concerning clean and unclean creatures draws to a close the importance of distinguishing between the clean and unclean is brought to our attention.

The rationale (11:41-43)

As a way of summing up the contents of the entire chapter, the rule concerning the creatures that move swiftly over the surface of the ground is reiterated: **'Every creeping thing that creeps on the earth shall be an abomination. It shall not be eaten'** (11:41; see 11:20,29). Interestingly, reference is made for the first time to whatever **'crawls on its belly'** (11:42), which would include worms and snakes. The phrase reminds us of the serpent who was cursed to move on its 'belly' (Gen. 3:14).[3] It may be that we are already being encouraged to see a sinister reason behind those creatures that are to be regarded as detestable. There are no exceptions within this grouping — all are unclean and not to be eaten. To eat any of these creatures would make that person detestable and unclean (11:43).

The cow, ox, sheep and goat are the only animals that can be used for sacrifice. They must of necessity be classed as clean because only what is clean can be set apart for God. These animals do not kill for food, so they are not associated with the polluting effects of blood. They also happen to be ones that chew the cud and part the heel. Thus they provide the norm for what is clean from among the land animals. Any other animal can be classed as clean if it has characteristics that belong to the ones that can be sacrificed to the Lord.

The same applies when ascertaining which flying creatures are clean and edible or not. The sacrificial birds are the pigeon and dove. There are no obvious physical features in these sacrificial birds for distinguishing birds that are clean. But the pigeon and dove are birds that do not live on dead carcasses or make their home in dark holes and desert places associated with demons, so this provides the norm. Birds of prey that feed on carrion are often found in such places and are therefore unclean. They eat flesh with the blood in it. Of the creeping, fast-moving creatures of the ground that may also fly, these are all banned except for types of locust or grasshopper that have features similar to a bird in that they have wings and hopping legs.

No provision was made in the law for offering fish; nevertheless, there was a clear method of distinguishing the water creatures that were to be considered clean and edible. In river, lake and sea the most frequent living thing they would see swimming in the water or catch in their nets would be fish with fins and scales. This was good food and thus set the norm of what was clean. As it happened, creatures of the water without fins and scales were more likely to be scavengers on the bottom of the river or seabed, or, like shellfish, notoriously prone to impart disease, or sea creatures that killed for food.

The law is not meant to be a modern scientific rule for discerning what is edible or not, but a rough and readily observable guide. It meant in practice that anything associated with decay and death, or which fed on blood and meat, or that reminded them of the serpent, was unclean. These dietary restrictions can therefore be seen as following a principle already laid down in the sacrificial legislation that the people must not eat blood (3:17; 7:26; cf. 17:10-15).

They also call attention to the fact that the creation is not as it once was. For God to call creatures he originally created good 'detestable' and 'unclean' indicates there has been a great disruption. Pain, suffering and death affect the whole created order as a result of that initial rebellion. Instead of the good order and life that we read of at the beginning, there is disorder and death. Because death is associated with sin and disorder it is the most unclean of states, the very opposite of the God who is life. All that is associated with God and life is clean and wholesome.

These laws concerning what is clean and unclean remained in force in Israel during the period when God's salvation was expressed in symbolic form. With the coming of Jesus Christ and the fulfilment of the Old Testament copy worship by his sacrificial death at Calvary, the old distinctions have served their purpose and are obsolete. Jesus Christ has dealt the final blow to sin, Satan and death. He has overcome these enemies and causes of disorder. Jesus said, 'I am the resurrection and the life. He who believes in me, even though he dies, he shall live. And whoever lives and believes in me shall never die. Do you believe this?' (John 11:25-26).

The reasons (11: 44-45)

Reasons are now given why God's people must not eat unclean meat, of which the detestable 'creepy-crawlies' provide the most obvious example as they belong to the pests that invade the home.

The first reason, introduced by the word **'for'**, is that *the Lord is their God*. **'I am the LORD your God'** occurs many times in the latter half of Leviticus (see particularly Lev. 18 – 19). Israel is called to observe God's ordinances simply because this is what their God commanded them to do. The same God who commanded Adam and Eve not to eat of the tree of the knowledge of good and evil now commanded Israel not to eat unclean food. 'There was nothing inherently evil about the tree, but it was off-limits simply because God had declared it to be so.'[4] Although we human creatures do not like the thought, God is the sovereign Creator and he has the right to say what we can and cannot do. We can be sure, however, from what he has revealed of himself, that he is not an almighty tyrant who enjoys being awkward and seeing his creatures bow to his every whim, but a wise and loving God who has good reasons behind his every command or prohibition.

A second reason is that *they are a redeemed people* (11:45). The Lord is their God because he has graciously come to their help and has brought them up **'out of the land of Egypt'** to be their God. They have been transferred out of Pharaoh's domain to God's. Instead of serving the King of Egypt they are now under new ownership. They have been set free to serve the Lord who has saved them in a most dramatic way. Likewise, Christians are those who have been redeemed by the blood of Christ and brought out of the kingdom of darkness and into the kingdom of light to serve the Lord. We are to be his obedient people (Rom. 6:20-22; Col. 1:13-14; 2:6; 1 Peter 1:18-19; 2:16).

The third reason has to do with *holiness*. Instead of making themselves unclean so that they will be 'defiled' (11:43), they are called to make themselves holy (**'sanctify yourselves'**) so that they will be **'holy'** (11:44). Holiness cannot exist where there is uncleanness. The detestable creatures have been deemed by God to be unclean; therefore in order to be holy the Israelites must obey God's command and not contaminate themselves by eating, or having contact with the carcasses of, these creatures and, by inference, all the other creatures like them. Furthermore, the call to

cleanness and to holiness is in order that they may imitate
God. They are to be holy, for the Lord says, **'I am holy.'**
This call to be holy as God is holy is repeated for emphasis
(11:44,45) and later in Leviticus it occurs again three more
times (19:2; 20:7,26). Holiness is what makes God so
unique. The Israelites are to reflect this uniqueness by their
life of obedience to God. Eating only the kind of meat that
was offered to God would remind the people of their need to
imitate God. They are to follow the sacrificial norm and eat
what is clean, and thereby show to the world their relationship to God.

Christians are called to be a holy nation, set apart for God.
Therefore, as obedient children of our heavenly Father, we
are to act differently from the ungodly world (see Rev.
18:2-4). As holy people we are not to make ourselves unclean by defiling ourselves through sinful activity and
associations. In order to sanctify ourselves we need to
'cleanse ourselves from all filthiness of the flesh and spirit,
perfecting holiness in the fear of God' (2 Cor. 7:1). Paul said
this after quoting passages from the Old Testament to support his call for the Corinthian believers not to be unequally
yoked together with unbelievers. Among them are the words
of Isaiah 52:11, in which the people are urged to be separate
from the idolatry and practices of the pagans. The command
to 'Touch no unclean thing' echoes the regulations of this
chapter of Leviticus.

Furthermore, as the call to Israel is to be clean and holy in
order to imitate God, so the church, the Israel of God, made
up of all those who are united to Christ, is likewise urged to
be holy like God. The apostle Peter writes, 'But as he who
called you is holy, you also be holy in all your conduct,
because it is written, "Be holy, for I am holy"' (1 Peter
1:15-16). Christians are to reflect the uniqueness of God and
show to the world whose side they are on. The Lord Jesus
put it like this: 'Therefore you shall be perfect, just as your

Father in heaven is perfect' (Matt. 5:48). The picture we are given of the holy city draws on the imagery of Leviticus. Neither the unclean nor anyone who does what is detestable will ever enter. The unclean 'dogs' are outside (Rev. 21:27; 22:15).

The purpose (11:46-47)

In this summary statement the purpose of the detailed regulations is given. It is **'to distinguish between the unclean and the clean'** and between what could and could not be eaten. These words echo the duties of the priests (see 10:10). By complying with these regulations, the people would be constantly reminded of God's grace and their calling to be a holy nation (Deut. 14:2,21). By following these dietary laws the people would be symbolizing their distinctiveness as a nation set apart for God. They were to distinguish between clean and unclean creatures because the Lord had separated them from the other peoples of the world to be his (20:24-26).

Nothing is said here or anywhere else in the law about hygiene and health, although for a mass of people living at first in tents in the hot wilderness climate without modern refrigeration and medical science some of these laws would have promoted a healthier society. But the health benefits can only be seen as a by-product of the purification laws and a testimony to the Lord's interest in their life and well-being. The fact that certain foods could be given to non-Israelites or sold to the Gentiles, as well as the removal of the distinctions between clean and unclean, edible and inedible in the New Testament, indicates that hygienic considerations were not the main purpose of these regulations. As Gordon Wenham puts it, 'Theology, not hygiene, is the reason for this provision.'[5]

These dietary laws served as 'boundary markers' distinguishing the Jew from the rest of the nations of the world. The New Testament reveals that in Christ the wall separating Jew from Gentile has been pulled down (Eph. 2:11-22). In preparing Peter for his encounter with Gentiles the Lord gave him a vision of a great tablecloth coming out of heaven to earth on which 'were all kinds of four-footed animals of the earth, wild beasts, creeping things, and birds of the air'. When told to 'kill and eat', Peter immediately objected, 'I have never eaten anything common or unclean.' Three times this happened and each time a voice replied, 'What God has cleansed you must not call common' (Acts 10:9-16). This would have reminded Peter of what our Lord had said during his earthly ministry. He made it clear that people were not contaminated by the food they ate, but by the sinful passions that came from the uncleanness at the centre of their beings. And Mark adds that in saying what he did Jesus was declaring all foods to be clean (Mark 7:14-23).

While Jesus' main point was to show that it is what comes from within 'that defiles a man' (Mark 7:20,23), Peter was being taught that he should not call anyone 'common or unclean' (Acts 10:28). Such laws dividing Jew from Gentile helped the Old Testament people of God to keep their identity so that the purposes of God for the salvation of the world might be realized. Now, with the establishment of the new covenant, those laws no longer apply. Paul states it very bluntly: 'I know and am convinced by the Lord Jesus that there is nothing unclean of itself' (Rom. 14:14). It may be necessary to abstain from certain foods in the interests of evangelism (see 1 Cor. 9:19-23), out of pastoral concerns (Rom. 14:15; 1 Cor. 8; 10:23-33), or for one's own spiritual well-being (1 Cor. 10:1-22). However, Paul's final word on this, in the context of a false teaching on the subject, is that everything created by God 'is good, and nothing is to be refused if it is received with thanksgiving; for it is sanctified by the word of God and prayer' (1 Tim. 4:4-5).

The call for holiness is not lessened in the New Testament, but the way we demonstrate it does not include the old-covenant dietary laws. The principle remains, however, that holiness is to affect the whole of our lives as Christians. We are not to live as the 'Gentile' world that practises every kind of impurity, but as the new people of God, for 'God did not call us to uncleanness, but in holiness' (1 Thess. 4:7; cf. Eph. 5:3-5).

13.
Uncleanness from giving birth

Please read Leviticus 12:1-8

What can be more delightful than to see a newborn baby in the arms of its mother with the proud father standing close by? So many family photograph albums have such happy scenes from a hospital maternity ward. Yet here in this chapter mothers of newly born babies are said to be unclean and unfit to worship at the tabernacle. Why should God's law appear so insensitive and cruel to mothers? And why are fathers let off the hook? After all, they are as responsible for the birth of children as mothers. What was the law teaching the people through what seems like sexual prejudice and unfair treatment?

First of all, we must be clear that the uncleanness mentioned in these chapters is not directly to do with sin and moral uncleanness. We saw in the previous chapter that the animals declared to be unclean were not ones considered morally blameworthy, but ones that had physical characteristics that did not conform to particular norms.

Secondly, there is no thought that sexual relationships within the marriage bond are dirty, sinful and unholy, or that they pollute a person morally and spiritually, despite what some misguided Christians have thought down the centuries.

Children are seen as a blessing from God. The original command of God made before the Fall was to 'Be fruitful and multiply', and this command was reiterated after the Flood to Noah and his family (Gen. 1:28; 9:1). It is a very sacred thing for human beings created in God's image to be able to reproduce other such beings capable of having a personal relationship with God and of acting as God's representatives on the earth, exercising authority over the created order (see Gen. 1:26-29).

Nevertheless, the entrance of sin into the world has brought about massive disturbance and trouble. God's curse affected human beings at every level. It brought suffering and hardship, decay and death. Even the blessing of bearing children would become burdensome. If we are within reach of modern medical equipment, we probably do not appreciate how dangerous giving birth can be. Even so, with all our sophisticated helps, the experience can still be harrowing and frightening as mothers bring new life into a world now marred by the Fall.

All these physical signs of being under the judgement of God point to the fact of sin and its ultimate penalty in the second death. Though the birth of a baby is generally seen as a happy event, God would have us all know that it is tinged with sadness. Human beings are reproducing creatures who are like themselves, corrupt and sinful. It was to this that David was referring when he wrote, 'I was brought forth in iniquity, and in sin my mother conceived me' (Ps. 51:5). He was not commenting on any moral misdemeanour on the part of his mother, but on the effect of that original sin which had been passed on to him and in which he stood guilty before God.

A mother's uncleanness (12:1-5)

Why is uncleanness through childbirth placed at this point between the laws concerning unclean creatures and those relating to unclean leprous conditions? Animal uncleanness is probably dealt with first, before human defilements, following the pattern of Genesis 1, where animals were created before humans. The importance of the leprosy legislation (Lev. 13 – 14) is heightened by its being introduced by and concluded with regulations on bodily discharges, including post-natal discharges (Lev. 12; 15).

Uncleanness due to the birth of a male child (12:2-4)

If the mother gives birth to a boy then she is to be considered **'unclean** [for] **seven days'**. We must emphasize again that the mother is not unclean because it was thought sinful to give birth. What makes her unclean is 'the flow of her blood' (12:7). During the first few days the post-natal discharge ('lochia' in medical terminology) is crimson red. This state of uncleanness is similar to the uncleanness associated with a woman's **'customary impurity'** or monthly period (12:2; see 15:19-24). It probably meant that during those seven days after the birth of her son she was contagiously unclean, as was the case when a woman started her period, so that her uncleanness affected other people or things through contact. After the seventh day the discharge would normally be brown and grow paler, but it could last in some cases for up to six weeks. This is possibly the reason why the law considered the woman to be **'in the blood of her purification'** for a further thirty-three days (12:4). She was still in an unclean condition although not to the same degree.

During the whole time of her ritual uncleanness she could **'not touch any hallowed thing, nor come into the sanctuary'**. This is an important statement for it shows clearly what is meant by uncleanness. Uncleanness is not to be thought of in terms of some vague cultural taboo, but in terms of worshipping God with his people. To be in a state of uncleanness meant that a person could not come with the assembled people to worship at the tabernacle. All these laws concerning cleanness and uncleanness have reference to approaching God's earthly sanctuary. They were meant to be visual aids to remind the people of spiritual realities. In particular, they spoke of that first great human rebellion that brought moral uncleanness when Adam and Eve were removed from God's holy presence and from the garden of life.

We have a saying in English that time heals. Here we find that time purifies: **'... until the days of her purification are fulfilled'**. It took forty days in all for a mother who gave birth to a son to be ritually clean again. We do not read of any ritual washings; time alone in the end brought about purification in a similar way that governments today use quarantine procedures for infectious diseases.

We are faced again with the biblical principle that uncleanness is incompatible with holiness. God is holy and 'of purer eyes than to behold evil, and cannot look on wickedness' (Hab. 1:13). The unclean cannot come into his holy presence. One children's hymn is for ever impressed on my memory:

> There is a city bright;
> Closed are its gates to sin;
> Nought that defileth,
> Nought that defileth
> Can ever enter in.[1]

Another possible reason why the initial period of contagious uncleanness was set at seven days for a boy was to enable the mother to witness her own son's circumcision. The law required that a baby son was to be circumcised on the eighth day after birth (12:3; see Gen. 17:10-14). The sign of God's covenant with Abraham was associated with the organ of reproduction, thus emphasizing God's promise to him that he would have many descendants and that they would become a great nation (Gen. 12:2; 17:6; 22:17). The 'seed' of Abraham is associated with a royal 'seed' of the tribe of Judah who would bring blessing to all nations.

But this passage in Leviticus not only reminds us of God's covenant with Abraham, it takes us back to the beginning and to the promise of a victorious 'seed'. The Hebrew word translated **'conceived'** (12:2) is not the usual one for becoming pregnant. A more literal translation would be 'produced seed', and the word comes from the same verb that is used of the herb 'yielding seed' (see Gen. 1:11-12). In the creation account yielding seed and yielding fruit are parallel expressions referring to what the trees and vegetables produce. Yet the same can be said of human beings. When God first blessed humans, he said, 'Be fruitful and multiply' (Gen. 1:28). Similar words are found in the Psalms, which speak of the 'fruit of the womb' and of a wife being like 'a fruitful vine' (Ps. 127:3; 128:3). Here in Leviticus the parallel idea of the woman 'yielding' or 'producing seed' is found. By using this more unusual expression — 'If a woman has produced seed' — Moses draws our attention to the promise of the woman's 'seed' gaining the victory over the root cause of all uncleanness and every detestable object (see Gen. 3:15).

When the first couple disobeyed the divine command, God pronounced a curse and a blessing, both of which involved the woman and childbearing. The divine punishment on the human pair did not result in withdrawing the blessing of being fruitful and producing offspring, but it did involve pain and eventual death. In particular, the woman would experience great pain in childbirth. Nevertheless a new blessing was promised in that the woman's 'seed' would crush the tempter's head (Gen. 3:15-16). This is the 'seed', or descendant, that lies at the heart of God's covenant promises to Abraham. The woman's part in bearing that 'seed' is alluded to here, but it is set in the context of the uncleanness that separates human beings from all that is holy and prevents their free access to worship the holy God. Paul refers to the promise of the woman being saved through childbearing. Suffering the curse of pain and possible death in childbirth does not exclude mothers from God's salvation if their trust is in the promised 'seed', Jesus the Messiah (1 Tim. 2:15).

At the time that a mother delivers new life she also loses life in that she loses blood. In the law, blood is a symbol of life. A discharge of blood can therefore be life-threatening. Losing blood after childbirth meant a diminution of life. Unless it stopped it could lead to death. Death was considered a most unnatural and totally unwholesome state. This flow of blood was quite incompatible with God, the source of life and of all that is wholesome. Anything suggesting death, therefore, was treated as unclean and unfit to come near God's presence.

Uncleanness due to the birth of a female child (12:5)

If a mother gave birth to a daughter her time of uncleanness was twice as long as for a son: in all eighty, as opposed to forty days. Instead of being contagiously unclean for one week, as in the case of a boy, she would be unclean for two weeks, and instead of a further thirty-three days to complete her period of purification, it would take sixty-six days. Scholars have scratched their heads over why the period of purification is longer for a baby girl than a baby boy. One suggestion that has been offered is that a female is less valuable than a male. But this cannot be so for, according to the laws of uncleanness, that would make humans less valuable than animals, since human corpses were far more unclean than, for instance, a dead pig (see previous chapter).

Part of the answer lies in the fact that a baby son was circumcised on the eighth day after birth and so the initial period of uncleanness is reduced to a week. But the longer period of a mother's uncleanness in the case of a female probably takes account of the fact that it anticipates the girl's own association with blood discharges when she is of age.

A mother's sacrifice (12:6-8)

At the end of the period of her purification, whether for the birth of a son or a daughter, the mother was instructed to offer two sacrifices — a burnt offering and a sin offering. We notice in passing that this instruction is one of the few places in the Old Testament that actually makes it clear that women could themselves make sacrifices at the tabernacle. In later Judaism women played no active part in synagogue worship. It is also worthy of notice that the sacrifices to be offered by the mother are the same whether the baby is a boy or girl. Clearly, whatever the reason for the doubling of the time of a mother's uncleanness in the case of a baby girl, it has nothing to do with 'the male chauvinism of the culture' which God is said by some commentators to 'go along with'.[2] Human beings, whether male or female, are equal in value before God. Both male and female are created in God's image (see Gen. 1:26-30).

The **'burnt offering'** on this occasion was to consist of **'a lamb of the first year'**. In the case of mothers who were too poor to offer such an expensive offering, two doves or two pigeons could be substituted (12:8; see 1:14-17). Because this was a required offering it was necessary to make this provision for poor families. This was the offering that Mary brought, emphasizing the poverty of Jesus' earthly parents (see Luke 2:22-24). Besides the propitiatory element, the sacrifice may well have been considered a thanksgiving offering for the gift of a child. Burnt offerings as well as peace offerings were brought as expressions of gratitude (see 22:18).

A pigeon or dove was required for the **'sin offering'**. This expiatory offering was the final act in the mother's return to the worship of God at the tabernacle. She was in the fullest sense ceremonially clean **'from the flow of her blood'** (12:7). By the presentation of these two offerings to the priest at the tabernacle, **'atonement'** was made **'for her, and she will be clean'** (12:8). These verses make it clear that it was blood discharge following a birth, not sexual misconduct or the process of giving birth, that made the mother unclean and unfit to worship at the tabernacle. Furthermore, the chapter shows that, while her *own blood* made her unclean, she could come near God's holy place with a *substitute blood sacrifice* that was acceptable to God for her complete purification. Gordon Wenham expresses the profound nature of what is being taught when he states that 'Blood is at once the most effective ritual cleanser ... and the most polluting substance when it is in the wrong place.'[3]

The cross of Jesus displays the greater mystery to which the old Sinai regulations point. At the very place where human sinfulness is seen in all its profound ugliness, there we see the amazing love for sinners. The cleanest of all people was found in the most unclean place bearing the uncleanness of sin so that sinners who look to him might be presented clean before God's holy presence. On Golgotha's hill — the place of a skull — amid ruin, decay and death, God's perfect sacrifice for human uncleanness was offered to bring cleansing to sinners the world over.

Through this very traumatic and dangerous experience in a mother's life God directed his people to spiritual realities. Sin has made us unclean and we are in the most unwholesome state because the wages of sin is death. How thankful we ought to be that God has provided such an amazing sacrifice in the gift of his own precious Son, Jesus Christ!

Jesus was conceived by the Holy Spirit, yet he was born into our world in the way all babies enter it. When the time came, Mary gave birth to 'her firstborn son' (Luke 2:6-7). He was, as Paul explains in Galatians 4:4, a mother's son ('born of a woman'), a real human being, born into a pious Jewish home where the law of Moses was respected ('born under the law'). This is why his parents had Jesus circumcised on the eighth day. Then, thirty-three days later, when Mary's period of purification was over 'according to the law of Moses', his parents came with Jesus to the temple to offer the necessary sacrifices both for his mother's ritual cleansing and in order to present their firstborn son to the Lord (Luke 2:22-24; cf. Exod. 13:2,12,15; 22:29; Neh. 10:35-36). All the requirements of the law were carried out, and it is in that same context of fulfilling 'all righteousness' that Jesus set himself to go to the cross. He did this to redeem those under the curse of the law, and whatever other slave masters we might be under, so that we may experience the blessing of sonship through the Spirit (Gal. 3:13-14; 4:4-6).

14.
Uncleanness from leprosy

Please read Leviticus 13:1-59

The way in which AIDS is often regarded in our modern world is similar to how leprosy was considered in former days. The English word 'leper' has become a pejorative word and is often used to describe a person who is shunned as being a danger to the good of society. Such a use of the biblical word is unfortunate and lacks a concern for true leprosy sufferers. Nevertheless, it has been Bible-believing Christians, motivated by the love of Christ, who have been at the forefront in helping leprosy sufferers both medically and practically.

Leprosy

This chapter and the next deal with uncleanness in human skin (13:2-46; 14:1-32), in clothes (13:47-59) and in the walls of houses (14:33-53). Clearly the word translated 'leprosy' cannot mean, in every case, leprosy as we know it (that is, Hansen's disease).[1] We shall, however, continue to use the traditional terms, 'leprosy' and 'leprous', to describe these various scaly or disfiguring conditions that are obvious on human skin, on clothing and articles made of leather and on the walls of houses.

It is interesting that in these chapters Moses and Aaron are not required, as in the case of almost all the other laws (see 11:1-2; 12:1-2; 15:1-2), to pass on God's instructions to the people (13:1-2). The skin disorders are not left for the people to diagnose themselves; they must come to the priests. The latter are the experts in calling for periods of quarantine and deciding whether the sufferers' condition renders them unclean or not.

While health and safety may be considered a by-product of these laws, their primary concern is religious. There are three reasons for this conclusion. They all arise out of the text.

Clean and unclean

Guidance is given to the priests concerning these skin complaints, not with a view to medical treatment, but to enable them to recognize what is clean and what is unclean (see 10:10-11). As the summary statement makes clear, the instruction for cases of 'leprous' skin, garments or houses was 'to teach when it is unclean and when it is clean' (14:57).[2] Even the quarantine periods are not stated to be for the purpose of isolating and treating the problem. All they do is allow time for the condition to develop or fade so that the priest can make an accurate pronouncement. Aaron and his sons were not early physicians, but priests who taught the people about God's holiness and its implications by what they said and by the ritual actions they performed.

Decay and death

These 'leprous' conditions in the skin, in clothes and in the walls of houses were evidences of unwholesomeness. A chronic skin condition that caused the skin to rot, flake, peel and weep with blood was a clear sign of decay and corruption. Aaron did not want his leprous sister Miriam to be like one born dead with the flesh half eaten (Num. 12:12). Nothing so unwholesome was fit to exist in the clean camp, and a person associated with such an unclean state was disqualified from worshipping the holy God who is set apart from all that is unclean and unwholesome. The same principle is being emphasized in chapter after chapter to bring home to Israel that they are a people set apart for God and that they cannot worship at God's sanctuary while in an unclean condition.

Plague and punishment

The Authorized / King James Version speaks of the 'plague' of leprosy (13:2,9, etc.). This Hebrew noun, which appears sixty-six times in these two chapters, is translated in modern versions with words such as 'infection' or 'infectious', 'sore' and 'disease'. Perhaps 'attack' would be nearer the mark, as, for example, when people speak of 'an attack of bronchitis' or influenza. In this chapter and the next it is not suggested that the 'plague' is necessarily a punishment for some known sin in an individual's life, even when God is expressly said to be the author of the attack, as we see in 14:34: 'I put the leprous plague in a house...' But more often than not in the Old Testament a 'plague' is seen as a punishment from God. Because Pharaoh took Abram's wife, we read, 'The LORD plagued Pharaoh and his house with great plagues' (Gen. 12:17), anticipating the great plagues at the time of the Exodus (see Exod. 11:1). The Lord punished Miriam with leprosy (Num. 12:9-10; Deut. 24:9), and when King Uzziah disobeyed, 'The LORD struck the king, so that he was a leper' (2 Kings 15:5).[3] Holiness was not merely a matter of ritual; it was about moral purity. This is what made true religious devotion in Israel so different from the idolatrous worship of the Canaanites, where sexual orgies took place within their temple precincts.

These chapters give the priests, firstly, instructions to determine and declare what conditions are clean and unclean; secondly, instructions concerning the actions to be taken if a person or object is declared unclean; and, thirdly, instructions concerning the purification ritual in cases where healing has taken place.

Scaly conditions in skin and clothes (13:1-59)

The symptoms described

First, seven skin conditions are presented, including a detailed description of symptoms, so that an accurate pronouncement on the state of the person could be made (13:2-44). As the text indicates, on inspecting the condition, the priest could make three kinds of pronouncements: he could declare the person **'leprous'** and **'unclean'** (13:3); he could **'isolate'** the person pending further examinations before declaring him or her **'clean'** or **'unclean'** (13:4-8); or thirdly, he could declare the individual **'clean'** immediately (13:38-40).

The mental state in which Israelites found themselves over their skin conditions would not have been dissimilar to that of people today when a growth has been detected. The waiting process can be unbearable. What relief there is when the doctor declares it non-malignant, but how devastating when it is found to be cancerous!

1. *Skin eruptions* (13:2-8)

In the case of pimples, rashes and spots, many would be of a minor and transitory nature, but they would still need to be examined before the all-clear could be given. If a person suspects he has a **'leprous'** attack he must show it to the priest. There are two initial tests applied by the priest. Firstly, has the affected area turned the hair white? Secondly, is it deeper than the skin? If the tests are positive, then the person is pronounced **'unclean'** (13:3).

Where these symptoms do not exist the person is isolated for a week and re-examined. The test now is whether the symptoms have progressed (13:4). If they have not spread the person is confined for **'another seven days'** (13:5). At the end of this fourteen-day period, if the affected area has faded and has not spread then the person is declared clean. A normal life could then resume after the person's clothes had been washed (13:6; cf. 11:25,28,40). The need for washing indicated that the skin condition, though in the end pronounced clean, was nevertheless considered potentially serious, making a token purification ritual necessary. Cleansing that required only bathing and washing clothes indicated that the impurities were of a minor nature.[4] However, if the skin problem starts to spread again after the all-clear has been given, the person must return to the priest and be pronounced unclean — **'It is leprosy'** (13:7-8).

2. *Chronic skin conditions* (13:9-17)

Two tests are applied when a person shows signs of developing a **'leprous'** complaint that can be described as **'an old leprosy'** or 'a chronic skin disease'. Firstly, has the swollen area become white and turned the hair white? Secondly, is there a **'spot of raw flesh in the swelling'**? The presence of 'ulcerated tissue' means there is no need for any quarantine period: the person can be pronounced unclean immediately (13:10-11,14-15). If the **'raw flesh'** turns white — that is, the open sore has healed — then the person can be re-examined by the priest and declared clean (13:16-17).

If the skin condition has covered the whole body and left the skin white all over, then the priest can pronounce the person clean (13:12-13). This has caused headaches to many people because they have understood 'white' to signify a leprous condition. The confusion has been caused by translators adding 'white as' when the word 'snow' is used of leprosy in Numbers 12:10 and 2 Kings 5:27. But the colour 'white' is not found in the original text of these verses. Sufferers from bad dandruff, when they comb their hair, find particles of dry skin on their clothes like flakes of snow. That is the point of the comparison. Both Miriam and Gehazi were leprous 'like snow', not in the sense that their skin became 'white like snow', but that it became 'flaky like snow'. One of the two miraculous signs that God gave Moses was that his hand became leprous 'like snow', in the sense of 'flaky like snow', and then was restored again like the rest of his skin (Exod. 4:6-7).

The whiteness of the skin in the present passage is therefore not a sign of leprosy but of clean skin after a leprous skin disorder. It is like new white skin after scabs have peeled off. I well remember a student being covered from head to toe in sores that resembled the cold sores that usually develop on the lip. The crust of the sores finally dropped off leaving the skin beautifully smooth and clean like that of a newborn baby, which is precisely how the flesh of Naaman is described when he was healed of leprosy — 'like the flesh of a little child' (2 Kings 5:14).

3. Skin trouble with boils (13:18-23)

Where a complication arises over a boil, so that a white swelling or a reddish-white shiny spot appears, the priest must examine it. If, as in the first case, the spot is deeper than the skin and the hair has turned white the person is pronounced **'unclean'** (13:19-20). Where these symptoms are not present and the brightness has faded then the person is to be isolated for seven days. If the shiny spot has spread the person is unclean, for he or she has the plague mark of the skin disease.[5] But if it has not spread such people can be pronounced clean (13:21-23).

We have two examples in the Bible where boils caused complications in the skin. The sixth plague to attack the Egyptians is described as boils that broke out in sores (Exod. 9:9-11). As for Job's state, his boils covered all his body so that his friends did not recognize him. He used a piece of broken pot to scrape his flaking skin (Job 2:7-8,12).

4. Skin trouble resulting from burns (13:24-28)

If the burn fails to heal properly and becomes a spot that is reddish or white, then the priest must inspect it. It is pronounced unclean if the familiar symptoms are present — the hair is white and the spot is deeper than the skin. It is a leprous 'attack' (13:25). If the symptoms are absent the person is isolated and re-examined seven days later. If the condition has spread in that time then the person is unclean; but if there has been no change and the colour has faded he or she is declared clean (13:26-28).

5. Skin trouble in the scalp or beard (13:29-37)

The condition described is sometimes translated 'itch' or **'scall'**. The word is probably referring to a 'scurfy patch' on the scalp or where the beard grows. A man or woman is pronounced unclean if he or she has a scurfy patch that is deeper than the skin and has turned the hair yellow and thin. But if the patch is only skin deep, yet still does not have normal black hair, the person is to be isolated and re-examined again in seven days' time. If the condition has not spread and there are no yellow hairs he is to shave himself, but not the area affected, and be confined for a further period of seven days. The priest can then pronounce him clean if there are still no signs that the patch has spread. But the presence of the scurfy patch has rendered the person unclean to a certain extent, so that he is required to wash his clothes (13:34; cf. 13:6). If there are indications that the patch is spreading, the person is to be pronounced unclean.

6. Harmless rashes (13:38-39)

If a man or woman has many obvious spots on their skin, yet these spots are dull white in appearance with no other symp-toms, he or she can be immediately declared clean. It will be clear from the above examples that it is skin which has hairs that are abnormal in appearance, that show signs of decay, that dig into the flesh or that produce raw flesh, that makes a person unclean.

7. Skin trouble with baldness (13:40-44)

While baldness itself (usually a male condition), whether of the entire head or forehead, does not make a man unclean, if a reddish-white swelling develops in the bald area and it resembles that of the other unclean skin conditions already mentioned, then the priest shall declare the man unclean.

The regulations for a person who is declared unclean

Secondly, regulations are set out for those found to be unclean due to the skin condition (13:45-46). They are instructed to tear their clothes, untidy their hair, cover their mouths,[6] cry out, **'Unclean! Unclean!'** and live alone **'outside the camp'** all the time they have the 'plague'. This public display emphasizes their state. The signs of death in their skin are mirrored in their appearance and in their accommodation. When people mourned for the dead, they tore their clothes and let their hair become unkempt (see 10:6; 21:10). When Jacob learnt of Joseph's supposed death he tore his clothes (Gen. 37:34). When his wife died, Ezekiel was told not to show the usual signs of mourning (Ezek. 24:17).

As a result of this chronic state of uncleanness, the leprous person was excluded from the clean area in and around the tabernacle. He or she was banished to a lonely existence far away from the presence of the holy God who made his earthly home in the tabernacle. This was a living death and it reminds us of what happened to Adam and Eve. When they sinned they were put outside the holy garden of God (Gen. 3:23-24). The punishment meted out on Cain included being banished even further from God's blessing and presence (Gen. 4:14,16).

Conditions that affect clothing

Third, a **'plague'** in clothing that resembles flaky skin diseases is now considered. Like the skin complaints it is a condition that is clearly abnormal and disfigures the surface of the material. The same procedures are put in place for inspecting and pronouncing on the condition of articles of clothing made of wool, linen or leather.

If a garment, or anything made of skin, is attacked by a greenish or reddish plague mark, it must be taken to the priest for examination. Some form of mildew or fungal growth is suggested. As with a skin condition, the article is to be set aside for seven days and re-examined by the priest. If the trouble has spread it is clearly not a surface problem. It has penetrated below the skin of the material, which is probably what the phrase **'the warp or ... woof'** indicates, as with symptoms that were 'deeper than the skin' in the section on skin complaints (see 13:3). The material must be declared **'unclean'** and **'burned in the fire'** (13:51-52).

On the other hand, if the 'plague' does not appear to have spread, the priest is to order that the item be washed and then examined again in a week's time. If there is no improvement in the colour of the plague mark, even though it has not spread, the article is unclean and must be burned (13:53-55). But if the mark has faded in colour after washing, the priest is to tear out the affected area and the rest of the material can then be reused. However, if the trouble reappears later in some other part of the article it means the 'plague' is still spreading and so the whole thing must be burned (13:56-57). If the plague mark has not spread after the affected part was torn out, then the material is to be washed a second time and pronounced clean (13:58).

The significance of these laws

Why all this detailed legislation on what to a modern reader seems so pernickety? The summary statement (13:59) provides the clue, along with all the other laws in this section (Lev. 11 – 15). The priests are instructed **'to pronounce it clean or to pronounce it unclean'**. As we saw earlier, their task is 'to distinguish between holy and unholy, and between unclean and clean' (10:10). This entire chapter on 'leprous'

conditions is about the priest declaring what is clean and
what is unclean. It was on the basis of the symptoms that the
person or material was declared clean or unclean. If the
trouble appeared to be serious and long-lasting, causing the
person or the material to appear abnormal and decayed, and
if it was deep-seated, it was unclean because it was incompatible with life and with what was complete.

In Leviticus we are taught that holiness is associated with
wholeness of life. Any visible permanent signs of degener-
acy and abnormality were incompatible with the most
wholesome, holy God, the author of life. They were clear
physical indications of impurity. To preserve the holiness of
the tabernacle that lay at the centre of the clean camp of
Israel where the holy God ordained that he would be present
with his people in a visible and felt way, it was necessary to
remove from the camp those individuals and articles which
were obviously and physically unwholesome. They spoiled
the wholeness of the camp. These outward requirements
reminded the people of what happened when the first human
couple sinned and were removed from the paradise of God.

The legislation also taught the people the deep theological
truth that only what is pure and wholesome can come near
the presence of the pure and holy God. This part of God's
Word speaks to us today, as we can sometimes become slack
in our view of who God is and casual in our approach to him.

> Eternal Light! Eternal Light!
> How pure the soul must be,
> When, placed within Thy searching sight,
> It shrinks not, but with calm delight
> Can live and look on Thee.[7]

15.
Restoring the outcasts

Please read Leviticus 14:1-57

The 'leprosy' referred to in these chapters was not considered incurable. We have, of course, examples of God miraculously healing people like Miriam and Naaman (Num. 12:12-13; 2 Kings 5:14). But there would be other cases where a skin disorder that rendered a person unclean would clear up through the natural healing processes of the human body. What we do not find in the Mosaic law is any indication of the way in which a leper could be cured. This chapter is not about how lepers can find healing, but how they can return to the camp when they find that they are healed. Can you imagine the feeling of people who realize that their skin no longer shows signs of the disease and that they can apply to re-enter the camp and be with their families? But there was no quick and easy way back into the community. Just as astronauts returning from space are subjected to rigorous tests and elaborate processes before they are allowed to mix again with family and friends, so the healed leper had to be patient and submit to close examinations and special rituals. The priest was responsible for ensuring that the outcast person was properly clean and fit to be among God's holy people.

Restoration rituals (14:1-32)

As the previous chapter indicated, the leprous person was considered to be in a state of living death. Death and death-like situations were viewed as being among the most unclean conditions possible. To return, therefore, from a deathlike state outside the camp to a position of life in the camp necessitated a special ritual process. The ritual did not bring healing. Israel's pagan neighbours engaged in all kinds of magical rites to obtain cures, but that was not the purpose of these regulations. Their sole design was to readmit into the holy community those whose unclean skin diseases had already completely healed.

The ceremony outside the camp (14:2-8)

The priest examined the individual and if he was satisfied that the person was indeed healed, there followed two distinct procedures on day one.

First, two clean live birds were brought. As on the Day of Atonement, when one goat was killed and the other released (see 16:8-10), so here one bird was killed and the other set free. The blood of the dead bird was caught and mixed with fresh running (literally, 'living') water in an earthenware pot. Using cedar wood, scarlet yarn and hyssop, the blood-and-water mixture was sprinkled seven times over the person healed, who was then pronounced clean. The second bird was also dipped in the blood and water before being allowed to go free.

Secondly, the healed person was directed to wash his body and clothes and shave completely. For the remainder of the week the individual was in a transitional state, being clean enough to enter the camp but not clean enough to live with the family: **'He shall come into the camp, and shall stay outside his tent'** (14:8).

The ceremony inside the camp (14:9-20)

This final part of the acceptance ritual, such as washing, sacrifice and the use of oil and blood, was reminiscent of the priestly ordination ceremony (see 8:1-36). Again, there were two main parts, only this time they are distinguished by particular days.

First, on **'the seventh day'** (14:9), the person was again to shave completely, including **'head'**, **'beard'** and **'eyebrows'**, and wash clothes and body. People shaved in this way would stand out a mile in a culture where a man would never be seen without a beard, nor a woman with a bald head. This part of the cleansing rite signified the complete eradication of the skin disease and presented the cleansed person like a newborn baby.

Secondly, on **'the eighth day'** (14:10), the healed person was to bring one female and two male unblemished lambs, along with grain and oil, to the priest at the entrance to the tabernacle. All the sacrifices apart from the peace offering were to be presented, commencing with the trespass offering. One of the male lambs became the trespass offering and, along with a quantity of oil, it was presented as a wave offering before being slaughtered. Some of the lamb's blood was collected and placed on the extremities of the right side of the healed person — the ear lobe, thumb and big toe.

The oil was poured into the palm of the priest's left hand and with his right hand he was to sprinkle it seven times before the Lord. With some of the oil remaining in his hand, the priest daubed it on the same extremities where the blood of the trespass offering had been placed, while the rest was poured on the individual's head. In this way, **'The priest shall make atonement for him before the LORD'** (14:18).

Only when this had been done could the more regular offerings be presented — namely, the sin, the burnt and the grain offerings, and in that order. Thus again, **'The priest**

shall make atonement for him, and he shall be clean' (14:20).

Provisions for poor people (14:21-32)

In the case of a poor person **'who cannot afford the usual cleansing'** (14:32), a smaller amount of oil and flour was allowed for the grain offering and two turtledoves or pigeons, **'such as he is able to afford'** (14:22), were accepted for the sin and burnt offerings. However, a male lamb was still necessary for the trespass offering and the same **'log of oil'** for the sprinkling and daubing ceremony (14:24; cf. 14:12).

Gospel truth

There are a number of ways in which this passage points us forward to the good news concerning Jesus Christ.

1. Jesus had power to heal leprosy

What the law could not do, Jesus Christ can do. The priest could not heal the leper. All he could do was to diagnose and monitor and wait for healing to take place. But Jesus, our great High Priest, when he was on earth ministering to people's needs, actually healed lepers. When they came up to him seeking help, Jesus even touched them. Far from Jesus being infected and made unclean, the opposite was the case. The lepers were instantly healed. Something new had appeared, bringing to an end the old ritual laws. Jesus did not do miracles for the sake of it. There was always a purpose in his actions. The miracles clearly displayed the power of God, as in the days of Moses and Elisha (Exod. 4:6; 2 Kings 5:7-8). But they were also signs of God's rule on earth which Jesus had come to establish, in anticipation of the end-time re-creation when sin would be eradicated, and with it all disease, distortion and death (Luke 7:22; Rev. 21:4-5; 22:3). Jesus preached the kingdom, or rule, of God and used stories and miracles to illustrate his message.

2. Jesus and the priests

During his earthly ministry, when Jesus healed lepers he upheld the law by telling them to go to the priest and offer the necessary sacrifices. He had not yet offered himself as the perfect sacrifice to end all blood sacrifices. But when the priests examined the lepers and pronounced them clean this would in itself have been a testimony to the unique power of Jesus (Luke 5:14; 17:14). The priests, who were often opposed to him, would have been forced to acknowledge that Jesus was in fact greater than Moses and the law.

3. Outside the camp

The cleansing ritual began with the priest going outside the camp. In the same way, Jesus our High Priest went outside the camp, and in order 'that he might sanctify the people with his own blood, suffered outside the gate' (Heb. 13:12).

4. The symbolism of the two birds

The two clean birds represented the Israelite sufferer. As we are told in the similar procedure for cleansing a leprous house (14:53), they were symbolic of the need for an atoning sacrifice as well as evidence of a complete work of cleansing. The two birds parallel the ceremony of the two goats on the Day of Atonement (see Lev. 16). However, the blood of the bird that was killed was sprinkled seven times over the healed leper. It was like a purification offering, but instead of cleansing the tabernacle from the uncleanness of the Israelites, as in the case of the goat's blood (16:14-19), it purified the body of the healed person so that the word 'clean' could be pronounced by the priest (14:7). Further, as the scapegoat symbolically carried away the nation's sin to indicate its complete destruction, so the live bird, closely identified with the dead bird by being dipped into its blood, was allowed to fly freely away, assuring the healed person that through the sacrificial death there was complete cleansing and life. Christ by his sacrificial death has procured cleansing and life for all his people. In rising from the dead on the third day and ascending into heaven, he was released from the chains of death, indicating that his life-giving, cleansing work was done. Jesus was 'delivered up because of our offences, and was raised because of our justification' (Rom. 4:25).

The cedar wood, scarlet and hyssop are objects frequently associated with purification rites in the law, the latter two particularly so as they point to sacrificial blood. The scarlet yarn, symbolic of blood, was probably used to tie the wood and hyssop together as a tool for sprinkling. Using hyssop, the posts and lintels were daubed with sacrificial blood at the time of the first Passover (Exod. 12:22). There was life and salvation for all who came under the sacrificial blood. This is the message of the cross.

As for the details concerning the bird's lifeblood mixed with 'living' or fresh water, both elements were used for purification. There would have been very little blood from a small bird, so that the water was needed to produce enough liquid to sprinkle the person. John bears witness to the fact that Jesus was truly human and really did die on the cross by mentioning that blood and water flowed from his sword-pierced side (John 19:34). Like the blood and water in the cleansing ritual, John is showing that life and cleansing flow from Jesus' death.[1]

5. The importance of 'cleansing'

The Gospel writers always use the word 'cleansed' when referring to lepers who were healed by Jesus. They do not write in this way when referring to people whose sight or hearing was restored by Jesus. By so doing they are drawing our attention to these chapters from Leviticus and to the spiritual pollution which the leprous conditions so graphically illustrated. The Bible can use a variety of human ailments to speak metaphorically of human sin, such as blindness, a stiff neck and hardness of heart. Other human physical disabilities and diseases are also used to illustrate the effects of sin, as we shall see in the next chapter. Not every type of disease is covered by these laws, for to make all sick people ceremonially unclean would have been quite impracticable. The leprous conditions, however, in which the skin or surface was disfigured, are obvious visual aids for what was unwholesome and unclean in the moral and spiritual sphere. 'Leprosy' was a clear symbol of human sin. The prophets followed Moses in using visible wounds and sores to speak metaphorically of the sin problem:

> From the sole of the foot even to the head,
> There is no soundness in it,
> But wounds and bruises and putrefying sores
> > (Isa. 1:6; cf. Jer. 30:12-15).

It was natural, then, that cleansing from these conditions became symbolic of the removal of sin and its effects. The elaborate cleansing rituals had no medical function; they were given to teach spiritual lessons. David saw the significance of these instructions, for in his prayer of repentance he refers to the hyssop of the cleansing ritual that took place outside the camp: 'Purge me with hyssop, and I shall be clean; wash me, and I shall be whiter than snow' (Ps. 51:7).

In the New Testament Paul urges fellow Christians: 'Let us cleanse ourselves from all filthiness of the flesh and spirit, perfecting holiness in the fear of God' (2 Cor. 7:1).

6. From death to life

The journey for a healed leper from a deathlike state outside his family and the worshipping community to a new life in fellowship with God and his people is one full of significance and meaning. The New Testament informs us that we are all by nature dead in trespasses and sins and far off from the blessings of God's family. It is by the washing of regeneration and renewing of the Holy Spirit that we are made alive and fit for God's presence (Eph. 2:1-6). This also is made possible through Jesus Christ's death for sinners. Water baptism is the sign and seal of that radical spiritual bath that has happened to all true believers (Titus 3:4-6; John 3:5; 13:10-11). Without that initial cleansing work by the Spirit we cannot embrace Christ's atoning work on the cross that is so essential for bringing us into fellowship with God. The rituals outside and inside the camp convey this need for inner cleansing and for an atoning sacrifice that will allow us to come near to God and to know that the debt we owe has been satisfied, that God's wrath has been removed and that we have been completely pardoned and cleansed of all our sins. How wonderful it must have felt for the former lepers to be back again within the family of Israel! The elaborate rituals gave these former outcasts all the assurance they needed that they were healed, restored and accepted. For believers in Jesus Christ, what an amazing fact it is that we 'who once were far off have been made near by the blood of Christ'! (Eph. 2:13). While the ordinances of baptism and the Lord's Supper are signs and seals of spiritual realities, our assurance comes through the Spirit by looking to Christ alone. 'Therefore, brethren, having boldness to enter the Holy Place by the blood of Jesus, by a new and living way which he consecrated for us, through the veil, that is, his flesh, and having a high priest over the house of God, let us draw near with a true heart in full assurance of faith, having our hearts sprinkled from an evil conscience and our bodies washed with pure water' (Heb. 10:19-22).

7. A new birth

The washing and shaving emphasized that the disease was gone completely. The person had no hair but appeared clean and white like a newborn baby. It was as if he or she had been born all over again. Here is another pointer to the new birth in the law of Moses which Nicodemus should have known.

8. A new start

Only on the eighth day was the restored leper able to come to the sanctuary with his offerings. This was the beginning of a new week and spoke of a new start, a new creation even. Like the infants of Israel who were circumcised on the eighth day and made members of the covenant community, so those cured of leprosy were restored as if from the dead. They had become 'as it were born again', to use Calvin's words.[2] The cleansing ritual on this day also included their being daubed with the blood of the trespass offering and with oil on the right-hand side of the person's bodily extremities, as well as being anointed with oil. The action with blood and oil links the healed person both to the altar and to the priest, thus bringing cleansing and consecration.

Regulations concerning contaminated houses (14:33-53)

This passage deals with a leprous growth in the walls of houses made of stone and covered on the inside with mud or plaster. It suggests some kind of fungal growth or mould. Unlike the verses dealing with 'leprosy' in fabrics and leather (13:47-59), this section on 'leprosy' in the walls of houses has a separate introduction of its own (14:33). While there are similarities with what has gone before, a fresh heading is understandable. These verses look forward to a time when the nation of Israel would be settled in **'Canaan'** and living in houses. What is more, it is acknowledged that the Lord is the one who will give them the land **'as a possession'**. Ultimately, the land belongs to the Lord and it is his gift to his people. It is probably in this light that we are to view the statement that the Lord is the one who puts (**'I put'**) the **'plague in a house'** (14:34). The plague may be due to natural wear and tear, but because God is over the whole natural order it can be said to come from him. This is more probable than to suppose that in this passage it means that God sends the plague as a punishment. We should also remember that the word 'plague' has already been used for leprosy in humans and garments with no suggestion of its being a judgement from God (see 13:2).[3]

The first signs of an outbreak

The symptoms for 'leprosy' in the walls of houses are similar to those affecting humans and fabrics. If the owner of a house detects trouble, he is to report it to the priest, who then orders the building to be emptied of its contents before examining it. If the house were to be declared unclean while the contents were in it, then everything would become unclean, which could mean financial ruin for the occupants. Hence the need to remove everything as a precaution. If the priest detects greenish or reddish marks on the inside or outside walls, the house is to be shut up for seven days. A second inspection is to be made a week later and if the marks have spread, the priest is to order that the affected material be removed and thrown into **'an unclean place outside the city'** (14:40). Clearly there were areas declared 'clean' and 'unclean' outside the camp or city walls (see 4:12; 6:11). New stones and mortar were to replace what had been removed. Every effort was made to save the house from being destroyed.

Subsequent outbreaks

If the leprous attack broke out again in the wall after all these efforts had been tried, then the house was declared **'unclean'** (14:44). It had to be pulled down and the stone and mortar thrown into **'an unclean place'** outside the city. All who entered the building during the quarantine period were **'unclean until evening'**, while those who slept or ate in it were required to wash their clothes as well.

On the other hand, if the leprous attack had not spread after the house had been replastered, then **'the priest shall pronounce the house clean, because the plague is healed'** (14:48). The house must then be subject to a purification ritual that is similar to the ritual that took place outside the camp for the healed leper and involved two birds, cedar wood, scarlet material and hyssop. This is probably the reason why the passage is placed after the cleansing of people who have been healed (see 14:1-7). The house is sprinkled seven times with the blood of the dead bird mixed with fresh water. As for the other bird, again it is dipped into the mixture of blood and water and released outside the city in the open field. In this way **'atonement'** is made for the house and it is cleansed (14:52-53). No sacrifices at the sanctuary are needed as the house itself has not sinned.

More gospel truth

1. Creation spoiled by sin

Just as 'leprosy' in humans is a pointer to the sad effects of
sin in spoiling our lives and separating us from God and
others, so 'leprosy' in houses is a reminder of the way
human sin has led to a disfigured and distorted creation. The
creation 'was subjected to futility' and under 'the bondage of
corruption' (Rom. 8:20-21). Not only do we humans need
rescuing, the very creation needs releasing from the effects
of sin and God's judgement.

2. Creation restored

Just as the purification ritual for the cleansing of a house and
its 'atonement' is similar to the ritual for healed humans to
be brought back into the holy community, so the atoning
death of Christ is effective not only for believing sinners to
be members of God's heavenly city, but for the very creation
itself to be reconstituted so that God may be as much at
home on the earth as in heaven (see Rev. 21:2-3,22-23;
2 Peter 3:13). By his cross, Jesus has reconciled all things to
himself (Col. 1:20). Our Lord died to bring about a new
heaven and earth. As we are delivered from the bondage of
sin and Satan, so creation is to be released from the bondage
of corruption. Believers groan, eagerly awaiting the redemption of the body, and the creation also groans, looking with
keen expectation for the new creation (Rom. 8:18-23).

3. God is in control

Not only is God the ultimate owner of this world, he is also
the one who governs and controls all things. We are not in
the hands of impersonal fatalistic forces. The good, wise

creator God is in charge, and he is the one who '[puts] the leprous plague in a house' (14:34), who gives life and takes it, who wounds and heals, who brings prosperity and creates calamity. 'I, the LORD, do all these things' (Isa. 45:7; cf. Deut. 32:39). We are inclined these days only to think of God bringing healing, wealth and life. But the Bible is clear that in a world where people are in rebellion against his loving rule, the true God, for good and gracious reasons, ordains to bring ill-health, poverty and death, both to warn sinners of the greater judgement to come and to restrain or remove evil people.

4. The need for purity in the home

As the New Testament uses the purification laws to urge Christians to be clean and holy in their living, so we can draw out a principle from the ritual cleansing of houses to challenge us. It reminds us of the need to make sure that our homes are free from impurity of every kind. When Jacob prepared himself and his family to worship God at Bethel he urged them to put away foreign gods, to purify themselves from their moral uncleanness and to change their clothes (Gen. 35:2). Are we harbouring unclean items in our homes, such as magazines and videos that pollute the mind? Are we watching television programmes that are unhelpful to our spiritual development, or using the computer to access pornographic sites? Clear out the unclean trash from your home and put it in the waste bin, and see to it that the Lord Jesus Christ has central place. Allow the Word of God to cleanse your thinking and life and that of your family.

16.
Uncleanness from genital discharges

Please read Leviticus 15:1-33

Not everyone would catch a leprous condition in their lifetime, but generally all adults would find themselves ritually unclean from some kind of genital discharge or emission. These secretions provided yet another opportunity to impress upon the people that uncleanness was incompatible with holiness. Holiness for the people of God involved separation *from* uncleanness as well as separation *to* the Lord's service.[1] While these ritual laws are no longer in operation now that the Messiah has come, the fundamental principle still applies to those redeemed by the blood of Jesus to serve the living and true God.

The passage is skilfully formed so that male discharges, both abnormal (15:2-15) and normal (15:16-18), are mirrored by the normal (15:19-24) and abnormal (15:25-30) female discharges.[2] This balance between the two halves of the chapter not only emphasizes the unity of the sexes, but makes it possible to affirm the 'one flesh' union of the man and woman in marriage at the midway point in the structure (15:18).

The uncleanness arising from these genital discharges is again ceremonial and therefore given to convey spiritual and moral truth. There is no suggestion that sex is sinful or dirty. Marriage is to be held in honour and there is nothing unclean about the marriage bed. What is sinful and dirty is sexual immorality (see Heb. 13:4), but that is not the point at issue in this chapter.

Sometimes abnormal secretions were seen as a righteous punishment for sinful behaviour. David pronounces a curse on the family of Joab, on account of Abner's murder, which includes people being afflicted with leprosy and discharges (2 Sam. 3:29). But, as with the leprous conditions, there is no thought in this chapter of these abnormal discharges being the result of particular sinful activity. Because the passage is about ceremonial uncleanness and purification rituals, it follows that any health, hygiene and other benefits detected here are secondary spin-offs and not the primary reason for the legislation.

Abnormal male emissions (15:2-15)

When the text speaks of a discharge from his **'body'** (literally, 'flesh') in contexts like this it is referring to secretions from the man's genitals (see 15:19 in the case of a woman). The rest of the chapter is specific in detailing discharges from the reproductive organs. Anal discharges such as diarrhoea or bleeding from haemorrhoids are not included.

Description and action (15:2-12)

The discharge could either be fairly runny or thick enough to cause a blockage. It has been the opinion among the Jews even before the coming of Christ that the abnormal, long-term complaint described here is gonorrhoea. But whatever disease it was, such long-term secretions made the man unclean, which meant that he was unable to participate fully

in the life of the community, particularly in its worship. It did
not necessarily mean his expulsion from the community.
Nevertheless, his uncleanness was very potent. Anything the
man touched or sat on became unclean. Any person who
came into contact with the man or his saliva, or an article
that the man had touched, became a secondary source of
uncleanness. Such persons would need to wash their clothes
and bathe in water and would remain unclean for the rest of
the day (15:5-11). Contaminated clay pots could not be
cleansed with water; they had to be destroyed (15:12; cf.
6:28; 11:33). The more expensive wooden implements,
however, could be rinsed in water and reused.

The exception (15:11) enabled the unclean man not only
to live at home but to experience some degree of normality.
If he washed his hands before touching anybody, or anything, his impurity was not passed on to others, but he still
had to be careful where he sat.

In Numbers 5:1-4 the law is more stringent. It directs that
not only male and female lepers, but 'everyone who has a
discharge, and whoever becomes defiled by a dead body'
was to be put outside the camp. Perhaps this further legislation applied where the unclean discharge had become long-
term and severe and when it was more difficult to find
enough water for washing continuously, as, for example, in
the wilderness wanderings.[3] According to Josephus, this is
how people with genital discharges were treated in New
Testament times; they were banished from the city like
lepers.[4]

Again, God used this very physical condition to teach
spiritual lessons. Just as these unnatural genital secretions
made a man unclean and unfit to come near God's presence
at the tabernacle, so our sinful natures, which produce all
those loathsome corrupt thoughts and actions, make us unfit
to have fellowship with the holy God. Jesus taught that out

of our corrupt innermost being come evil things (Matt. 12:34-35).

Furthermore, sin is contagious. Minds already depraved by the sin virus can be further polluted and ruined by the corrupt lifestyles and attitudes of the people with whom we mix, or the things we see, hear or read.

Purification rituals for the cured male (15:13-15)

There are two parts to the purification process. They are not as elaborate as in the case of healed lepers. Firstly, the man must wait seven days after the discharge has stopped and then wash his clothes and bathe his body in fresh or **'running water'**.[5] Secondly, on the eighth day the man is to present himself at the door of the tabernacle with birds as an offering, either two turtledoves or two pigeons. These are the least costly offerings allowed (see 1:14-17) and are token offerings to establish the truth concerning the continuing need for blood sacrifice. The priest offers the one as a sin offering and the other as a burnt offering **'to make atonement for him before the LORD because of his discharge'** (15:15).

The purification rituals could not cure the disease, but they are given to point the people to the reality presented in the gospel. Washing with water is symbolic of the need to be cleansed at the centre of our being from the dirtiness of our sinful condition. It is by the power of the Holy Spirit in regeneration that we are cleansed (see Titus 3:5). This is the new birth that Jesus spoke of to Nicodemus (John 3:3-7). Instead of the old washing ceremonies, water baptism is now ordained as the New Testament sign of this once-and-for-all spiritual washing. The eighth day, the beginning of a new week, also suggests a new beginning, a new creation (cf. 12:3; 2 Cor. 5:17). In addition, the sacrifices symbolize the atoning work of Christ that pacifies the divine wrath and cleanses God's spiritual temples from all sin (1 John 1:7).

Normal male emissions (15:16-18)

Involuntary emissions

The law is very down to earth and in a matter-of-fact way draws our attention first to those spasmodic and involuntary emissions of semen that can happen quite naturally in an adult male. They usually take place while the man is sleeping and are popularly known as 'wet dreams'.[6] Even these normal emissions brought ritual uncleanness. The man was directed to wash his whole body with water and to be considered unclean until evening. Likewise, any affected fabric or leather had to be washed and only became clean in the evening (15:16-17).

Voluntary emissions

During sexual intercourse both the man and the woman became ceremonially unclean through the emission of semen. Cleansing again required bathing in water and remaining unclean until evening (15:18). It was for this reason that sexual intercourse was not permitted when a person had religious duties to perform (see Exod. 19:15; 1 Sam. 21:4-5). As with other normal emissions, sacrifice was not required, but the couple were ordered to wash and wait till the close of the day before being considered ceremonially clean.

How different was the religion of Israel compared with their ancient neighbours! At the pagan sanctuaries sexual activity was commonly practised. The boundaries were set very firmly for the people of God. All sexual activity was to be seen to be completely separate from the sanctuary and the worship of God. The sins of Eli's sons not only concerned crimes against the people of God but sacrilege of the worst order. They 'lay with the women who assembled at the door of the tabernacle of meeting' (1 Sam. 2:22). Church leaders must be careful not to bring the gospel into disrepute through sexual misconduct. Christian gatherings for fellowship or evangelistic outreach must not give the impression, or lay themselves open to the charge, of anything suggestive of sexual orgies.

Though verse 18 continues the subject of normal male emissions, it is made to stand out from the rest of the chapter. Instead of beginning, as one might expect, with a man lying with a woman, it is the woman who is the subject of the sentence, as if the second half of the chapter, dealing with female discharges, had already begun. At the very place where the chapter is about to cross from male to female discharges we have this distinctive law that is made the central point of the passage.[7] It is 'the only case of impurity that is under the complete control of the individuals in-volved' and thus highlights 'the equality of the responsibility in the sex act'.[8] It was God who ordained marriage and the sexual relationships bound up with that union (Gen. 2:23-25).

Though there is nothing sinful or dirty about sex in the context of marriage, nevertheless the persons became ritually unclean through engaging in the act of intercourse. This apparent anomaly follows the principle that uncleanness is associated with lack of wholeness and life. Semen, like blood, was associated with life and, although the loss of semen did not normally make a man ill or pose a threat to life in the way that a woman's loss of blood might do, it did suggest a giving up of life. Even in the natural union of procreating the emission of semen was suggestive of the essence of life being discharged.

Normal female discharges (15:19-24)

The woman's monthly loss of blood balances the man's normal genital emissions. This made her unclean for seven days even though the flow might only last for three or four days (see 12:2,4). Anyone who touched her in this state would be unclean for the rest of the day (15:19). Whatever she lay on or sat on would become unclean, and all who touched anything she had sat on would become unclean and would need to wash their clothes, bathe and consider themselves unclean until evening. Rachel used a similar ruling to deceive her father Laban (Gen. 31:33-35). If a woman started her period while a man was engaged in sexual intercourse with her, he would be in the same position as she was.[9] He too would be unclean for seven days and all he touched would become unclean (15:24). This uncleanness incurred no guilt and therefore, as with the normal male emissions, no sacrifice was required. It does not mention washing but that is probably taken as read (see 15:16-18). We know in the case of Bathsheba that she was washing herself after her monthly impurity when King David saw her (2 Sam. 11:2-4).

This monthly seven-day exclusion from society might seem very unfair and there are those who wish to use such passages as evidence that the Bible discriminates against women. But the legislation has nothing to do with unfairness and gender and everything to do with the kind of discharges that are described. Both men and women become unclean through genital discharges. A woman is unclean longer from her natural discharges because her menstrual flow lasts longer.

Blood is a symbol of life. Menstrual blood was being discharged from the body and this suggested loss of life and depicted an unwholesome condition. It was therefore incompatible with God, the source of life and all that is wholesome. No one in that condition was fit to come near God's presence.

The preachers of the Old Testament period were very bold in describing Israel's sinful condition. Ezekiel would have shocked his congregation by stating that Israel's defiled ways and deeds were 'like the uncleanness of a woman in her customary impurity' (Ezek. 36:17). Isaiah went further and considered that his people's righteous deeds were like 'filthy rags' (literally, 'soiled menstrual cloths', Isa. 64:6). On the other hand, they also proclaimed that there was a fountain opened 'for sin and for uncleanness' (Zech. 13:1).[10] A vile sinner like the repentant thief on the cross looked to that fountain and was assured that he was cleansed from all his sins and fit for paradise.

Abnormal female discharges (15:25-30)

A flow of blood that extended beyond the normal period, or was distinct from the menstrual bleeding, made the woman unclean for as long as the condition lasted. As with the abnormal male discharges, uncleanness was communicated to others through contact. Those who touched her bed or seat became unclean until evening and needed to wash their clothes and bathe in water. When the bleeding stopped she was required to wait seven days. If she was truly cured her restoration rites were the same as those for a man. She brought to the priest two pigeons or doves as sin and burnt offerings on the eighth day. The text does not mention her need to wash her clothes and bathe but that, again, is probably assumed from the parallel male case. It is notable that a woman's place in the life of the community is equal to the man's. The man does not represent the woman at the tabernacle door but the woman herself presents her own offerings to the priest. It was because the discharge was abnormal that there was need for offerings to be made.

In the New Testament we have the remarkable incident of a woman with the kind of abnormal discharge found here (Matt. 9:20-22; Mark 5:25-34; Luke 8:43-48). Instead of the woman defiling our Lord by her touch, she became whole and clean through his power. Here was another indication that with the coming of the Messiah the old Sinai covenant had had its day and a better covenant was being established. Jesus was able to do what the law could not do. The law could not make people whole, but he could. He came to undo all the effects of sin and Satan and to make people clean and whole and acceptable to God.

By drawing attention to the uncleanness of genital emissions the law symbolically emphasizes that in the very procreation of life, human beings are impure. Sinners can only produce sinners. None of us is born neutral. Before we are sinners in action we are sinners in nature (Ps. 51:5). Purification from genital emissions first of all indicates the need for a washing that can deal with our sinful natures. The one common cleansing rite was the washing with water. Even in the case of normal sexual relationships bathing in water was necessary. Our human natures are polluted and only the washing of regeneration can make us clean. It is by the power of the Holy Spirit that this inner cleansing takes place. For sinful actions or sins of omission we need the blood of Jesus to cleanse us from all sin.

Summary (15:31-33)

As the contents of the chapter are summarized the people are reminded that they are not to be in an unclean state when they go to the tabernacle. To pollute God's holy house with their uncleanness was a serious offence. Wilful desecration of the sanctuary would result in direct action from God. This severe warning at the end of the chapter was necessary because, unlike the leprous conditions where the priest was involved, these unclean situations were very personal and private, so that the people were themselves responsible for carrying out the requirements of the law.

The Bible's insistence on purity is not confined to the Old Testament or to the law of Moses. God remains holy, and unclean lips and lives cannot approach the holy presence. All must cry with the prophet, 'Woe is me, for I am undone! Because I am a man of unclean lips...' (Isa. 6:5). Or with Peter we must confess, 'Depart from me, for I am a sinful man, O Lord!' (Luke 5:8).

Let us praise God, as Matthew Henry reminds us, that we are not under the burden of these regulations concerning ritual uncleanness. In Christ, we are not only delivered from sin and Satan and have the victory over death itself, but we are free from these ceremonial rules. Nothing but sin itself can make us unclean. Those who under the old covenant were prevented from appearing at the tabernacle because of physical disabilities can come boldly before God's presence through Christ. Furthermore, the uncleanness that we contract on account of our sins can be cleansed and forgiven, not by coming to an earthly priest, but by coming to Jesus, our great High Priest, in faith and with a repentant spirit.

17.
The Day of Atonement

Please read Leviticus 16:1-34

In parts of North London where Jews have settled in sizeable numbers it is impossible not to be aware of the Day of Atonement. The roads are reasonably quiet; many of the shops are closed, and smartly dressed men and women are seen walking the streets. For Jewish people Yom Kippur, or the Day of Atonement, is the most important and solemn day of the year. Although they observe the holy day they cannot carry out the elaborate, unique rituals mentioned in Leviticus, for they have been without temple or priests for the whole of Christian history. In fulfilment of prophecy the Romans destroyed Jerusalem in A.D. 70 because the temple and its rituals had outlived their purpose.

Atonement

Two important words keep on appearing in this chapter and we are indebted to William Tyndale for inventing the English terms to convey the Hebrew originals. The first is the noun **'mercy seat'**. It is related to the other important word that has already appeared a number of times, translated into

English by the phrase **'to make atonement'**. Older commentators took this verb to mean 'to cover', but it almost certainly belongs to the same word family as the term 'ransom' (see Num. 35:31). Thus the verb 'make atonement' (16:6,10,11,16,17,18,20,24,27,30,32,33,34) means 'to pay a ransom', or 'rescue by means of a substitute'.

'Mercy seat', or 'place of atonement', describes the slab of gold 'on top of the ark' (Exod. 25:17-21) at either end of which was a golden cherub with outstretched wings. This was the place where God ordained that he would meet his people (see Exod. 25:22), and where the redeeming blood was sprinkled. To express something of the greatness of God, the place became a figure of speech for God's footstool, with the whole area between the cherubim viewed as God's throne (see Ps. 99:1; 1 Chr. 28:2). The 'mercy seat', resting on top of the ark in which the Ten Commandments were placed, marked in a symbolic way the boundary between the 'glory cloud' of the exalted Lord and God's covenant people. Here God's wrath was appeased (propitiation) and amends were made for human sin (expiation).[1] It spoke of gospel truth where, in the words of the hymn writer, 'mercy met the anger of God's rod'. It was here that God's ancient people worshipped through the high priest, their representative (see Ps. 99:5; 132:7). Imagine the horror of seeing this symbol of God's mercy destroyed and the judgement of God falling on the people, as it did when the Babylonians destroyed the temple:

> How the Lord has covered the daughter of Zion
> With a cloud in his anger!
> He cast down from heaven to the earth
> The beauty of Israel,
> And did not remember his footstool
> In the day of his anger

> (Lam. 2:1).

Thank God that no enemy can destroy the true temple. It is prophesied that the ark of the covenant will not be made any more and the people will not miss it, for the new Jerusalem will itself be called 'the Throne of the LORD', the place where God makes his home (Jer. 3:16-17; Rev. 21:2-3,22; 22:1-3).

A special day

Burnt offerings and sin offerings were presented on a regular basis at the tabernacle, but what was done with them on this day marked it out as special. This one most holy day in the year directs us to the real Day of Atonement, when Christ died for our sins 'according to the Scriptures'. That was indeed a remarkable day and one that ended the need for further atonement days. While the chapter acts 'like a hinge for the whole book of Leviticus',[2] which is itself the central book of Moses, the contents direct us to the central point of history. The Old Testament people of God looked forward and the New Testament people look back to *the* definitive Day of Atonement. The first Good Friday was not only the unique day of that year but of every year, in every century and in every millennium.

The context

The chapter begins with a reference to what happened to Aaron's sons when **'they drew near before the LORD'** (16:1, ESV; see 10:1-7).[3] It reminds us again that the laws were given in the context of a historical narrative. Leviticus, like the other books of Moses, is first of all concerned with the history of God's people. In the light of the redemption from Egypt and God's special arrangement with them at

Sinai, it seeks to show how this special people were to worship and live.

The regulations for the Day of Atonement are directly related to the tragic deaths of Nadab and Abihu. That episode serves as a warning to the high priest to be very careful how he conducts himself when coming into God's presence. Approaching God is not a natural right for sinful humans and not something to take for granted. Though Aaron and his sons had been specially set apart for this purpose, this privileged position still remained a dangerous one. Aaron had to realize that he could not go **'at any time'** inside the veil where God appeared in the cloud above the mercy seat where the ark was (16:2, ESV). Only after taking the proper precautions, was Aaron, the high priest, allowed to go once a year into the Holy of Holies.

Whether God's fearful presence is revealed on Mount Sinai or more permanently among his people, he is still the same holy God who demands the same respect. This is not something about which twenty-first-century Christians seem concerned. Yet the New Testament reminds us that God remains 'a consuming fire' and that it is 'a fearful thing' to fall into the hands of the living God (Heb. 12:29; 10:31).

While other priests of Aaron's line could offer the daily sacrifices, on this one day of the year the high priest had a special job that only he was allowed to do. It is important that we understand, as the New Testament directs us, that both Moses and Aaron are used in their varying unique functions to symbolize the work of the Messiah. Jesus the Messiah is the Word of God made flesh, the supreme spokesman for God and the unique mediator between God and human beings. But he is also the one great Priest who has appeared once for all at the end of the ages to represent his people and to atone for sin.

The atonement ceremony

In typical Hebrew fashion the chapter presents an introduction and outline of the ritual (16:3-10), followed by a more detailed description of what was to take place (16:11-28), concluding with instructions for the people (16:29-31).

Basic requirements (16:3-5)

Besides the animals that he received from the people — **'two kids of the goats as a sin offering, and one ram as a burnt offering'** (16:5) — the high priest was required to bring a **'young bull'** for his own sin offering and **'a ram as a burnt offering'** (16:3). Aaron was a sinner like the people he represented. The writer to the Hebrews is not slow in showing how Jesus' priesthood is so much better than that of Aaron. Our great High Priest did not need, like the old Levitical high priests, 'to offer up sacrifices, first for his own sins and then for the people's' (Heb. 7:27).

In addition, the high priest was directed to wash and then to wear, not the rich robes of his office (see Exod. 28), but plain, linen clothes and a turban like the other priests. On this atonement day, when he entered the holiest place of all, Aaron divested himself of the symbols of honour and dignity and clothed himself with simple ordinary attire more like that of a servant. Only when he had completed his work in the inner sanctum was he allowed to put on his glorious garments (16:23-24). As he engaged in this special work of atonement his clothing demonstrated the need for a humble, lowly spirit. By this simple action, the high priest expressed the attitude to be adopted by priests and people on that solemn day as they humbled themselves and expressed sorrow for their sins. Not only that, but it pictures for us our great High Priest who emptied himself by taking the form of a servant, humbling himself in order to make real atonement for his people's sins, before coming to his highly exalted position (see Isa. 52:13 – 53:12; Phil. 2:5-11).

A brief summary of the day's events (16:6-10)

In these verses the most important parts of the special atonement ceremony are highlighted.

The first is the reference to the bull as a sin offering **'for himself and for his house'**, meaning for the high priest and all the other priests (16:6). It is what happened to the blood of the bull that is significant.

In the second place, the sin offering for the people consisted of two goats. What happened to each goat fills out the meaning and purpose of this unique sin offering. One goat was sacrificed and again it is where the blood was sprinkled that is significant. As for the other goat, it was **'presented alive before the LORD'** and then allowed to go free into the wilderness. The part played by each goat in the ritual was determined by casting lots.[4]

Tyndale, who was the first to translate the Bible into English from the original languages, also coined the word **'scapegoat'** when he came to the Hebrew term *Azazel* (16:8,10,26). He accepted the traditional understanding of the word as 'a goat that goes away'. Other ideas have not found wide support.[5] It is clear from the text that this goat provided the people with a powerful visual aid.

The ritual in detail (16:11-28)

There are three important stages to the ceremony.

1. The sprinkling of blood

The blood-sprinkling ritual had two parts to it and lies at the heart of this special day's activities.

First, in order to make atonement for himself and the priests, the high priest slaughtered the **'bull of the sin offering'**, took some of its blood and sprinkled it before the mercy seat. The blood was to be sprinkled once *on* the mercy seat and seven times *before* the mercy seat (16:15). This signified complete cleansing and holiness (16:16,19). But making atonement also involved appeasing the wrath of God. Blood sprinkled on the mercy seat, above the ark where God's law, the symbol of God's covenant, was stored, and the meeting point between the holy God and the representative of God's people, spoke of the way that God and his sinful people could be united.

This was not the usual way of dealing with the sin offering on behalf of the priests. What normally happened was that the blood was sprinkled on the outside of the veil or curtain that separated the Holy Place from the Most Holy Place and on the incense altar (see Lev. 4). But on this occasion the high priest went through the veil into the Holy of Holies.

With the death of Nadab and Abihu still in mind, the high priest must take proper precautions when going into the Most Holy Place — **'lest he die'** (16:13; cf. 16:1-2). To protect himself from the presence of the holy God who ordained that he would meet with his people at this symbolic spot, the high priest was directed to take a censer and fill it with hot coals from the altar of burnt offering. Two handfuls of fine incense were dropped on the hot coals to create billows of smoke. This helped to conceal the mercy seat. The mercy seat lay on **'the Testimony'**, a term used here to describe the ark of the covenant because it drew attention to the Ten Commandments, the most important of the items stored in the coffin-like box (see Exod. 31:18; 40:20). The smoke also served in time to symbolize the glory cloud of the divine presence when God no longer visibly appeared in a cloud at the tabernacle and later the temple. When the prophet Isaiah saw the Lord in the glory of the heavenly sanctuary, smoke filled the place (Isa. 6:4).

Secondly, the high priest went through the same procedure with the slaughtered **'goat of the sin offering'** on behalf of the people (16:15). It is stressed that only the high priest was allowed to be in the tabernacle when he was involved in making this act of atonement in **'the Holy Place'**, that is, the Holy of Holies (16:16-17).[6]

Thus on this special day, the high priest was allowed to go twice into the Holy of Holies, first to make atonement for himself and the other priests, and then for the rest of the people. Atonement was necessary because of the people's uncleanness and **'because of their transgressions, for all their sins'** (16:16).

It is interesting that the emphasis falls on cleansing the whole tabernacle. Not only the Most Holy Place, but the rest of the tabernacle and the bronze altar were cleansed with the blood of both the bull and goat (16:18-19). Human sin soils everything, even the place where God chose to reside on earth among his people. God's special presence would no longer be able to dwell there and God's people would be under God's wrath. In this unique ceremony there was an all-embracing cure for treating the effects of ritual and moral uncleanness.

The blood of bulls and goats, as Hebrews reminds us, could not really atone for human sin and cleanse from sin's polluting effects, but it was given in preparation for the coming of the promised King (Heb. 10:4). This special ritual is a pointer to the Lord Jesus Christ, who shed his precious blood at Calvary to make atonement. When he died that atoning death, he did not go into a temple made with hands, but into the real sanctuary (Heb. 9:24-26). As the risen, glorified Lord and our great High Priest, he represents all his people in the heavenly throne room. Our sinful uncleanness can never pollute heaven because of the Saviour's work on our behalf. All who belong to Jesus Christ can come near to God on account of his sacrificial atoning death. Now that the real atoning work has been accomplished, the shadows and symbols have given way to the reality. When Christ died, the veil of the temple was torn in two from top to bottom, demonstrating the effectiveness of his atonement (Matt. 27:51). All whose trust is in the Saviour have a right to enter God's heaven. We can also be assured in the present that, though our prayers and worship are imperfect and soiled by sin, they are cleansed through Jesus and we are accepted by God (Heb. 10:19-22).

2. The scapegoat

The scapegoat ritual portrays in a vivid way the other aspect of this special sin offering. Taking the live goat, on whose head the high priest had placed his hands as he confessed **'all the iniquities ... all their transgressions ... all their sins'** (16:21), to **'an uninhabited land ... in the wilderness'** (16:22) pictures not only the transfer of sin to a substitute, but the removal of sin's burden and guilt. 'As far as the east is from the west, so far has he removed our transgressions from us' (Ps. 103:12).

Again, the law prepares us for Christ, who was led out of the city to that place of desolation where he experienced the curse of God for us. 'He made him who knew no sin to be sin for us' (2 Cor. 5:21). All the sins of his people were laid on Jesus and he took them away. John the Baptist rightly declared as he saw Jesus coming, 'Behold! The Lamb of God who takes away the sin of the world!' (John 1:29). He has taken the guilt; he has paid the penalty. The Christian can sing:

My sin — O the bliss of this glorious thought! —
My sin, not in part, but the whole,

Is nailed to His cross, and I bear it no more:
Praise the Lord, praise the Lord, O my soul![7]

3. The washing with water and other rituals

More cleansing rituals were necessary in case the camp and sanctuary became recontaminated.

First, the high priest was required to remove the special linen clothes, wash himself **'in a holy place'** and put on his normal priestly robes of office.[8] Then he was to offer burnt offerings for himself and the people, burning the fat of the sin offering at the same time (16:23-25). These burnt offerings were also to atone for himself and the people.

Secondly, the person who took the scapegoat into the wilderness was required to wash himself and his clothes before coming into the camp (16:26). This, as we have seen, was standard procedure for someone who had become impure (see Lev. 15; Num. 19:8).

Finally, the parts of the bull and goat that were not burned on the altar — namely, **'their skins, their flesh, and their offal'** — were to be carried outside the camp and burned (16:27). The person responsible for doing this was also required to wash his body and clothes before re-entering the camp.

All who were in any way associated with sin and death became ritually unclean and in need of cleansing to enable them to be fully involved once again in the life of the holy society. Although Christians do not need a second washing of regeneration when they sin, they do need daily cleansing from moral impurity, as Jesus explained to Peter (see John 13:10-11). We have not only the cleansing blood of Christ, but the benefits that come from 'the washing of water by the word' (Eph. 5:26).

Directions for the people (16:29-31)

While the instructions up to this point have mainly concerned the high priest's activities, the law turns to the
people's part in this holy day. These are the requirements
that Jews today are able to observe. Three matters are raised:

1. Calendar

This most holy day is to be kept during the holiest time of
the year, **'in the seventh month'** on **'the tenth day of the
month'**.

2. Cost

The people are to **'afflict'** themselves and **'do no work at
all'**. As a **'sabbath of solemn rest'** it is to be kept like the
weekly Sabbath (cf. 23:3). The word **'afflict'** is used in the
context of fasting and prayer (see Isa. 58:3; Ps. 35:13) and
suggests a submissive, contrite attitude (as in Exod. 10:3,
where the word translated 'humble' is literally 'afflict').

3. Continuance

Enveloping what is demanded of the people is the emphasis
on the permanence of the ruling. It is **'a statute for ever'**
(16:29,31).

These demands not only indicated the importance of the
day, but reminded the people that the ritual on their behalf at
the sanctuary was to be attended by their own humble,
repentant spirits. Likewise, the benefits of Christ's atoning
sacrifice apply to those who are of a submissive, repentant
spirit, as exemplified in the self-effacing tax collector and the
repentant thief (Luke 18:13; 23:40-42).

Summary

The concluding verses (16:32-34) emphasize that this Day of Atonement is to be an annual event where each successor to Aaron who is **'anointed'** and **'consecrated'** to serve as high priest is to carry out the special requirements at the tabernacle. Dressed in those simple **'linen'** clothes, which were like those of a servant and yet were **'holy'**, the high priest was to make atonement, first for **'the Holy Sanctuary'** (that is, the Holy of Holies), then for **'the tabernacle of meeting'** (that is, the rest of the tabernacle structure) and, finally, for **'the altar'** of burnt offering in the tabernacle courtyard. All parts of the tabernacle where sinful human beings had set foot needed to be cleansed. It also emphasized that he was to make atonement for **'the priests'** and for all the Lord's people (**'all the people of the congregation'**). Again, the purpose is reiterated: **'to make atonement for the children of Israel, for all their sins'**.

We praise God for our Lord Jesus Christ, who has become 'high priest for ever according to the order of Melchizedek' (Heb. 6:20). 'Not with the blood of goats and calves, but with his own blood he entered the Most Holy Place once for all, having obtained eternal redemption' (Heb. 9:12). In order to do this, our Saviour laid aside the splendour of his divine appearance and became a human being, taking the position of a holy, humble servant that he might 'give his life a ransom for many' (Mark 10:45; Phil. 2:6-8). In this way sinners who put their faith in Jesus are 'justified freely by his grace through the redemption that is in Christ Jesus, whom God set forth to be a propitiation by his blood' (Rom. 3:24-25).

Part 4.
Obeying the holy God:
rules concerning moral purity (17:1 – 27:34)

LORD, who may abide in your tabernacle?
Who may dwell in your holy hill?
He who walks uprightly,
   And works righteousness,
   And speaks the truth in his heart...

(Ps. 15:1-2).

18.
The sanctity of life

Please read Leviticus 17:1-16

Holiness for the Israelites was to mean more than ritual purity and physical wholeness. It was about obeying the holy God, whether it concerned matters of worship or personal morality. This last section of the book emphasizes that God is the standard for what is wholesome, pure and good, and that his laws are an expression of his holy character.

Most of the legislation in this chapter has already been considered, but it is brought together here to stress its signifi- cance and the seriousness of disobeying God's commands (17:4,10,15-16). It is the subject of **'blood'** that is brought to our attention: blood-guilt, bloodshed, sprinkled blood and the ban on consuming blood. This is certainly not the kind of topic polite Western society finds attractive. Nevertheless, its importance for understanding the heart of the Christian message cannot be overemphasized.

Shedding blood (17:1-9)

The two rules concerning the slaughter of animals from the herd and flock deal with the same subject, but the first

(17:3-4) has in mind **'peace offerings'** (17:5), whereas the second (17:8-9) covers all the sacrifices — **'burnt offering or sacrifice'** (17:8). One reason — **'to the end that...'** (17:5-7) — does duty for both laws even though it has specific reference to the first.

What the law requires

We immediately face a problem of interpretation. Do these laws require every domesticated animal to be killed at the entrance to the tabernacle before it can be eaten, or do they only require that animals offered as sacrifices be slaughtered there? The first view would mean that the Israelites were to regard the slaughter of every animal from among the flocks and herds as a sacrifice. This interpretation has led some conservative scholars to assume that the ruling only applied to the wilderness period when the people lived in close proximity to the central sanctuary. When they were in the land of Canaan it would have been practically impossible for those living at great distances from the tabernacle to eat lamb, goat or beef in their own homes if they were required first to bring the animal to the tabernacle to be slaughtered. Commentators therefore assume that this law was later relaxed before Israel entered Canaan (see Deut. 12:21-22).

There are difficulties with this position. Matthew Henry comments that 'It is hard to construe this as a temporary law, when it is expressly said to be a *statute for ever.*' While there are some regulations that apply during the wilderness wanderings and others which can only come into effect when they settle in the land of promise, this stipulation is specifically stated to be **'a statute for ever'** (17:7).

It will also be seen that both regulations speak of offerings made **'to the LORD'** (17:4,5,9). These are not animals slaughtered for the purpose of providing ordinary meals, but are sacrificial offerings presented to the Lord, as in Leviticus chapters 1-7. The very word used for the slaughter of the animals — **'kills'**, (17:3) — is the term generally used for ritual killing in sacrifice.

Furthermore, if these laws required all slaughter to be carried out at the tabernacle, does it not seem strange that no regulations are given concerning what to do with animals found to be defective? They could not be presented at the tabernacle. Were such animals never to be killed for food?

A further factor favouring the view that domesticated animals could be killed for food without the necessity of bringing them to the tabernacle is the freedom that is given to kill clean wild animals in the open field (17:13).

Thus the whole paragraph suggests that it is animals that are to be offered in sacrifice that are the subject of this legislation. It is blood sacrifices that need to be regulated. Up to this point, individual worshippers had offered sacrifices at various places, as we see from Genesis. Now it is being stipulated that all animal sacrifices are to be carried out at the officially recognized place, at the altar by **'the door of the tabernacle of meeting'** (17:5,9), and involve the properly appointed priests, who carry out the appropriate rituals (17:6). Deuteronomy 12:1-32 stresses the same point, namely, that all sacrificial slaughter is to be done at the central sanctuary and nowhere else. At the same time Deuteronomy also clarifies the position concerning the killing of non-sacrificial domesticated animals. This can be done at home and is to be seen as being no different from the killing of clean wild animals like the deer and the gazelle (Deut. 12:15,21-22). Thus there is no conflict between Leviticus and Deuteronomy and there is no need to suggest any change in the law.

The reason for the law

1. Illicit worship

It had been, and would continue to be, a temptation for people offering sacrifice to the Lord **'in the open field'** (17:5) to think in pagan or semi-pagan, syncretistic terms. This law was given in order to direct the people away from sacrificing to false gods: **'They shall no more offer their sacrifices to demons'** (17:7). The actual term for **'demons'**, which is also translated 'goats' in the account of the ritual of the two goats on the Day of Atonement (16:7-8), signifies 'hairy' or 'shaggy' creatures. It is applied to the hairy animals that inhabited desert places (see Isa. 13:21; 34:14) and they are often compared with the satyrs of Greek mythology. According to Walter Kaiser, goat worship was part of Egyptian religion and he suggests that Joshua was referring to this when he spoke of Israel's ancestors worshipping false gods in Egypt (Josh. 24:14). Just as idolatry was associated with the bull calf from Israel's early history and remained a constant temptation, so it was with these hairy creatures of the wilderness. When Jeroboam introduced worship to rival that of the temple in Jerusalem it included not only calves but goats (see 2 Chr. 11:15, where the term is again translated 'demons', or 'goat-gods').

The link between false gods and demonology is made explicit in the Song of Moses (Deut. 31:30 – 32:43). When the Israelites sinned at Baal Peor and sacrificed to Moabite gods (Num. 25:1-3) they were sacrificing to demons (Deut. 32:17). Paul makes the same point as he warns against participating in pagan worship. Though 'an idol is nothing', when the pagan world sacrifices to idols 'they sacrifice to demons and not to God' (1 Cor. 8:4; 10:19-20). There are still professing Christians who live in fear of demonic forces. Some even seek to pacify ancestral gods by pouring out libations and offering gifts of food. This passage directs us to the true God and points us to the deliverance that Christ has brought from superstitious fears and demonic influences. He himself was tempted to worship the devil, and his reply must be ours: 'You shall worship the LORD your God, and him only you shall serve' (Matt. 4:10; see Deut. 6:13). It also encourages us to have nothing whatever to do with pagan practices and warns us against dabbling in any form of demonic activity. Neither does the passage provide any warrant for marrying Christianity and paganism. This legislation is simply an obvious application of the first great command, where God insists: 'You shall have no other gods before me' (Exod. 20:3). God demands total allegiance and there could be no rival worship in Israel to that laid down by God through Moses.

2. Infidelity

The dangerous attraction of paganism is expressed by the words: **'after whom they have played the prostitute'** (17:7). The law of Moses is very aware of the temptation faced by the people to turn to other gods. Sacrificing to other gods is an act of spiritual infidelity and a breach of their covenant relationship with God. The concept of marriage as a metaphor for Israel's relationship to the Lord is implied in the language of prostitution and is a theme that is later developed by the prophets, particularly Hosea. Already in Exodus 34:14-16 the Lord warned of this danger after the golden-calf incident. He reminded his people that worshipping other gods is tantamount to playing the harlot and, like a husband jealous over his wife, so, 'The LORD, whose name is Jealous, is a jealous God.'

3. Instruction

By bringing their sacrifices to the central sanctuary for the priests to carry out the required procedures, the people were also taught that there is only one way of salvation, only one means of access to the true God, only one place where sin can be atoned for and pardon obtained. Furthermore, it reminded Israel that they were to be a united people and that their unity lay in belonging to the Lord. It provided them with a point where that unity could be expressed and encouraged, and at the same time helped to keep them from straying into false ways.

Now that Jesus has offered himself as the one true sacrifice for sin, our acceptance before God is only through him. In him we are united to God and with fellow believers. 'To set up other mediators, or other altars, or other expiatory sacrifices is, in effect, to set up other gods,' comments Matthew Henry. While Christians are no longer bound to one earthly sanctuary, we are encouraged to assemble together and express our unity in the Lord. There is no encouragement in either the Old or New Testaments for the kind of individualism that is so prevalent in some Christian circles.

The punishment for offenders

To go against the ruling meant that a very serious offence had been committed. To offer an animal in sacrifice away from the sanctuary meant that its blood had been poured out needlessly. The offence is equivalent to murder. This is made clear both by the legal pronouncement that blood-guiltiness is imputed, or reckoned, to the person and by the statement that blood has been shed (17:4). To **'shed blood'** is used specifically to denote the intentional murder of a human being (see Gen. 9:6; 37:22; Num. 35:33). Not only are the people warned against committing spiritual prostitution when they sacrifice wherever they please, but the very act of ignoring this ruling and continuing their former practices, even though their sacrifices are exclusively to the Lord, is now considered a major crime. As Matthew Henry puts it, 'Idolatrous sacrifices were looked upon, not only as adultery, but as murder.'

The punishment is severe, for those who disobey are to be **'cut off'** from among their people (17:4,9). It is not given to human courts to execute the offender, for this is not the murder of a human being, nor a case of badly treating an animal. It is God who accounts this offence to be equivalent to murder and it is God who will punish them. The guilty person has forfeited the right to be counted among God's people (cf. 7:20-21). When the whole nation committed spiritual prostitution and provoked the Lord to anger he banished them from the land of promise. The New Testament makes it very clear that wilful, sustained rejection of God's gospel after receiving the knowledge of the truth demands the severest of penalties (Heb. 10:26-31).

Applicable to all

These laws (and the ones that follow in 17:10,12-13) were not confined to the Israelites themselves, but to all foreigners who took up residence among them — **'the strangers who sojourn among you'** (17:8). While Israel is directed not to mistreat or oppress aliens (Exod. 22:21), they on their part were to respect this ruling and abide by it. The Israelites would not be tempted to indulge in pagan worship if those from other nations were prevented from performing their rituals in the community of God's people. It would have the effect of hindering the spread of idolatry in the promised land. The kingdom of God on earth at that time was confined to the Israelite nation and the principle contained in this law is now only applicable in the context of God's covenant people worldwide. Those once strangers to the common-wealth of Israel who become members of the family of God must not seek to introduce items foreign to the worship of God as revealed in the Bible.

Eating blood (17:10-16)

Many people today, as in ancient times, consume the blood of animals in a variety of ways, from actually drinking blood to eating black pudding. For the Israelites such practices were strictly forbidden (3:17; 7:26-27). In fact, when God first sanctioned the eating of meat after the Flood, he or-dained that humans should refrain from consuming meat that had not been drained of blood (Gen. 9:3-4).

It is repeated for emphasis that no one in Israel is to consume any blood (17:10,12). Again a severe warning that applies to both Israelites and resident aliens accompanies the first ruling, in which God speaks not indirectly but directly: **'I will set my face against that person ... and will cut him off...'** (17:10). Instead of God's face 'shining' in blessing (see Num. 6:25), the person would come under God's curse (cf. 20:3,6; Ezek. 14:8; 15:7). It is interesting that Cain's punishment for killing his brother involved being 'hidden' from God's face and being driven from the ground to be-come 'a fugitive and a vagabond', as it were, cut off from land and community (see Gen. 4:14).

This is followed by a rule dealing with the right way of killing clean wild animals (17:13). Again the concern is about not consuming blood and it is accompanied by a similar warning of being 'cut off' (17:14).

Finally, a ruling is given for anyone who eats an animal found dead (17:15). Such an animal that had died naturally from disease or old age, or had been killed by other wild creatures, would not have had its blood properly drained from the flesh. Eating it would make an Israelite ritually unclean and would necessitate a special cleansing procedure before the person could be clean again (see 11:40). While God's holy people should not deliberately make themselves unclean (see Deut. 14:21), necessity or ignorance might result in their not only touching the carcass (see 11:39-40) but eating the flesh. The crucial thing was that they should quickly perform the necessary rituals to make themselves clean again. Not to carry out the proper cleansing process would betray a rebellious spirit for which the person would bear full responsibility: **'he shall bear his guilt'** (17:16). In other words, as in the previous cases, the person would face God's curse and be cut off from the covenant community. What started out as a minor uncleanness would end up as a major disaster.

The significance of blood (17:11,14)

The early chapters of Genesis first alert us to the seriousness of this subject. Murder is spoken of as blood spilt on the ground and justice required that the murderer's blood should be shed (Gen. 4:10-11; 9:4-6).

Blood was not to be eaten (17:12,14) and if it was not used in the sacrificial rituals at the tabernacle it was to be poured out on the ground and covered with dust (17:13). Of course, it was impossible to drain away completely the blood from the flesh, but the action of pouring it out and the prohibition against eating it applied to the main blood-flow that runs through the body. All flesh was created by God from the ground and the act of draining the blood out onto the ground and covering it symbolized the return of that life to God who first gave it (Gen. 3:19). The blood of murder victims was considered to be uncovered and cried out to God for vengeance (Gen. 4:10).

Two reasons are given why care should be taken not to consume blood.

Blood represents life

This commentary is being written in the year that celebrates the 400th anniversary of Harvey's discoveries concerning the circulation of the blood in the body. Since then we have learnt much more about its amazing properties. The life and well-being of the whole body is the blood and, as everyone knows, loss of blood can lead to loss of life.

Breath and blood are two very obvious evidences of life that people can observe. Genesis refers to 'the breath of life' (Gen. 2:7; 6:17; 7:22) and then to 'flesh with its life, that is, its blood' (Gen. 9:4). Using slightly different wording, the close relationship between life and blood is stated repeatedly (17:11,14; Deut. 12:23).[1]

There are no magical powers attached to blood, but where there is no blood there is no life in the flesh of any creature. To shed blood meant the ending of the life of that human or animal. Because of this strong link between blood and life, to honour the ruling not to consume blood implied respect for life.

The strong implication is that animal life, as well as human, is sacred (see Gen. 9:4). Draining the blood from the body of the animal before it was eaten acknowledged this. To make a sport out of killing is therefore contrary to the spirit of this regulation. That which represents the life of the creature must be treated with respect. Humans are not allowed to do as they like with the life that God has given. The same is true of human life even in its earliest stages in the womb. It is not merely a piece of matter that can be tossed from test tube to trash in the interests of medical science.

In the early days of the church, Gentile believers were asked to refrain from consuming blood so as not to offend Jewish converts (Acts 15:20,29). Drinking blood was often associated with pagan rituals and Gentile converts also needed to be warned.

Blood makes atonement

Another reason why blood was not to be eaten was that God ordained the shedding of blood upon the altar 'to make atonement' for the people, **'for it is the blood that makes atonement for the soul'** (17:11). The theological importance of this verse cannot be overestimated. Many scholars, including an increasing number of evangelical ones, make heavy weather of it. There was a popular liberal view that suggested that the people's sins were atoned for through the life of the animal. As the blood represented life the argument was that when the blood was shed its life was set free and this was how the blood atoned for sin. This was a strange conclusion to draw and suggested a pagan rather than a Hebrew way of thinking. There continues to be strong opposition to using this verse to support penal substitutionary atonement.[2] But it is difficult to ignore the plain meaning of the text that the animal's blood atones, or ransoms, and that one life is substituted for another. It is interesting that the term 'soul' or 'life' is used three times. The verse speaks of the **'life'** (or 'soul') of the animal being offered to make atonement **'for your souls; for it is the blood that makes atonement for the soul'**. It is soul for soul, or life in exchange for life. The offender deserves to die but his or her life is spared because another life has been substituted. 'Had not the life of the substituted victim intervened, exposure to the divine wrath would mean certain death to the offender.' The sacrificial lifeblood of the victim on the altar 'comes between the offender and the wrath of God to rescue the offender from the just penalty for the sin'.[3] This blood offering is not something that the people are said to give to God. Rather, it is God who gives it to the people. The text reads, **'I have given it to you upon the altar.'**

All this was in preparation for the coming of Christ, whose 'precious blood' redeems us to God (1 Peter 1:18-19). It was 'with his own blood [that] he entered the Most Holy Place once for all, having obtained eternal redemption' (Heb. 9:12; cf. Eph. 1:7). The blood of Jesus speaks better things than the blood of Abel, for though Jesus was unjustly put on the cross instead of crying out for justice to be done, justice was done, and all who belong to God through Christ are free from the coming wrath of God. God presented Christ Jesus 'to be a propitiation by his blood' (Rom. 3:25). Jesus startled the people when he spoke of the need to drink his blood (John 6:53-56). By this he meant 'not participation in his life but appropriation of the benefits of his life laid down'.[4]

19.
The sanctity of sex

Please read Leviticus 18:1-30

There was a time when most people in the Western world would have found the perversions named in this chapter too shocking and embarrassing to mention. All that has changed as a result of the 'swinging sixties'. Though the sinful world in its better moments can detest some of the sexual perversions that exist, the more they are tolerated, the more acceptable and appealing they become.[1]

The opening exhortation (18:1-5)

The legislation is introduced and concluded by short sections of sermonic material in which the people are urged to obey God's laws (18:1-5) and warned against following the depraved customs of the pagan nations (18:24-30).

Life

'Life' in this context is the blessing of a full, satisfying, contented existence in the land of promise. Like the tree of life in the Garden of Eden, these concrete expressions of the life that God promises in the land come to be symbolic of that fulness of life that comes from knowing God and 'walking with God'. It is the sort of life that Enoch experienced in his fellowship with God and which death could not touch (Gen. 5:22-24; cf. John 8:51). Jesus said that he had come so that those who receive him might have life in all its fulness (John 10:10).

The phrase, **'... if a man does, he shall live by them'** (18:5), is quoted by Ezekiel as he denounces Israel for failing to practise God's statutes and judgements (Ezek. 20:11,13,21; cf. 18:23; 33:11). Jesus alluded to it in his conversation with the lawyer who asked him what he must do to inherit eternal life (Luke 10:28). In addition, Paul quotes the words as he takes issue with those who look to the law for justification (Rom. 10:5; Gal. 3:12). Life is not something that sinful human beings can achieve by their efforts. The phrase points us to Christ, who is the only one who has kept the law perfectly — and therefore he deserved to live, not die. Yet he experienced the curse of death for sinners like us. Those who are righteous live by faith in the promises of God, which means embracing Christ our righteousness and substitutionary sacrifice.

Nevertheless, the faith that trusts Christ for salvation is a faith that shows itself in obedience to God's commandments. Paul teaches that godliness has the 'promise of the life that now is and of that which is to come' (1 Tim. 4:8). Furthermore, as Israel was urged not to do **'according to the doings of the land of Egypt ... and ... of the land of Canaan'** (18:3), so professing Christians are told, 'If you live according to the flesh you will die; but if by the Spirit you put to death the deeds of the body, you will live' (Rom. 8:13).

God's people were directed not to **'walk'**, or live, according to the objectionable rules of the pagan land they had left, or those of the land where they were going, but to keep God's rules and legal decisions and **'to walk in them'**

(18:3-4). Paul reminds the Ephesian Christians that they 'once walked according to the course of this world'. Now they are urged not to 'walk as the rest of the Gentiles walk, in the futility of their mind' (Eph. 2:2; 4:17-19). Christians must resist the pressures to conform to the present age (Rom. 12:1-2).

'I am the LORD'

'Authority' is a nasty word in the minds of many. It is often associated with repression, violence and the abuse of human rights. To keep reading, both here and in the following chapters, **'I am the LORD'** (18:2,4,5,6,21,30), may tempt some to think that God is laying down the law like an oppressive dictator.

These laws, however, come from a good and wise Creator who has the right to make the rules that define the boundaries and to warn of the consequences of transgressing them. Gordon Wenham rightly points out that ' **"I am the LORD"** is sufficient motive for keeping them.'[2] He does not need to justify himself. The phrase occurs at the close of particular decrees (18:5,6,21) and is similar to the refrain, '... says the LORD', that is often found at the end of prophetic oracles (e.g., Amos 1:5,8,15; 2:3,16). The Lord has spoken and we do well to listen and obey. Nevertheless, God does point out the dangers of violating his decrees (18:24-30).

But there is more to this phrase, especially in its longer form. The issuing of religious and ethical demands is never isolated from God's redemptive grace. The abrupt opening — **'I am the LORD your God'** (18:2) — is similar to the words that introduce the Ten Commandments. It reminds us that the context is the redemption from Egypt (Exod. 20:1-2; cf. Lev. 11:45). As God gives this legislation the people are not allowed to forget what the Lord has done for them nor his commitment to them. The sovereign Lord is Israel's God.

He is **'your God'** (18:2,4,30). The God who identified himself with their ancestors as the God of Shem and the God of Abraham, Isaac and Jacob is the God of the Israelite nation. God, whose name is **'the LORD'** (Jehovah/Yahweh), has not only redeemed them, but has entered into a special relationship with them. What an incentive to walk in God's ways!

Incestuous relations (18:6-17)

The legislation deals with forbidden relationships and practices that are in one way or another destructive of the family. They either produce unacceptable offspring (18:6-18) or they result in no offspring (18:19-23).

Incest is defined as 'sexual intercourse between persons too closely related to marry'.[3] Most societies have laws governing the subject, not necessarily because of what the Bible teaches, but on account of the effects of such unions on the health of families. Too much inbreeding leads to genetic problems, as is well known from the blood disorders that have afflicted members of Europe's royal families.

Because of the break-up of family life in so much of modern Western society, coupled with the capabilities of medical scientists, it is possible for incest to occur without the parties realizing it. Ancient Israel had its own problems that made incest more likely. The law did not allow individuals to marry outside the covenant community (Deut. 7:3) and land inheritance was to remain within the family or clan (Num. 36). Such restrictions necessitated incest laws.

Many of the rules listed here forbid what seems to have been accepted practice in earlier times. In the nature of the case it must be assumed that at the dawn of human history close relatives married to produce offspring (see Gen. 4:17,26; 5:4). Beside the shocking offence committed by

Lot's daughters when they took advantage of their drunken father (Gen. 19:30-38), there are four obvious instances where the founding fathers of Israel committed acts that the Mosaic law now prohibited. Abraham married his half-sister, Sarah (Gen. 20:12; cf. Lev. 18:11); Jacob married Rachel when her older sister Leah was already his wife (Gen. 29:28; cf. Lev. 18:18); Judah unwittingly was seduced by Tamar, his daughter-in-law (Gen. 38:18; cf. Lev. 18:15); and Reuben committed a double violation by his adulterous relationship with Bilhah, Jacob's concubine (Gen. 35:22; cf. Lev. 18:8).

One's closest blood relations (18:6-11)

The opening verse of this paragraph introduces us to the terms used for defining incest. A relative, or one who is **'near of kin'** (18:6), is more literally 'any flesh of his flesh'. This is an expression that means the closest of relatives. Some have wondered why in the following list there is no mention of the father's daughter or a brother's full sister. But this opening directive covers all close relatives, even those missing from the list. It is spelled out in detail in 21:2-3 who one's closest relations are: mother, father, son, daughter, brother and unmarried sister.

Discreet expressions are used to describe sexual activity. The word **'approach'** in this context means to make sexual advances, and for a person to **'uncover ... nakedness'** is a euphemism for sexual intercourse. It is the head of the family group who is addressed. Close blood relatives would be under his direct authority. If he himself behaved indecently towards them, they might feel intimidated and the man would not be brought to justice. **'I am the LORD,'** reminded the head of the house that the Lord would see that justice was done.

The paragraph details the kind of incestuous relations that are forbidden.

Mother

The close relationship between a man and his wife is the reason why **'the nakedness of your father'** (18:7) is mentioned in a prohibition against a son having an illicit relationship with his mother. In marriage the two become 'one flesh' (Gen. 2:21-25).

Stepmother

For the same reason, in a polygamous situation a son may not have sex with other wives or concubines of his father. The term 'nakedness' used on its own refers to a person's private parts and by extension to the close relationship that exists between the parties. For a son to have sex with his father's wife, even if she is not his mother, is as bad as having sex with his father, for she is one flesh with his father (18:8). Such a case of a man having committed incest with 'his father's wife' is highlighted by Paul (1 Cor. 5:1).

Half-sister

While full sisters are covered by the general prohibition in verse 6, the law also rules out sexual relationships with half-sisters, whether they are brought up within the family household or another family (18:9). The half-sister is blood-related to one's father or mother, and therefore to have sex with her would be as bad as having sex with either parent.

Granddaughter

This is a blood relation as close as a parent and child (18:10).

Step-sister

Some translations do not make it easy to distinguish between the sister mentioned in verse 9 and the person mentioned in verse 11. The difficulty lies with the phrase translated **'begotten by your father'**, which some modern translations give as 'of your father's family'. The same Hebrew word for 'begotten' is translated 'born' or 'family' in verse 9. It is better to render it as 'clan' or 'family' and therefore it does not mean that one's father is related by blood to this daughter of his wife. What the verse seems to be saying is that though the girl might originally be from a different, totally unrelated 'family', she nevertheless now belongs within the clan, or family household, of the person addressed because the person's father has married her mother. Though she is only a step-sister, sexual relationships with her are out of bounds because both parties are within the same family household, having the same father figure.

People related through the parents (18:12-14)

This paragraph deals with blood relatives who do not necessarily live within the same family group. Sexual relations with one's aunts on both sides of the marriage — **'father's sister ... mother's sister'** — are prohibited (18:12-13). Jochabed, Moses' mother, was his father Amram's aunt (see Exod. 6:20). The ban also extends to wives of one's uncle on the father's side (18:14). To make sexual advances towards his wife would be as bad as having sexual relationships with one's uncle. The wife must be treated like a blood-related aunt. Uncles on the mother's side are not mentioned because they are not part of the father's extended family and therefore their wives are not considered to be blood-related. Thus, while sexual activity is prohibited with one's mother's sister because of the blood tie, the same does not apply to sisters-in-law on the mother's side.

People related through marriage (18:15-16)

The ban on sexual relations extends to a daughter-in-law — for she is, after all, **'your son's wife'** (18:15) — and to a sister-in-law — because of her marital union to the blood brother (18:16; cf. 18:7-8). It cost John the Baptist his life when he verbally attacked Herod Antipas for stealing Herodias, his own brother Philip's wife (Matt. 14:1-12). An exception to this latter prohibition was the legislation concerning levirate marriage.[4] Where a woman was widowed before she had a son, her brother-in-law was directed to marry her for the sake of his deceased brother's name and inheritance (see Deut. 25:5-7).

People related through the wife (18:17)

Also prohibited are sexual relations with a step-daughter or with granddaughters of one's wife (18:17). A man, for instance, could marry a woman or her daughter but not both because, through marriage to the woman, the girl has become a close relative (**'near of kin'**; see 18:6). This is condemned as **'wickedness'** or depravity.

Unacceptable practices (18:18-23)

The prohibitions in this new section[5] are presented in such a way that the most depraved cases are mentioned last.

Prevention (18:18)

This law prohibits a man marrying (**'nor shall you take'**) his wife's sister while his wife is still living. We might consider this to be similar to the previous verse, but no reference is made to an incestuous relationship. The reason this time is contained in the word translated **'rival'**.[6] It conveys the idea of the strife and hostility that arise in bigamous marriages where wives vie with each other for their husband's affection. Samuel's father had two wives, and Peninnah provoked Samuel's mother, Hannah (1 Sam. 1:1-7). The pressure could easily become greater and the rivalry more intense where the wives were sisters, as in the case of Jacob's marriages to Leah and her sister Rachel (see Gen. 29:28-35; 30:1-2,14-24). It was to prevent unnecessary tension and distress that this law was included. Bigamy and polygamous marriages were tolerated but not encouraged. It was because of the hardness of the people's hearts, as Jesus showed, that much of this legislation was included to curb immorality and regulate the results of sinful behaviour. From the beginning the pattern was set that marriage was to be between one man and one woman.

Pollution (18:19-20)

Two cases of moral pollution are considered. First, sexual relationships are prohibited during a woman's menstrual period (18:19). No reason is given here, but it presumes earlier legislation where it is stated that a man becomes unclean through contact with a woman during her normal discharge of blood (15:19-24). While that ruling is in the context of ritual uncleanness that could arise accidentally, this decree makes deliberate violation a moral offence. This law benefited a woman at a point when she was psychologically and physically low and it still needs to be remembered by husbands today.

The second case involves a man engaged in sexual relations, not with a blood relative, as in the incest cases, but with someone else's wife (18:20). Adultery, the most prevalent of the crimes listed in both ancient and modern times, is strongly condemned throughout the Bible. It is viewed as a senseless act that destroys the person (see Prov. 6:32) and as 'an assault on the nuclear family'.[7] It breaks the Seventh Commandment (Exod. 20:14) and means that the man is morally unclean: **'... to defile yourself with her'**.[8]

Perversion (18:21-23)

For the last three crimes Romans 1:24-32 provides the best commentary.

Dedicating children to be sacrificed to Molech (18:21) may seem out of place in a list that concerns sexual matters. However, the word used for children or **'descendants'** (literally, 'seed') is found in the previous verse, where the translation **'lie carnally'** or 'lie sexually' is, literally, 'your lying for seed'. Wasting 'seed' is a common factor in this section and, whatever the precise fate of these children was, whether employed in pagan worship, actually sacrificed on a pagan altar or, as often translated, allowed to **'pass through the fire'** in some pagan ritual, it meant the child was lost to the family. 'Seed', as we see from Genesis, has important implications concerning the fulfilment of God's promises in undoing the effects of the Fall.

But the practices connected with the worship of Molech are prohibited more fundamentally because of the syncretism involved. Molech, a god worshipped by the Ammonites (1 Kings 11:7), was being honoured with sacrifices that were recognized as being among the most precious gifts of the Lord, as Genesis consistently teaches. By so doing they '**profane the name**' of God. To '**profane**' means to make unholy that which is holy. God's name is holy, as the following chapters will emphasize (see 19:2; 20:3), but God's name in this context does not mean some label by which he is called. It stands for the very essence of his being. For people who have been brought into a special covenant relationship with the living God to engage in such practices is to associate the nature and character of God with the worship of Molech. This 'tarnishes God's reputation among the nations (Ezek. 36:20-21)'.[9] In other words, profaning God's name involves giving God a bad name. That is why Israel was to have nothing to do with such pagan practices.

The principal point made in this verse is something that Christians need to be aware of more often. What effect are we having on the watching world? Are we giving God a bad name by the way we live and act? Are we serving God and materialism in the way we handle our children, driving them to get on in life as if this present world order and its goods were everything? Jesus said, 'You cannot serve God and mammon' (Matt. 6:24).

The second item in this paragraph relates to homosexual activity, otherwise known as sodomy (cf. Gen. 19:5), where a man engages in sexual intercourse with a male '**as with a woman**' (18:22). While other ancient Near-Eastern cultures produced laws to regulate such practices, the Bible is unique in allowing for no exceptions. God hates and detests it. It is described as an '**abomination**', something abhorrent. Because this practice runs counter to God's initial blessing of producing children and the promised hope through the seed of Abraham, there are those who argue that the text is concerned not so much with the activity itself but with its consequences: the man's 'seed' is wasted. Seeking to bring the law up to date, it is then argued that 'gay partners' in a stable relationship who adopt children would not be violating the intention of this prohibition.[10] But, as other passages make clear, it is the act itself that is denounced as detestable, in the same way as the syncretistic worship associated with child sacrifice is morally unacceptable. The consequences concerning offspring are important but secondary to the main concern.

The final item in the list concerns the even more repulsive practice of bestiality (18:23; Exod. 22:19). Sexual activity with animals is strictly prohibited. Because bestiality in Babylonian and Canaanite texts is limited to acts between the gods and animals it is claimed that we should not suppose it reflects human behaviour in these cultures. But if mythology 'does not mirror society's norms, it surely reflects society's ideals'.[11] A man is not to lie with **'any'** kind of animal. It was necessary to emphasize that all animals are included because in Hittite society, for instance, while bestiality was not permitted with an ox, sheep or dog, it was allowed with a horse or mule. A woman too, must not **'stand before'**, in the sense of deliberately putting herself at the service of, an animal. **'It is a perversion'**, which means that it is 'confusion'. The boundaries between humans and animals are crossed. Purity involves 'keeping apart what God has created to be separate'.[12] Evolutionary theories that suggest that we are merely 'naked apes' obliterate the biblical distinctions between humans and animals and encourage such perversions to thrive.

Final exhortations (18:24-30)

Warning to the newly formed nation (18:24-28)

Violating any of the statutes listed is to engage in practices that God hates — **'these abominations'** (18:26,27). They contaminate nation and land and the punishment is banishment from the land (18:24-25). It was because of their vile sexual practices that the Canaanites were to be removed from the land and the same would happen to the Israelites if they engaged in similar immoral activities. To describe inhabitants of the land as vomit that needs to be spewed out shows how repugnant these sinful actions are in God's sight. Jesus uses similar graphic language in his letter to the Laodicean church (Rev. 3:16). Modern ecologists are rightly concerned about pollution from gases that can cause devastating consequences for the earth, but there is little concern over moral pollution. That human sin affects the land is not a new thought. The ground was cursed as a result of human sin (Gen. 3:17-18; 6:13; 8:21) and banishment from the land is a regular punishment for the disobedient (Gen. 3:23-24; 4:11-12). The final end-time punishment will be exclusion from God's new creation (see Rev. 22:15). To avoid God's judgements Israel is called to keep God's ordinances so that the land, cleansed of the Canaanite filth, might remain clean.

Warning to individuals (18:29-30)

Individual Israelites are warned that those guilty of committing any of the **'abominable customs'** will be **'cut off from among their people'**.[13] These are warnings from a God who loved them and had redeemed them: **'I am the LORD your God.'** Paul warns Christians: 'Do you not know that the unrighteous will not inherit the kingdom of God?' He later urges them to 'Flee sexual immorality' and reminds them that they 'were bought at a price' (1 Cor. 6:9-11,18-20).

20.
Living the godly life:
an introduction

Please read Leviticus 19:1-37

At the beginning of the twentieth century holiness was a hot topic among many devout Christians. A 'holiness' movement had developed and 'holiness' churches were formed. But holiness is not meant to be the preserve of a particular church, society or monastic order. Holiness is to be the concern of all God's people.

Before examining in more detail the contents of Leviticus 19, we shall look at the chapter as a whole.

The call to holiness (19:1-2)

The Lord ordered Moses to speak to the entire Israelite covenant community about the holiness of God and how it should affect their lives (19:1-2).[1] **'You shall be holy, for I the LORD your God am holy'** (19:2). When the people first heard this call to holiness it was in the context of ceremonial cleanness. They were to sanctify themselves and be holy by not defiling themselves through eating unclean meat (11:44-45). Now the call heads a list of commands and prohibitions where ethical issues predominate. The apostle

Peter, when challenging the new-covenant chosen people not to be conformed to their former sinful passions, issues the same challenge: '… as he who called you is holy, you also be holy in all your conduct, because it is written, "Be holy, for I am holy"' (1 Peter 1:14-16).

What is holiness?

Holiness is not just a mysterious, awesome power associated with God. It does include that, as we see from the way the priests were set apart for God's service and from the tragic results that occurred when they offered what was unauthorized (8:35; 9:23-24; 10:1-3). Neither is it to be confined to a list of ceremonial taboos that priests and people are to respect. Holiness is not only about ritual cleanness and bodily wholesomeness; it concerns moral wholeness — clean, healthy behaviour. The Hebrew word suggests 'being separate and distinct', so that holiness includes the idea of separation from all that is morally unclean and unwholesome (see 20:26).

The standard of holiness

The reason why God's people are to be holy is because their God is holy. Jehovah/Yahweh is the absolute standard for measuring holiness and the source of all holiness. In God holiness is to be found in its purest form. His name, the very essence of his being, is holy (see 20:3; 22:32). Holiness is what makes God the mysterious and glorious being that he is. It is not possible, then, legitimately to talk about holiness without first considering what God has revealed about himself.

God's holiness includes his separation from everything and everybody else. It distinguishes him from every other being, as Hannah's prayer reminds us: 'There is none holy

like the LORD, for there is none besides you...' (1 Sam. 2:2).
Therefore when God says, 'I am holy,' he is indicating his
'total otherness'.

Holiness is also associated with life, wholeness and
completeness of being. God is the immortal one, the fountain
of life. Nothing savouring of death or corruption is found in
him. He is wholesome in every way. God is the absolute
standard of perfection. There is nothing incomplete or
imperfect about God. This is why, as we have seen, nothing
associated with decay or death was allowed near God's
tabernacle (see Lev. 13 – 15). It is also the reason why
physical wholeness and normality were expected of those
who served at the tabernacle (see Lev. 21).

Moral qualities

In calling Israel to be holy as God is holy the implication is
that, as God is different from his creation, so God's holy,
'set-apart' nation should be different from all the other
nations (20:26). God's 'statutes' and 'judgements'
(19:19,37) that are presented here for the people to observe
express the kind of holy God he is and provide concrete
examples of what holiness means when it is applied to
people living in this world. It becomes clear that holiness
cannot be separated from ethics. Righteousness is an essential element of holiness, as Isaiah indicates: 'The Holy God
shows himself holy in righteousness' (Isa. 5:16, ESV), and
the requirements of this chapter make this very clear.

God's holy name was proclaimed to Moses when the
Lord passed before him: 'The LORD, the LORD God, merciful
and gracious, long-suffering, and abounding in goodness and
truth, keeping mercy', and who both forgives and punishes
sin (Exod. 34:6-7). By keeping God's laws Israel would not
only be imitating a God very different from the gods of the
surrounding nations, but would be expressing something of

the holy character of God which they themselves had experienced. For instance, their attitude towards the resident alien is to be similar to God's compassionate love towards them when they were aliens living in Egypt (see 19:33-34).

Christians too are challenged to reflect and embody the love and glory of God. It is part of what being made in the image of God means. The image has been marred as a result of human rebellion against God, but in Christ we are being renewed according to the image of God's Son. In seeking to be holy as God is holy we shall be those who reflect God in this world, just as Israel was called to be but never was. Jesus is the true reflector of God. He practised what he preached and in the Sermon on the Mount he calls those who are his to be like him and to be perfect, just as God their heavenly Father is perfect (Matt. 5:48).

It need hardly be said that, in seeking to be holy like God, there is no thought that Israel can be as holy as God. God is superlatively holy, as Isaiah's experience revealed in the seraphic threefold repetition of the word 'holy' (Isa. 6:3). There are degrees of holiness, as we have observed in the ceremonial laws. This needs to be remembered when considering the religious and ethical demands. Keeping God's commandments will lead to being like God, not in the sense of being divine, but in being godly.[2]

Separate but not withdrawn

Though God is separate and transcendent he is not withdrawn from the world. The God revealed to Israel is not like the god of the Deists, who does not concern himself with his creation. He revealed himself to Israel with the aim of benefiting the whole world (Gen. 12:3). Likewise, Israel is to be separate from other nations but not withdrawn. Obeying the commandments of God would not only set Israel apart from the nations; it would enable Israel to be a light to the nations and a witness to the character of the true God. Similarly, Christians are not called to live in holy ghettos such as monasteries or communes, cut off from the world, but by their clean living are to witness to the holy God and Saviour and to act as salt and light in society, to the glory of God and the blessing of the watching world. Jesus indicated in his prayer that those who belong to him should be in the world but not of the world (John 17:15-16).

Uniting the list of laws

Attempts to understand the way the laws are set out have failed and all efforts to arrange them into neat subject divisions prove to be unsatisfactory. It is not that there is no order; it is just that it is not the order we are used to or expect. There are a number of ways in which this body of law is organized and held together.

'I am the LORD your God'

This phrase appears in the introduction (19:2) and is repeated so frequently throughout the chapter, in its longer or shorter form, that it helps to bind together the wide-ranging collection of laws. **'I am the LORD your God'** appears three times in the first half (19:3,4,10) and four times in the second half (19:25,31,34,36), while the shorter form, **'I am the LORD'**, is found four times in the first half (19:12,14,16,18) and three times in the second (19:28,30,32). This results in the refrain being found seven times in each part, and the occurrences of both the full and short forms, when each is added up, also come to seven. Seven is certainly a significant number in the books of Moses and points to the completeness and holiness of the subject matter. There is symmetry here after all, and it is used to keep our minds focused on the holiness of God and what it means to be holy like God.

Halfway through the list the exhortation, **'You shall keep my statutes'** (19:19), has the effect of dividing the collection into two parts. It appears again at the close (19:37), along with the refrain, **'I am the LORD'**, thus providing a suitable and powerful conclusion.

By this phrase, our attention is drawn continually from the laws themselves to the God who gives them. The author of these laws is not a well-respected religious leader or social reformer but, as Isaiah so frequently puts it, 'the Holy One of Israel' (e.g. Isa. 1:4).

When someone issues us with orders our instinctive reaction is one of resentment as we mutter to ourselves, 'Who does he think he is? Who does she think she is?' Before Israel had time to frame such a question God told them who he was. The one giving these orders is not some self-styled autocrat, but the living God who had shown them mercy and had kept the promises he had made to their ancestors (see Exod. 2:23-24). He had rescued them from their slavery to the Egyptians and entered into a special agreement with them at Sinai that they should be his people and he would be their God. God's covenant people are therefore called to please and serve him. The reasons and motives are no different for God's new-covenant people, only now they are intensified through God's revelation and redemption in Jesus the Messiah.

No doubt there is also a veiled threat in the refrain. If these laws are broken, then the people are to beware, for it is the Lord who gives them. The next chapter will say more on the penalties for non-compliance, but there are already hints in this chapter (19:8,20).

The Ten Commandments

Another way in which this list of laws is bound together is through the use of the Ten Commandments. They are not slavishly followed, nor are they always explicitly mentioned, but the collection of laws does have the effect of expounding them and concludes by drawing our attention to the introduction to the basic principles for living: **'I am the LORD your God, who brought you out of the land of Egypt'** (19:36). The following chart shows the links:

Ten Commandments	verse
1. No other gods	19:4a
2. No graven images	19:4b
3. No wrong use of God's name	19:12
4. Remember the Sabbath	19:3b, 30a
5. Honour parents	19:3a
6. No murder	19:16b
7. No adultery	19:20
8. No stealing	19:11a
9. No false witness	19:11b,16a
10. No coveting	19:17-18

Order and balance

There are other ways in which we see order and balance in this list of laws. Gordon Wenham has pointed out that the command to love one's neighbour as oneself (19:18) is expanded in the second half of the chapter to include the resident alien (19:34). The call to **'fear your God'** is a motive in both halves when the law considers the physically disabled and elderly (19:14,32). Again, in the first half children are urged to honour their parents and keep the Sabbaths (19:3), while in the second half parents must respect their daughters and honour God's Sabbaths (19:29-30).[3]

An overview

A miscellaneous list

The list moves quickly from not eating blood or practising divination to banning shaving and tattoos, prostitution, keeping God's day holy and respecting the elderly. The point is that Israel was not allowed to think of separating what many in the West have tended to split up. Religious life was not to be kept in a separate compartment from ordinary, everyday concerns. The whole of life was to be set apart for God. 'At every step in life', writes Walter Kaiser, 'the call to holiness confronts us: in the field, at home, in business, with friends, with aliens and foreigners, in acts of worship, and in the family.'[4]

An extensive list

This comprehensive collection of moral, ceremonial and religious laws covers all areas of life, both public and private. It concerns attitudes towards God (19:4-8,26-28,30-31), the family (19:3,29) and various members of society, from the poor and vulnerable (19:9-10,14-15,20) to the immigrant (19:33-34) and the aged (19:32). The law deals with a person's thoughts (19:17-18) and words (19:14-16) as well as actions. Holiness is expressed in obedience to parents, respect for the elderly, care of the needy, speaking the truth, justice in court and in business dealings, separation from paganism and sincere devotion to God.

Love, respect and justice sum up what these laws teach about our relationship towards others, which will also indicate a love and respect for the God who gave them and who demands our wholehearted allegiance, manifested in doing his will and keeping ourselves from every pagan impurity.

An enduring list

It is especially in relation to this chapter that concerns are raised about the continuing validity of these laws for the new-covenant people of God. As the list is surveyed, there is so much of it that fair-minded people of different religions, or none, would wish to implement, let alone Christians. In fact a number of the laws are quoted or alluded to in the New Testament, but not all of them. The question is, do we only accept what is specifically mentioned in the New Testament and forget the rest? Are Christian farmers to leave grain in the corners of their field for gleaners? Are we all to keep a strict eye on the label the next time we buy an item of clothing to make sure it is 100% cotton or 100% wool?

These laws are set within the covenant that God made with the people at Mount Sinai and were specifically designed to remind Israel that they were to be a people separate from other nations, not only in moral standards but socially and culturally. Something of God's rule was to be seen on earth in the holy nation of Israel. That covenant was a temporary arrangement and looked beyond itself to something more substantial and permanent. With the coming of Christ and all that he has accomplished through his atoning death, the Sinai covenant has had its day and, with it, all that served to prepare for the coming of Christ. But the written Law has not been consigned to the rubbish heap of history. It remains part of God's revealed Word that needs to be interpreted in the light of Jesus Christ and the new covenant.

These rules and regulations for the ordering of Israel's personal and national life witness to basic standards that are of continuing significance. The Ten Commandments are unique even within the Old Testament, being clearly set apart from the other laws. Most would agree that they are themselves foundational and are not tied, like so many of the other rules, to a particular social and cultural environment or period of history. Other social and moral laws are often examples of the Ten Commandments applied to specific cases. Our Lord taught us to see, even with the Ten Commandments, the need to keep the true spirit of the law as well as the letter (Matt. 5:21-22,27-28). This encourages us to look for the principles behind those ceremonial and social laws that have had their day since the coming of Christ. The spirit and principle of all the laws listed remain unchanged, even if their formal expression may change.[5]

21.
Living the godly life: the challenge

Please read again Leviticus 19:1-37

When one earnest and respected preacher came to a coal-mining community near Wrexham, North Wales, in 1904, the Christians were so affected by his messages on Isaiah 6 concerning the holiness of God that the churches of the area experienced a spiritual awakening and many hundreds of people were converted. Such was the spiritual and moral transformation that the streets were quiet from drunken brawls, the crime rate dropped dramatically and home life was revolutionized.

People who have experienced God's holy presence and salvation are urged to express God's holiness by observing all God's statutes and judgements (19:37). This is what the God and Saviour of his covenant people demands.

The first set of obligations (19:3-18)

Respect for parents and keeping the Sabbath

Each person is to revere his or her mother and father as they would honour God[1] and is to observe God's Sabbaths (19:3).[2]

The mother's influence in the home is stressed by giving her pride of place, something which is contrary to the norm (cf. Exod. 20:12; Deut. 5:16; Prov. 6:20). King Lemuel was instructed in God's truth by his mother (Prov. 31:1), as was Timothy (Acts 16:1; 2 Tim. 1:5; 3:15). The fourth and fifth of the Ten Commandments are cited here in reverse order to show how closely they belong together. Later, when the law deals with the responsibility of parents to children, this is again followed by a reference to the Sabbath (19:29-30). Holiness begins in the home and the Sabbath law benefits family life. It is Jesus who teaches how the Sabbath should be kept, which is strange if, as some believe, it has been abolished under the new covenant.

No idolatry or images of God

They are not to turn to worthless gods, or make images of the true God (19:4; cf. Exod. 20:3-4). This is what Israel did when they made the golden calf (Exod. 32:4,8). God did not reveal himself to his people in a form which they could reproduce and then fall down before in worship (Deut. 4:12,15-19). When the representatives of Israel 'saw the God of Israel', all that could be expressed was what was under his feet, and even then the description is by way of analogy (Exod. 24:10). Moses, in his special experience, got no further than seeing the afterglow of God's presence (Exod. 33:18-23). Though God has revealed himself supremely in the person of his Son, we are not to make pictures or sculptures of him to pray before, or to worship. We do not know what Jesus looked like when he was on earth and the descriptions of the glorified Jesus that we are given in the book of Revelation defy pictorial representation. Particularly in times of prosperity and peaceful existence, the Christian can succumb to the temptation to make material possessions, pleasure and success a substitute for God.

A generous spirit and a right attitude to worship

They must carefully observe the rules of the peace offering and at harvest time they must leave some crops and grapes for the poor and the immigrant to gather up (19:5-10). These two laws probably follow one another because they encouraged a generous spirit, something the disciples of Christ are urged to possess (see Acts 20:34-35). While those with privileges are to remember their responsibilities to the needy, the less fortunate are to be helped in ways that are not degrading. Gleaning in the field and picking up fallen fruit meant that the poor could 'hold their heads high', for they too had worked for their food.[3] Ruth was one poor immigrant who made use of the gleaning laws to provide for herself and Naomi (Ruth 2), while Boaz went beyond the letter of the law in his generosity and eventually married Ruth, which resulted in descendants that led to the Saviour who came for poor sinners like us.

The **'peace offering'** (see 3:1-17; 7:11-21) was the only type of sacrifice where the offerer was given back a portion to eat. As the sacrifice had to be consumed within two days, or else be burned, it encouraged the people to share with the less well off these meat joints that were too large for one family to consume in a couple of days. For anyone to eat the holy meat on the third day would mean that the whole offering would be unacceptable. It would become rotten meat (19:7; cf. 7:18).[4] Any who ate it would be held accountable and would be 'cut off' from God's people, because they had desecrated (**'profaned'**) what was set apart (**'hallowed'**) for the Lord (19:8). In their enjoyment of the meal, they were not allowed to forget that it was sacrificial meat they were eating and they could not do what they liked with it. God does not automatically accept offerings. They must be presented in the way he has ordained. Christians are to have a similar attitude when partaking of the Lord's Supper. This symbolic sacrificial meal is to be eaten in a way that is respectful of our Lord's atoning death and of our unity with others in Christ. Otherwise we too shall be held accountable and fall under God's judgement (1 Cor. 11:17-34).

Honesty and respect for the possessions of others

They are not to steal, deceive one another by denying a truth or affirming a lie, or swear falsely using God's name (19:11-12). The Eighth, Ninth and Third Commandments (Exod. 20:7,15-16) are presented here and stress the need for honesty and honouring other people's possessions. Failure in this area has already been mentioned as unfaithfulness to the Lord (6:1-7). Those belonging to the new covenant are each called to put away lying and 'speak truth with his neighbour, for we are members of one another'. And, perhaps with a view to the previous section concerning a generous spirit, Paul goes on to say this: 'Let him who stole steal no longer, but rather let him labour, working with his hands what is good, that he may have something to give him who has need' (Eph. 4:25,28; cf. Col. 3:9).

When a false statement is made under an oath that uses God's name, it means that God's good and holy nature is sullied. Swearing falsely in God's name is, in effect, to make God an accomplice and give him a bad name. When we pray, 'Hallowed be your name', let us be sure we mean it by not acting in a way that pollutes the holy name by which we are called. God's name includes not only the Father, but Jesus the Son and the Holy Spirit (Matt. 28:19).

No exploitation of the vulnerable

They are not to exploit or rob a member of the covenant community; hired servants must be paid promptly, and they are not to harm the deaf and the blind (19:13-14). The strong, in other words, must not take advantage of the weak by misusing their position of power or influence. It is another type of robbery to use an employee's time and energy and not to pay up the agreed wage on time. (This law is also applied to immigrants in Deuteronomy 24:14-15.) The New Testament is forthright in its condemnation of this type of crime (James 5:4). Defenceless people like the physically disabled are not to be mistreated. To swear an oath in front of the deaf, to do them harm, or to put literal or figurative obstacles in the way of the blind, to abuse or exploit them, are despicable practices that witness to the depths of human depravity.

While various forms of disability are used in the ceremonial laws to symbolize lack of wholeness and unfitness to enter God's presence, this did not mean that disabled people were to be treated with disrespect. Jesus reached out to the deaf and dumb, the blind and the maimed, and healed them. It not only expressed his care and authority but it indicated that a new era was dawning and signalled the end of the old symbolic system that included the disability rules (see Isa. 35:5-6; Matt. 11:1-6).

The Israelites are commanded to fear God. The deaf and blind have a God who sees and hears everything. Great evils are done when there is no fear of God (Ps. 36:1; Rom. 3:18). The Christian is ever to live conscious not of CCTV cameras, but of the all-seeing eye of God. This will help restrain us from committing evil acts. Peter and Paul both encourage Christians to 'fear God' (1 Peter 1:17; 2:17; Phil. 2:12).

Impartiality and justice in dealings with others

They are neither to pervert the course of justice by showing favouritism and spreading malicious gossip, nor to endanger the life of a covenant member (19:15-16). Those responsible for justice in the community must be impartial in their decisions. In carrying out their legal duties, they must not be influenced by the rich and powerful, on the one hand, or, on the other, show special favours, other than the ones specified in the law, to the disadvantaged. This would rule out the modern policy of positive discrimination that has become popular in some quarters. Each member of the community is to be judged **'in righteousness'**. God is a righteous, or just, God and is the ultimate standard for what is fair and right.

Associated with justice in the courtroom is the instruction that a person must not go about spreading slander, which is a form of bearing false witness (Exod. 20:16). James urges Christians not to show partiality (James 2:1,9). To **'take a stand against the life** [literally "blood"] **of your neighbour'** is a difficult expression. It probably means that a person is not to stand idly by when a fellow citizen is in danger, especially in the case of refusing to give evidence in support of someone falsely accused of a crime that deserved the death penalty.

This legislation is weighted in terms of obligations rather than of rights, which is the emphasis of the New Testament as well. Christians are called to have the mind of Christ, who did not stand on his honour and rights, but made himself nothing for our sakes (Phil. 2:4-8).

Love for others, not hatred

They are not to hate in their hearts fellow members of the covenant family, but wrong-doers are to be faced with their actions, otherwise the witnesses will share their guilt. And they are not to seek revenge or bear a grudge, but they are to love fellow-citizens of the covenant as they would like to be loved (19:17-18). This list of moral obligations reaches a climax with the call not to hate but to love the people of God. Instead of harbouring hatred in the heart, an offended person is encouraged to rebuke, or argue the case openly with, the offender (see Prov. 27:5). This is the way of love, and the offended person would then **'not bear sin because of him'**, meaning either that the offended party's own feelings would not boil over into sinful action, or that the offended one would not be party to the offender's wrong by keeping silent. The law is not confined to externals, but considers sin **'in your heart'**, an important point to which Jesus drew attention (Matt. 5:28).

Instead of seeking revenge and nursing grudges, God's people are to **'love your neighbour as yourself'**. This is not an invitation to be preoccupied with ourselves before we consider others, but a call to self-giving love, where we treat others just as we would like to be treated. Love can be commanded because it is not merely an emotion but an action. God is loved when his commandments are kept (Deut. 11:1) and love for Jesus is shown when we keep his commandments (John 14:15,23-24). James calls the command to love the 'royal law' (James 2:8) and it was named by Jesus as the second great commandment that embraces all our duties to others (Matt. 22:39-40). Paul also quotes the law of love as a summary of the second half of the Ten Commandments (Rom. 13:8-10). In addition, in his teaching concerning the one who is weak in the faith, the law of love is in his mind. He prompts strong believers not to please themselves but to bear with the weak. 'Let each of us please his neighbour for his good, leading to edification. For even Christ did not please himself' (Rom.15:2-3).

Those who claim to love God are urged by John to love fellow members of the Christian community, bearing in mind God's love in sending his Son to be the Saviour of the world (1 John 4:7-21). Jesus showed that such love was to be extended to one's enemies (Matt. 5:43-48) and Paul highlights the fact that God's love for believers in Christ was when they were still sinners and enemies of God (Rom. 5:6-8,10).

The second set of obligations (19:19-36)

This is what the God and Saviour of his covenant people demands:

Holiness in every area of life and respect for the rights of owners

They are not to mix different types of animal, seed or fabric, and the rights of owners must be respected, both in the case of sexually abused slave girls and of the harvesting of fruit trees (19:19-25).

Three quite distinct situations are addressed in this paragraph. The people are first reminded that holiness is about being set apart and that in every area of life they were to be a holy, separated people for God. Unnatural mixtures were seen as out of keeping with the creation order that everything was made 'according to its kind' (Gen. 1:21,24,25). These laws that helped to emphasize the distinction between Jew and Gentile have no place in the church, for in Christ the various walls separating them are broken down (Eph. 2:14-15; Gal. 3:26-28).

Again, with the law concerning slaves and their owners, the gospel of Jesus Christ knows no such distinctions (Gal. 3:28; Col. 3:11) and provides principles that led to the emancipation of slaves. What this law does in regulating sinful behaviour is to allow an exception to the rule governing the death penalty for adultery. It concerns the case of a free man who has had a sexual relationship with a slave girl assigned in advance of redemption and freedom to be married to another (the word **'concubine'** in some translations is an unwarranted interpretative addition). Since the girl had not yet gained the status of a free married or betrothed woman, she still belonged to her master. This meant that the offence was not technically adultery, for under the legislation, adultery was sexual intercourse with a married or betrothed woman (Deut. 22:22-27). Though the death penalty did not apply in this case, the action was still a serious sin and, after proper 'investigation' (this is a better translation than **'scourging'** or 'punishment'),[5] the guilty man was required to bring the most costly type of sacrifice, a trespass offering (see 5:14 – 6:7), for the priest to make atonement on his behalf. And this grave sin **'which he has done shall be forgiven him'**. Certain situations were tolerated because a perfect, ideal society did not exist and this law encourages respect for what belongs to others and restrains those who would take unfair advantage of other people's rights. It was because of the hardness of the people's hearts that such laws were necessary. Jesus makes it clear that every lustful look means that the adultery law has been broken (Matt. 5:27-28). There is, nevertheless, forgiveness for repentant sinners who look to Jesus Christ.

The third item of law in this paragraph points to the time when they are settled in the promised land. After they have planted fruit trees they are forbidden from eating the fruit for the first three years, and even in the fourth year they must offer all the produce to the Lord. Only from the fifth year onward are they allowed to eat the fruit which, God promises, will **'yield to you its increase'**. The law recognizes that it takes time for a tree to yield its full potential. In those first three years the fruit of such trees must be regarded as **'uncircumcised'**, a derogatory term (see Gen. 34:14; Judg. 14:3) which graphically conveyed the point that this is forbidden fruit.[6]

While **'uncircumcised'** (often translated 'forbidden') is how the Hebrew reads in the second part of the verse, the previous clause, commencing, **'then you shall count their fruit as uncircumcised'**, is literally, 'You shall foreskin its foreskin with its fruit,' which suggests plucking the buds before the fruit has formed. The branches of the young trees are not pruned, as some suppose, but the pollinated fruit-bearing buds are removed before they develop, which is good gardening policy.[7]

Because the fruit of the first three years is unworthy of God, it is the entire crop of the fourth year that is to be regarded as **'holy'** and offered to the Lord. It is not described as a first-fruit offering here (see 2:14; 27:26,30; Exod. 23:19), but as **'a praise to the LORD'**. Setting apart the first good year's crop for God is another aspect of the holy, godly life. By keeping this law they acknowledged that God was the owner of the land and the provider of the harvest and at the same time it enabled them to express their gratitude in praises to God. There is a principle here that the wisdom teacher picks up:

> Honour the LORD with your possessions,
> And with the first fruits of all your increase;
> So your barns will be filled with plenty,
> And your vats will overflow with new wine
> (Prov. 3:9-10).

No pagan customs or abuse of the body

They are not to follow pagan customs such as eating the blood of animals, practising divination and soothsaying, cutting their hair and beard in certain ways, or mutilating or tattooing their bodies (19:26-28). Unlike the laws already given about consuming blood (3:17; 17:10-14), there is a slight variation. Instead of eating **'with the blood'**, it literally reads, 'eating on the blood', suggesting that pagan fortune-telling practices are in mind here.[8] All attempts to predict the future by interpreting omens (**'divination'** or augury) and fortune-telling (**'soothsaying'**) are prohibited. God would reveal to his people what they needed to know through dreams, the high priest's Urim and God's prophets, without their resorting to pagan methods (see Deut. 18:9-22; 1 Sam. 28:6).

While customary expressions of mourning were acceptable, such as tearing one's clothes and putting on sackcloth and ashes, mourning rites associated with paganism were prohibited (see Deut. 14:1). These included cutting the hair round the temples and trimming the beard in some way. To this day the ultra-orthodox Jew will be seen wearing ringlets of hair each side of his face.

Finally, God's people are not to gash themselves, as the prophets of Baal did on Mount Carmel, neither are they to tattoo or paint their bodies, as the pagans did in their rituals. Such activities disfigured the body. 'This law', as Wenham remarks, 'conforms to other holiness rules which seek to uphold the natural order of creation and preserve it from corruption.' Wholeness of body is used to symbolize the perfection of holiness. Christians are encouraged not to abuse their bodies because as human beings they are made in God's image and their bodies are temples of the Holy Spirit (1 Cor. 6:18-20).

The sanctity of family life, the Sabbath and the sanctuary

They are not to degrade their daughters by forcing them into prostitution; rather, they are to observe God's Sabbaths and reverence his sanctuary (19:29-30). When people get into heavy debt, desperate times often call for desperate measures. The temptation for a father to sell his daughter into prostitution would be considerable. From different parts of the world we still hear sad stories of poor parents using their daughters in this way to eke out a living. The practice 'degrades' (literally 'desecrates/profanes', as in 19:12) the girl, depriving her of her right and duty to live a godly, holy life. Such a solution for making quick money, however obscene and degrading, encourages others to follow, leading to the prospect of the promised land becoming polluted with prostitutes and their clients, a situation that, sadly, did develop in Israel (see Hosea 4:14; Jer. 3:2). However desperate life becomes, it never warrants depraved activity that causes one's children to sin and only breeds further revolting practices.[9]

Again the keeping of the Sabbath is mentioned (see 19:3), along with reverencing the sanctuary. The word **'reverence'**, used already in reference to God (19:14) and parents (19:3), is attached to the place where God ordained that he would meet with his people. It applies here particularly to the tabernacle precincts where the people were allowed to enter (see 12:4). Here is one place where the special day is associated with gathering at the special place for worship. The coming of Christ has not done away with the need for God's people to come together on a particular day for communal worship. Under the new covenant the principle of a sacred time and place remains, only now Christians the world over are encouraged to assemble together on the Lord's Day to worship God in praise, prayer, hearing his Word read and proclaimed, partaking of the Lord's Supper, encouraging and supporting one another and in evangelism. They are to do this not in some central earthly sanctuary, but in their various localities, as when the disciples met with the risen Lord in 'the upper room'.

Interestingly, in this context, the holy day of the week and the holy place are brought together after the call not to make their daughters unholy. Ezekiel uses this verse in his prophecies against Israel and also refers to the way they are sacrificing their children to idols. They thought nothing of engaging in practices involving the worship of Molech and then on the same day entering God's sanctuary to profane it (Ezek. 23:37-39). Christians too must be careful not to bring dishonour to God and his people through modern forms of idolatry that spoil family life and injure children.

No consultation of the dead

They are not to resort to mediums or spiritists to defile themselves (19:31). It is forbidden to consult the dead. Necromancy was practised through those considered expert in the art, such as mediums and spiritists. It was very prevalent in the ancient world, as it is today, and was often associated with ancestor worship. Everything associated with death and the dead, as we have seen, was unclean, the very opposite of the living God. Those who seek ghosts and departed spirits pollute themselves, thus making it impossible to be holy. Only those who are clean can live the holy life. Besides being spiritually unhealthy, it can be mentally damaging. Saul turned to a medium to consult the dead when God refused to communicate with him. In judgement and to the consternation of the medium, God allowed Samuel to appear and pronounce Saul's end (1 Sam. 28).

Respect for the elderly and the fear of God

They are to stand in the presence of the aged, show respect for the elderly and revere God (19:32). Like the disabled (19:14), the elderly are among that class of vulnerable people of which the unscrupulous seek to take advantage. When a society ceases to fear God it soon degenerates in its respect for those whom it considers a drain on the system or an inconvenience, such as the unborn child, the mentally and terminally ill and the very old. It happened in Israel as part of God's judgement on a society about to collapse, when the 'child' became 'insolent towards the elder, and the base towards the honourable' (Isa. 3:5). People who revere God under the new, as under the old, covenant will respect **'the grey-haired'** as they would a president or member of the royal family.

Fair treatment for foreigners

They are to treat foreigners living among them as if they were native-born, not oppressing them but loving them as they themselves would like to be loved (19:33-34). The 'stranger' is someone who is not a descendant of one of the Israelite tribes but who comes to live and work among them. This designation included individuals like Doeg the Edomite (1 Sam. 21:7), Uriah the Hittite (2 Sam. 11:3) and Ittai the Gittite (2 Sam. 15:19-22). As in other countries of the ancient Near East, such people were kept ethnically apart and were only subsequently absorbed into the society through intermarriage.[10] Since such immigrants might at first not be so familiar with local customs it would not be too difficult to take advantage of them and cheat them.[11]

This law is remarkable in urging Israel to treat such foreigners among them like their own community members and to love them as people like themselves (19:34; cf. 19:18). This command is motivated by the memory that the Israelites had once been foreign residents in Egypt. Knowing what it was like for their ancestors to be at best second-class citizens, and then later to be treated like slaves, should make them eager to do right by them and not mistreat them. When Christians from the West Indies came to Britain after the Second World War to settle and work, they were in large measure shunned by the white British churches. It was a disgrace. Holiness in practice for a Christian means welcoming strangers of whatever background and colour. Christians, after all, are themselves strangers and pilgrims in this world (1 Peter 2:11) and often know what it is like to be ostracized and treated badly by the worldly powers. 'Let brotherly love continue. Do not forget to entertain strangers…' (Heb. 13:1-2).

Honesty and integrity in business dealings

They are not to use dishonest standards in business (19:35-36). The requirement begins in a familiar way: **'You shall do no injustice in judgement'** (cf. 19:15), but whereas earlier the focus was on courtroom justice, this concerns justice in the market-place. In scales, weights and measurements of capacity and quantity, they must have righteous, or **'just'**, standards. Double standards might help increase profits, but they are not legitimate for those who would live the godly life. This is a particular challenge to Christians in the cut and thrust of business life, but in all our dealings with other people honesty, integrity and faithfulness must be practised.

May the Lord help us all to please this God, who has rescued us from slavery to sin and Satan, to become slaves of God, presenting ourselves as slaves to righteousness leading to holiness, for without holiness no one will see the Lord.

22.
Death: the punishment for disobedience

Please read Leviticus 20:1-27

Some are appalled at this list of what they consider to be barbaric punishments, even though these may seem humane in comparison with the brutality meted out to offenders in other ancient Near-Eastern societies. However, we should be more outraged than we often are that human beings created in God's image could commit such terrible crimes.

The question is often asked whether the harshness of these punishments is against the spirit of Jesus and the New Testament. It would appear so at first sight, for we read that Jesus did not come to condemn the world but to save it (John 3:17) and did not condemn the woman caught in the act of adultery (John 8:1-11). However, Jesus and his apostles warned of God's coming judgement day when the punishments inflicted in this life will be as nothing compared with the eternal torment of the second death.

Crime and punishment

It would appear that capital punishment represented the maximum rather than the minimum penalty. The law that strictly forbids accepting a ransom for the life of a murderer (Num. 35:31) would seem to imply that in other cases it was possible for the death penalty to be commuted to some form of ransom or compensation. Walter Kaiser states that 'The death penalty showed how serious the crime was, and the provision of a substitute, either of money or of some other reparation, allowed the individual's life to be spared.'[1]

As we have seen with the laws, so the penalties are set in the context of a certain culture and period. But if the laws contain principles of living that are of lasting value and importance, so too it must be said of the punishments. In our permissive society it is important to remember that the wrath of God is already being revealed from heaven and that those who practise the kind of sins mentioned here and by Paul in Romans 1:18-32 'are worthy of death'.

Within the Christian community it is not for the church to punish criminals. That is left to the state (Rom. 13:1-7). However, the New Testament, while it encourages the need for compassion and understanding, does not support an easy-going attitude towards the breaking of God's laws. For the sake of the purity of the church and the eternal well-being of offenders, it urges local churches to discipline members and to put out of fellowship the unrepentant who persist in sinful activities (1 Cor. 5:1-8). It also suggests that God sometimes intervenes directly to remove sinful members, either for a time through sickness, or permanently through their death (1 Cor. 11:29-30).

While the application is primarily to Christians, as the Israel of God, we cannot ignore the bearing of this teaching on the wider world. The Canaanites were punished for the sins listed (20:23) and the nations of the world are judged according to the light they are given. They are not punished for rebelling against God's specially revealed will, as in the case of Israel and Judah, but for crimes against humanity (see Amos 1 – 2). The prophets make it clear that God rules the nations and they are accountable to him. Empires rise and he uses them for his purposes and they fall because of their corrupt customs and obnoxious crimes. As Kellogg observes, 'All history witnesses that moral corruption and relaxed legislation, especially in matters affecting the relations of the sexes, bring in their train sure retribution, not in Hades, but here on earth.'[2]

Structure

The chapter calls to mind many of the sins of Leviticus 18 and both chapters enclose and highlight the important collection of laws in Leviticus 19. As for this chapter, the contents are arranged so that the penalties for religious crimes (20:2-6,27) surround those for family crimes (20:9-21) and the second half of the chapter is a mirror image of the first.[3] After the introduction (20:1-2a), we have:

  A. Penalties for religious crimes (20:2b-6)
    B. A call to holiness (20:7)
      C. A call to obedience (20:8)
        D. Penalties for family crimes (20:9-21)
      C^1. A call to obedience (20:22-25)
    B^1. A call to holiness (20:26)
  A^1. The penalty for religious crimes (20:27)

Penalties for religious crimes (20:2-6,27)

The use of children in the worship of Molech and necromancy are two serious sins found together in the list of rebellious acts committed by King Manasseh (2 Kings 21:6). Both are referred to as committing **'prostitution'** (20:5-6; cf. 17:7). It is spiritual infidelity, for God had entered into a

covenant relationship with his people that is similar to the
marriage bond. The law pertains to **'a man or a woman'**
(20:27), to the immigrant or resident 'stranger', as well as to
the native-born Israelite (20:2; cf. 18:26).

The worship of Molech (20:2-5; see 18:21)

The Lord gives reasons for the condemnation of this revolting practice. To engage in the worship of Molech is **'to
defile my sanctuary and profane my holy name'** (20:3).
Far from hallowing God's name, it does the very opposite.
At the same time it soils the place where God has chosen to
live among his people (see 19:30). Even though sacrificing
their children to Molech took place outside the temple,
Ezekiel declared that it desecrated God's sanctuary.

Instead of knowing the blessing of having God's face
shining upon them, they would experience having his **'face
against'** them in judgement. The punishment is death by
stoning, which was the usual form of execution for religious
and family crimes, such as Sabbath-breaking, blasphemy,
idolatry and adultery, and for incorrigible children. It was the
responsibility of **'the people of the land'** — that is, the
ordinary Israelite citizens (cf. 4:27) — to see that the sentence was executed, but it was the witnesses to the crime
who were required to cast the first stones (Deut. 17:2-7).

If the people failed to do their duty and engaged in 'a
cover-up' — if they **'hide their eyes'** (20:4) — God would
act decisively and not only would the guilty party be punished, but the entire extended family (20:5). Being **'cut off'**
(20:3) implies more than a premature death, for that is what
the stoning accomplished (20:2). It suggests that the family
line was cut off and/or the person was cut off from the future
blessing associated with Abraham, Isaac and Jacob. The
punishment fitted the crime. As the guilty had given their
'descendants' (literally, 'seed') to Molech, so God would

end their 'seed', or family line, and they would have no part in the promised 'seed' about which so much is said in Genesis.[4]

Necromancy (20:6,27; cf. 19:31)

King Saul resorted to ghosts and familiar spirits when he received no communication from God (1 Sam. 28:3,7,9). It was the final rebellious act that tipped the scales and brought his downfall. Because of his unfaithfulness the Lord 'killed him, and turned the kingdom over to David' (1 Chr. 10:13-14). Saul's line was 'cut off' and he himself had no part in that divine rule associated with David and the coming Messiah.

Penalties for family crimes (20:9-21)

This list of prohibited unions, with the punishment for each, is headed by the case of a person dishonouring his parents. The assumption is that a breakdown in children's obligations to their parents will lead to a breakdown in relationships with other family members.

Dishonouring parents (20:9)

The previous chapter called on children to 'revere ... mother and ... father' (19:3). To 'curse' (literally, 'to make light of') one's father or mother is the very opposite of to 'honour' them (literally, 'to make [them] heavy'). Instead of recognizing their parents for who they are, the children are regarding them as nonentities, without weight or significance. The shocking nature of the sin is indicated by the repetition of the crime: **'He has cursed his father or his mother.'** It demands the death penalty. **'His blood shall be upon him,'** means that the person deserves to die and that those who carry out the penalty are free from any charge of murder.

The law applied not only to children when they were young, but to the responsibilities of children to look after their parents in their old age. This is clear when Jesus attacked the tradition of the Pharisees and accused them of cursing, rather than honouring, their parents. He called them hypocrites, play-actors, for under the appearance of great piety they were using human tradition to break God's law. Are we guilty of the very same thing when we use legitimate Christian activity as a pious excuse to get out of our responsibilities to our parents?

Adultery (20:10)

Adultery is another great cause of breakdown in family life (see 18:20). The law is directed against a man having sexual relations with **'another man's wife'**, even the wife of a covenant community member (**'his neighbour's wife'**). For breaking this Seventh Commandment the penalty is death both for the adulterer and the woman involved. Jesus made it clear that adultery also included lustful looks, as well as divorce and remarriage for the wrong reasons (Matt. 5:27-28; 19:3-9; Mark 10:2-12; Luke 16:18).

Incest and unnatural unions (20:11-21)

This list of penalties for incest is not an exact parallel to the list of offences in chapter 18. There are differences in the order and the cases covered. Here the order is according to the type of punishment described. Even though the woman is also culpable, the law is directed to the man, as he is the dominant partner who initiates the sexual activity. It prevents the husband and other males 'from taking advantage of the woman'.[5]

1. Crimes demanding community action (20:11-16)

Crimes where the penalty is death by stoning include sexual relations with:

- *A mother or step-mother* (20:11; cf. 18:7-8). The law assumes the mother's encouragement or consent, for both are declared responsible: **'Their blood shall be upon them.'**
- *A daughter-in-law* (20:12; cf 18:15). The act is considered a confusion, or **'perversion'** — a term applied to bestiality in 18:23.
- *Another male* (20:13; cf. 18:22). Homosexual activity is described as something abhorrent, **'an abomination'**. Both partners are held responsible.
- *A mother-in-law* (20:14). The case is where a man marries or cohabits with[6] **'a woman and her mother'**, which is similar to that of 'a woman and her daughter' (see 18:17). Not only the man but the women are held responsible, suggesting that they have collaborated together. It is depravity, or **'wickedness'**, and the punishment involved 'burning' their bodies, probably after being stoned, to prevent them from being buried (cf. Josh. 7:15,25; but see also Gen. 38:24; Lev. 21:9). Fire is a purifying agent (Isa. 4:4; 6:6-7) and is probably used on this occasion to press home the need to cleanse the depravity from among them.
- *An animal* (20:15-16; cf. 18:23). Both the person and the animal were to be put to death. Executing the animal as well as the man or woman incurs no guilt, for the animal is involved in a crime worthy of death. An ox that gores someone is similarly put to death for its action, even though it is not morally responsible (Exod. 21:28-32; cf. Gen. 9:5).[7]

2. Crimes demanding direct divine action (20:17-19)

In the following list, human action in carrying out the death sentence is not mentioned. The penalty of being **'cut off'** refers to direct punishment by God (see 20:3). The crimes demanding this punishment include sexual relations with:

• *A sister*, either by his father or his mother (20:17; cf. 18:9,11). For a man to cohabit with or marry his sister or half-sister is a disgrace (**'a wicked thing'**).[8] They are both equally involved and equally guilty, as the euphemisms 'sees her nakedness' and 'sees his nakedness' suggest. The covenant community will witness their punishment even if this secret affair has not been publicly recognized (literally, 'in the sight of the sons of their people'). Interestingly, it is the man who is principally to blame — **'He shall bear his guilt'** — for it is his responsibility to guard his sister's honour.[9]

• *A woman ill through bleeding* (20:18; cf. 18:19). This is the only case in this paragraph that does not concern incest. This situation is more comprehensive than the one described in 18:19, where it refers only to a woman's monthly period. Here it speaks more generally of **'her sickness'** and covers all blood loss whether after childbirth, as a result of a chronic condition or a menstrual period (see 12:2; 15:19-25). Though this law has physical advantages for the woman, it is because of **'her blood'** that sexual relations between the couple are treated so seriously. Both are held accountable, for the man has laid bare what the woman has revealed. While the original reasons concerning blood have now been annulled with the coming of Christ and the shedding of his blood, concern for the wife should always be in the husband's mind during times of such 'sickness'. Love for one's neighbour surely includes protection of women during periods of weakness. Peter urges husbands to live with their wives 'with understanding, giving honour to the wife, as to the weaker vessel' (1 Peter 3:7), while Paul adds a further dimension by demanding that husbands should love their wives 'as Christ ... loved the church and gave himself for it' (Eph. 5:25).

3. A crime where the penalty is unspecified (20:19)

Only one item is listed:
* It concerns sexual relations with *an aunt* (20:19; cf. 18:12-13). The aunt is a blood relative, the sister of either a mother or a father. **'They shall bear their guilt'** tells us that both parties are responsible for their actions and will experience the consequences. What form the punishment will take is left unstated, but punishment is certain.

4. Crimes demanding the penalty of childlessness (20:20-21)

To have no children was considered a great calamity and disgrace, as we see in the case of Rachel and that of Hannah (Gen. 30:23; 1 Sam. 1:5-11). There are many instances in Genesis where this caused much heart-searching and grief, as indicated in the stories of Abraham and Sarah, Isaac and Rebekah, and Jacob and Rachel. We should not forget the context for the people of God in the Old Testament era of the promised seed through the descendants of Abraham and Israel. Having children, particularly sons, was seen as a blessing from God: 'Behold, children are a heritage from the LORD, the fruit of the womb is his reward' (Ps. 127:3; cf. 128:3-4). Not to have children was therefore a sign of God's judgement (Gen. 20:17-18) and that is what is conveyed here. God will frustrate those who hope to have children through engaging in sexual relationships that are banned. Marriage was the means of continuing the family name and line. Absalom laments: 'I have no son to keep my name in remembrance' (2 Sam. 18:18).

The punishment of being childless does not necessarily mean that God intervened to cause barrenness, as he did in the case of the women in Abimelech's household (Gen. 20:17-18). The expression is used in the case of King Jehoiachin — called Coniah or Jeconiah (Jer. 22:30) — even when he had several sons (see 1 Chr. 3:17-18). Besides the specific meaning of being 'childless' it does have the more general meaning of 'stripped'. It suggests being stripped of honour, which is what happened to Jehoiachin's sons. They became eunuchs in Babylon (see Isa. 39:7). Now that Jesus Christ, God's promised 'seed', has arrived, childless couples need feel no shame as they come to terms with their situation.

Two more cases of incest are included, which concern sexual relations with:

• *An aunt by marriage* (20:20). This law relating to one's uncle's wife was not given in chapter 18 (but see 18:14). The wife is related through the marriage union in which the two become one flesh. In having sexual relations with his uncle's wife he has in effect had relations with him. The bond is close. The man and the woman involved are both held responsible and will die in dishonour, through having no children to support them, or give them a future.

• *A sister-in-law* (20:21; cf. 18:16). A man who seeks to marry his brother's widow, other than on the legitimate grounds of raising 'seed' for his dead brother (connected with the levirate law of Deuteronomy 25:5-6), has committed a 'repulsive' or **'unclean'**[10] act and they will both bear the consequences.

A call to obedience (20:8,22-25)

This call to observe God's statutes and ordinances picks up the challenge heard in 18:4-5,26. It also includes the same graphic language, describing the promised land as being made to **'vomit'** them out (20:22; 18:28), just as God was **'casting out'** the Canaanites who had been committing all the filthy habits listed (20:23; cf. 18:3,27). God loathed, or 'abhorred' (20:23), the Canaanites for their disgusting practices in the same way that ungrateful Israel was soon to loathe the manna that God provided (Num. 21:5). God again identifies himself as Jehovah/Yahweh their God (20:24), who has promised to give his people the land of Canaan as a gift.

They are encouraged to think well of the land, for it is **'a land flowing with milk and honey'**, a description first heard by Moses when God appeared to him at the burning bush (Exod. 3:8,17). It speaks of rich resources, of life and plenty — a little taste of the Garden of Eden (Deut. 8:7-9). This land not only looks back to a lost garden, but forward to the wonderful hope of a new creation when God's people will inherit a transformed earth.

God called his people to be a **'separated'** people from all the other **'peoples'**. As separation was an important factor in the creation account (dividing light from darkness, day from night, waters from waters — see Gen. 1:4,6-7,14,18), so it is in the creation of Israel. These ceremonial and separation laws that we find strange are to be seen against this background. They begin to make some sense to us when we understand that in distinguishing the clean from the unclean creatures Israel is being reminded at every meal table to be like their creator God, who had separated them from the other nations to live separated lives. The distinctions that they are constantly to make in everyday life encourage them to be God's set-apart people.

These distinctions and divisions are broken down with the coming of Christ. The people of God are drawn from all races to belong to a new worldwide family where the old rules distinguishing Jew from Gentile have had their day. Nevertheless, the principle behind the separation laws still applies, as well as those laws that clearly show the moral character of God. Christians are called to imitate God by showing through their clean, moral living something of what God is like. 'Be followers of God as dear children' (see Eph. 5:1-5). There is a constant appeal throughout the New Testament for Christians to be separate from the world in the way they live and act. Paul speaks of having no fellowship with the unfruitful works of darkness (Eph. 5:11). James includes in his definition of pure and undefiled religion 'to keep oneself unspotted from the world' (James 1:27). Peter calls believers to 'abstain from fleshly lusts which war against the soul' (1 Peter 2:11), while John writes, 'Do not love the world or the things in the world' (1 John 2:15).

A call to holiness (20:7,26)

In this renewed call for the Israelites to **'sanctify'** themselves and **'be holy'**, and so imitate the Lord their God who is holy (see 19:2), holiness is clearly identified with separation. Not only does the word **'holy'** itself suggest separation, but God spells it out that they are to be holy because the holy God has **'separated'** Israel from the nations to belong to him. This phrase, **'separated you from the peoples'** (20:26), is a repetition of the words at the end of 20:24. In this way we learn very clearly that sanctification (holiness) cannot be divorced from the separation that God demands. Holiness involves separation *from* all that is unclean and separation *to* what is clean. Israel is to be separate *from* the immoral practices of the pagan cultures — symbolized by abstaining from unclean foods — and be separate *to* God by keeping his statutes that display his moral characteristics.

In this call to be holy we have the essence of Israel's election. God speaks of them as being holy **'to me'** and of being separated from other nations **'that you should be mine'** (20:26). Holiness and separation are brought together again when Moses gives his final sermons to the people before they enter the promised land, but instead of the verb 'separate' being used there, the actual term 'choose' is found: 'For you are a holy people to the LORD your God; the LORD your God has chosen you to be a people for himself...' (Deut. 7:6; 14:2). This status of being elect, set apart, brings with it the responsibility of living in a way that reflects the God who has created them for his glory. Christians are God's chosen, set-apart people. They have this holy status with the responsibility of proclaiming the virtues of him who has called them out of darkness into his marvellous light (1 Peter 2:9).

Holiness is not something we can earn or achieve by our own efforts. It is, first of all, a state created by God which we are then called to maintain. Christians are called to live differently because God has sanctified them through his Son and Spirit. Nobody can become holy if he or she has not been set apart by God through the Spirit's regenerating work and Christ's atoning blood. The call to obedience is set in this context of the Lord who sanctifies. We then sanctify ourselves through obedience to God's revealed Word.

23.
Holy priests

Please read Leviticus 21:1-24

While all God's covenant people were called to be holy, and therefore separate from the pagan world around them, the priests were in a special position within the Israelite community. Beside the separation laws that applied to all the Israelites, the priests were called to express a degree of holiness that would even separate them from the rest of the nation. The priests were to be unique examples of the high standards that God required from his holy people. In addition, the high priest was to exhibit an even higher grade of holiness commensurate with his office. The division of Israel into three distinct classes — the people, the priests and the high priest — coincided with the three sections of the tabernacle: the outer courtyard, open to the people to come with their sacrifices; the Holy Place, where only the priests were allowed to enter; and the Holy of Holies, where only the high priest could enter once a year. The closer a person was to the symbol of God's presence, the greater the degree of holiness (see Lev. 8 – 9).

Though these instructions were addressed to the priests in particular (21:1,17; 22:2), **'all the children of Israel'** were to hear and understand the reasons for the stringent measures and were to be involved in helping to keep the priests in their specially holy state (21:8,24; 22:18). The New Testament likewise teaches Christians the high moral and spiritual standards expected from their leaders.

The sons of Aaron

Priesthood in Israel was to be hereditary and limited to the descendants of Aaron, thus making it unique and distinct from the practices of the surrounding nations. In Egypt, for instance, ordinary citizens could take up the office for a limited period and then return to their secular occupations. The priesthood in Israel could not be obtained through money or influence, or appointments made on the whim of a ruler. Israel's priests had solemn tasks to perform requiring extensive preparation. They were not only required to carry out religious ceremonies within the sanctuary away from the people's gaze, but to live in the community as set-apart people, familiar with all the purification laws and able to teach the people all the revealed statutes and ordinances (see 10:10-11; Mal. 2:7-8).

Our Lord brings this office to a grand climax and close. The priestly descendants of Abraham's line acknowledged a greater priesthood through the symbolic action of Abraham when he offered gifts to Melchizedek (Gen. 14:20). Jesus is priest after this order and was prepared for his work through the first thirty years of his life. Luke, who begins his Gospel against the background of the temple, its priests and its worship, tells us of one incident from Jesus' youth when, as a twelve-year-old, he was in the temple listening to the teachers and asking them questions (Luke 2:41-52).

This set of laws concerns priests when they are off duty with their families. Because of their status they must be careful to maintain their clean, holy position.

Preserving priestly purity (21:1-15)

This first main section restricts the priesthood in how they should behave when family deaths occur and regarding whom they should marry. There are rules for the priests and additional rules for the high priest.

The priests (21:1-9)

1. Rules for mourning (21:1-6)

While Christian pastors play a leading role in ministering to families who have lost loved ones and in officiating at funerals, the old-covenant priests were strictly prohibited from coming into contact with dead bodies. The only funerals an ordinary priest was allowed to attend were those of **'relatives who are nearest to him'** (21:2), such as his mother, father, son, daughter, brother, or unmarried adolescent sister (21:3).[1]

Missing from the list of 'blood' relatives is any reference to a priest's wife. Some consider that it is taken for granted that she is included, for a wife is one 'flesh' with her husband (cf. 18:6-17, where the father's daughter is missing from the list, although she is clearly included in the prohibition, as verse 6 suggests).[2] Ezekiel, who was also a priest, was specially forbidden to mourn for his wife as a symbolic gesture to shock the people (Ezek. 24:15-18). Others use the obscure phrase **'a chief man among his people'** (21:4) to mean that, although he is a husband[3] in the community, he must not become unclean even in the case of his wife's death. Most conservative scholars think this too extreme and understand the phrase to forbid a priest from becoming unclean by participating in a funeral, not of his wife herself, but of any of her close relatives.

He is not to **'defile himself ... to profane himself'** (21:1,4). This reminds us that the priest has been brought, through the cleansing rites of his ordination, into a holy state. To defile, or pollute, is the opposite of to cleanse and, as uncleanness is incompatible with holiness, the priest's action means that he is making himself unholy, which is what to 'profane' means. A dead body was one of the worst sources of pollution. All who came into contact with a corpse were immediately unclean for seven days (Num. 19:11-22). Holiness is associated with life, health and wholeness. Death is the very opposite and is connected with God's judgement on human rebellion. The Lord is the living God, the author and sustainer of life. He is not 'the God of the dead but of the living' (Luke 20:38). All those associated with this God must keep far away from anything resembling the antithesis of life, but, as we have seen, a special concession is made in the case of blood relatives.

In mourning for them, like the rest of the people, they are not to follow the customs of the pagan nations (21:5; cf. 19:27-28). Shaving the head, cutting the beard and slashing the skin were all part of pagan rites in honour of the dead (see Isa. 15:2; Jer. 41:5). As Milgrom rightly observes, shaving areas of the head and trimming parts of the beard were not the 'impulsive, anguished acts of grief' that we find in Ezra 9:3, but deliberate, carefully performed acts, and it is possible that the hair, symbolic of life, was offered to the gods of the dead.[4] In any case, defacing their bodies meant that they would be less than whole, and any obvious blemish or disfigurement, as is indicated later in this chapter, would be inconsistent and incompatible with holiness.

They must refrain from anything connected with paganism because the priests, like the people, are to **'be holy to their God'** (21:6; cf. 20:26). But the priests' holiness is of a higher order in that they are closely associated with God and minister in the sanctuary, receiving the sacrificial food, or '**bread of their God**' (21:8; cf. 21:17,21; 3:11,16 for the meaning of this expression). Actions that '**profane the name of their God**' (21:6) drag God's holy name in the dirt and dishonour the God whom the priests are called to represent and serve.

2. Rules for marriage (21:7-9)

Priests are also to be careful whom they marry, remembering again that they are holy to their God (21:7). Marriage to a woman who is a prostitute, or has been raped ('**a defiled woman**', better translated 'desecrated')[5] or is divorced is therefore out of the question. This means they were only allowed to marry virgins or widows. There must be no question marks over the woman's moral or ritual state, for she was about to become one flesh with a priest who was '**holy to his God**'. Though the priest was separated from the rest of the covenant community through his specially holy status, in order to receive the sacrifices made to God, the community had the duty of 'sanctifying him' (21:8), which included treating him as holy and making sure that he did not enter into forbidden relationships. The holy God who had set Israel apart and who continued to make them holy ('**I ... who sanctify you**') called upon his people at this point to recognize the holy status of the priest: '**He shall be holy to you.**'

As an appendix, the law states that a daughter of a priest who '**profanes herself**' by becoming a prostitute also '**profanes her father**' (21:9). Her action reflects on the rest of her family. Drastic measures are needed to clear up this unholy state of affairs. Burning is the only way of cleansing such defilement. This law is probably placed here to show that it applies to the high priest as well as the ordinary priests.

The high priest (21:10-15)

1. Rules for mourning (21:10-12)

The highest of standards are expected of the priest who is pre-eminent among his fellow priests.[6] He is more closely associated with the holy, living God than even the other priests, for he only is allowed to enter the most holy part of the tabernacle on the Day of Atonement. Death is the very antithesis of all that God stands for, and so the high priest must not come anywhere near a dead body or show any signs of mourning over the dead. His distinguished holy position is symbolized by the anointing oil on his head and his unique robes of office (21:10; see Exod. 28:1-39; 29:5-7; Lev. 8:7-12). Whereas all the priests had their clothes anointed with oil, only the high priest was anointed on the head (see 8:12,30). He must not show the customary signs of mourning, such as tearing his clothes and throwing dust on his head (cf. Josh. 7:6), for to do so would, as Wenham puts it, 'serve to nullify his consecration'.[7]

It is because of the anointing on his head that he must **'not uncover his head'**, which would involve removing his special turban and allowing his hair to be untidy (cf. 10:6). His holy robes were not to be spoiled by tearing them. Furthermore, the high priest was not to go to the place where there was a dead body. He was not even to make himself unclean by going to the funeral of his parents (21:11). Other members of the family were to be called in to bear the responsibility of burying them (cf. 10:4).

When the text declares that he must not **'go out of the sanctuary'** (21:12), it does not imply that he was to be imprisoned in the tabernacle for life. It means that his duties in the sanctuary came first, even above the normal responsibilities expected of sons. If, therefore, a death occurred at his home while he was officiating at the sanctuary, he was to

remain at his post. Because all in the home of the dead would
be ritually unclean for seven days, it would also be necessary
for the high priest to remain in the sanctuary for that period
until all the rituals for purification had been carried out (see
Num. 19:14-19). Otherwise, he would desecrate or **'profane
the sanctuary of his God'**. He is to remember that the
'consecration of the anointing oil of his God is upon him'
(21:12).

The term for **'consecration'** comes from the same word
group as 'Nazirite', and conveys the idea of being 'distinct,
set apart', as in the word for 'holy'. These verses show the
human cost of being appointed to this office of high priest.
But it was open to ordinary Israelites to place themselves in a
similar position by taking a Nazirite vow. A Nazirite was not
allowed to be contaminated by the dead, not even 'for his
father or his mother' (Num. 6:6-7). This is the background to
what appeared to be a most shocking thing for Jesus to say to
a would-be disciple who asked if he could first go and bury
his father. Jesus replied, 'Let the dead bury their own dead,
but you go and preach the kingdom of God' (Luke 9:59-60;
cf. Matt. 8:21-22). Do you claim to be a disciple of Christ?
What comes first in your life? All Christians are set apart for
God, and under God's rule only one thing matters. Consecration to God is not an optional extra for Christians; it is their
position and calling. Of course, duties towards parents come
under that, as we have seen, but those who love family more
than Christ are not worthy of him (see Luke 14:26). Those
called to the Christian ministry must understand their position in these terms, following the great High Priest and being
examples to the rest of the covenant community.

2. *Rules for marriage* (21:13-15)

Before the rules for marriage are mentioned a short line is drawn under the previous rule with the by now familiar words, **'I am the LORD'** (21:12; cf.18:2,4-5).

The high priest is also more restricted than the ordinary priest in whom he is allowed to marry. As one commentator observes, 'The purity and singleness of this devotion to God are to be reflected in the purity and singleness of his marriage relationship.'[8] It is mentioned twice for emphasis that he can only marry a girl of marriageable age who is living on her own in her father's house (21:13,14; cf. 21:3). She must be someone who has had no previous sexual relationships with men, whether legitimate (**'a widow'**, or **'divorced'**) or illegitimate (**'defiled'**/'desecrated', as in the case of a rape victim, or a **'prostitute'**). In addition, he must only marry a girl from **'his own people'**, in the sense of his own family clan. By these means the holiness of the priestly line is maintained (21:15). In particular, it would ensure that there would be no question mark in anyone's mind over the legitimacy of his first child who, if a son, would be in line for his father's office. While a priest's daughter would figuratively desecrate her father by prostitution (21:9), a high priest must see to it that he does not literally desecrate his offspring (**'posterity'**). The Lord who sanctifies his people (21:8) also sanctifies the high priest. God continues to sanctify those he has already sanctified by calling upon them to refrain from committing acts that would desecrate them and by encouraging them to do God's commandments.[9]

Preserving priestly perfection (21:16-24)

The second section, introduced again by a reference to God speaking through his chief spokesman, Moses (21:16), concerns those disqualified from being priests.

Defects that disqualify

Aaron is informed that not one of his descendants who has a physical defect is qualified to offer sacrifices to God (21:17).[10] This is pressed home later in the paragraph for emphasis: **'No man of the descendants of Aaron the priest, who has a defect, shall come near to offer the offerings... He has a defect; he shall not come near to offer ...'** (21:21). Between these two strong banning orders twelve blemishes are listed that exclude an otherwise ritually and morally clean member of Aaron's family from officiating at the altar.

Not all the defects mentioned can be identified with certainty, but they include being blind or lame, having a facial disfigurement,[11] being deformed,[12] having a broken foot or hand, being a hunchback or a dwarf, having an eye defect, a scab or unsightly nodules,[13] or having crushed testicles (21:18-20). These blemishes correspond to the blemishes that disqualify an otherwise clean animal from being offered as a sacrifice (see 22:22-24).

Though these blemishes prevent a priest from offering sacrifice, they do not prevent him from partaking of the priestly food, comprising **'the most holy'** as well as **'the holy'** (21:22). 'Holy' food included the priest's share of the peace offering (7:31-34), while the 'most holy' food referred to the priest's share of the grain, sin and guilt offerings (2:3,10; 6:16-18,29; 7:1,6) and the tabernacle bread — i.e., the 'shewbread' or 'Bread of the Presence' (see 24:8-9). This meant that any priest with a blemish who was otherwise clean was not barred from the sanctuary, for the most holy food had to be eaten there (see 10:12,17), but he was not to go near the inner veil or the incense altar, **'lest he profane my sanctuaries'** (21:23).[14]

Gospel truth

It seems outrageous to modern readers that a person should be debarred from the work he was intending to do on the grounds of physical disability. Even listing the disabilities would be regarded today as insensitive. That this was a deliberate policy set up by the God of the Bible makes it appear even worse and a very good excuse for having nothing to do with God or Jesus Christ. We do need to get things in perspective. These rulings have nothing whatever to do with the value and worth of people. The law has been quite clear on the need to respect all life, and especially human beings, treating others as we would like them to treat us. That includes people with various physical blemishes and disabilities.

We must understand these regulations in the context of those times and against the whole background of the holiness legislation. The people were taught important lessons through symbolic actions and taboos. Holiness, as we have seen, meant wholeness, fulness of life, completeness and purity. It was expressed not only in moral perfection, but in physical wholeness and normality. A human body that does not noticeably display any defect is one expression of this holiness. Because the priests were in this position of representing the holy God, their physical appearance had to display something of the perfection of God's creation.

We need to see things from a yet higher perspective. God created everything perfect but human rebellion has marred that perfection. Despite protests to the contrary, it is not normal for any human to be disabled or to have debilitating blemishes or to be ill with diseases. These things witness to a world that is fallen, imperfect and unholy. That is not how things were created and it is not how things are in God's heaven; nor is it what God has in store for the future. The restrictions therefore taught the people that all physical defects and illnesses are ultimately incompatible with God's holiness.

All these symbolic restrictions, along with the priesthood itself, have been abolished with the coming of Christ our great High Priest. His miraculous healings can only be understood against the background of these old-covenant symbolic laws relating to disability and purity. When he was on earth he cured disabilities and made people whole, an indication of what he would accomplish through his atoning death. On the cross Jesus dealt with the fundamental causes of all our blemishes, disabilities and imperfections, whether physical, moral or spiritual. All who are united to Christ by faith have no divine banning orders. Whatever physical and mental problems they may have, they are spiritually whole and can have free access into God's holy presence. Isaiah has this in mind when he refers to foreigners and eunuchs finding a place in God's house (Isa. 56:3-4). Furthermore, we can look forward to the end of all physical and mental disability in the new creation. This is a theme begun with prophets like Hosea and Isaiah and completed by John in his vision of the new universe.

The physical perfections demanded of the holy priests in the offerings they made to God were deliberately ordained by God to prepare and point forward to Jesus Christ, our High Priest, and his moral and physical perfection. He knew no sin, though he was tempted in all points like we are (2 Cor. 5:21; Heb. 4:15). He is the High Priest who is 'holy, harmless, undefiled, separate from sinners' (Heb. 7:26).

A challenge to church leaders

The passage becomes a challenge to all in positions of leadership in the church of Jesus Christ. There is no priestly caste system, but God does call men to the ministry of the Word and authority in the church of God. Paul becomes an example to all elders, pastors, ministers of the gospel: 'But in all things we commend ourselves as ministers of God ... by purity, by knowledge, by longsuffering, by kindness, by the Holy Spirit, by sincere love...' (2 Cor. 6:4-7). The highest standards are demanded of church leaders, as we see from Paul's lists in his writings to Timothy and Titus (1 Tim. 3:1-13; Titus 1:5-9).

Derek Tidball writes, 'It is all too easy to settle into a professional mode which slots into gear and accelerates away in evangelistic or pastoral ministry when the occasion demands it. But once the assignment is over — the visit made, the sermon preached, the prayer offered, or the meeting conducted — they change back into spiritual neutral and become something else. The public front is one of zealous spirituality; the private reality is one of spiritual mediocrity.'[15]

24.
Holy sacrifices

Please read Leviticus 22:1-33

From restrictive regulations designed to preserve priestly purity and perfection, this chapter moves quite naturally to restrictions intended to preserve purity and perfection in the sacrificial food (described as 'the bread of ... God' in 21:22). The various paragraphs close with the refrain, **'I the LORD sanctify them'**, or **'I am the LORD who sanctifies'** (22:9,16,32), a feature that helps to link the chapter with the previous one (see 21:8,15,23).

Preserving the purity of the sacrifices (22:1-16)

The priests (22:1-9)

1. Set apart for God

All the priests are urged to **'separate themselves from the holy things'** of the people (22:2). In dealing with all the sacred sacrifices that the Israelites give to God, whether holy or most holy, they must truly set themselves apart.[1] In other words, they must be scrupulously careful not to touch or eat

these holy offerings when in a ceremonially unclean condition. Otherwise, by handling what the people have set apart
for God ('**... which they sanctify to me**') they would be de-
sanctifying, desecrating God's person and character: '**... that
they do not profane my holy name.**'

The sacrifices are so closely associated with God himself
that to treat them without due respect would be to treat God
likewise, and so to diminish his holiness in the eyes of the
people. Thus the priests are warned that if they go near the
sacred offerings in a state of uncleanness they will be '**cut
off**', not 'from their people', as in the case of ordinary
Israelites (see 19:8), but from '**my presence**' (22:3). They
will die a premature death (22:9) and will no longer be in
that favoured position of ministering in the tabernacle. This
is what happened to Aaron's sons Nadab and Abihu, and by
it God was glorified in the presence of the people (10:1-3). '**I
am the LORD**' (22:3,8) reminds them yet again that this is
what the God and Saviour of his people demands (see 19:3).

2. Clean priests

While all priests, including those with blemishes (21:22),
were allowed to eat parts of the sacrificial offerings, none of
them could eat if they were in an unclean, impure condition.
The list of unclean situations includes, first of all, serious
conditions such as skin disease ('leprosy'; see Lev. 13 – 14)
and bodily discharges (15:1-12). Until he was better and had
carried out all the cleansing regulations, the priest was not
allowed to eat the sacred food (22:4). Four cases are then
presented of temporary uncleanness where a priest touches
anything that has been made unclean by a corpse (see
11:8,11,24-28,32-40), or by a man who has had an emission
of semen (see 15:16,18), or by unclean creepy-crawlies (see
11:29-30,41-45), or by contact with someone who passes on
some other uncleanness (see 15:2-12). In these situations the

priest is unclean until evening, when he must wash his body and after sunset will then become clean and free to partake of the sacred food to which he is entitled (22:4-7).

3. Clean sacrifices

A priest, like an ordinary Israelite, is not to eat the flesh of an animal that dies naturally or is torn by another beast (22:8; cf. 17:15). Perhaps this is emphasized here to indicate that this would be true even if a sacrificial animal awaiting slaughter in the tabernacle courtyard died of natural causes, or was fatally wounded by another. The blood would not have been drained out properly and so to eat it would make the priest ceremonially dirty. The whole paragraph (22:1-8) is concluded with a call to keep the order (**'ordinance'**) that God has given in the regulations, otherwise the priests will bear the consequences of their sin. They will die (22:9). That is the penalty for disobeying God and desecrating what is holy. On the other hand, through keeping this order they will continue to be holy, for God has given these rules to sanctify them.

All that is unclean must be kept strictly apart from what is holy. That is the lesson God was teaching the people through these laws. It is a lesson that Christians need to remember. We cannot offer to God acceptable sacrifices of praise, prayer and thanksgiving if we are living worldly, unclean lives.

A priest's household (22:10-16)

While the priest's family was allowed to eat some of the food set apart for the priests, it was necessary to make it clear how far this extended. No one outside the family was allowed to eat the holy food. This included hired labourers who happened to reside with them. This is repeated for emphasis (22:10,13). Slaves purchased by the priests or who were born into the household, however, were regarded as part of the family (22:11). Interestingly, these slaves would have been from other nations, for only non-Israelites could be bought with money (25:39-44). But, as in the case of the slaves Abraham purchased, they were part of the family and would have been circumcised (Gen. 17:12-13). Once a priest's daughter married **'an outsider'** — that is, someone outside the priestly circle — she was not allowed to eat **'the holy offerings'** (22:12; cf. 7:28-36). On the other hand, if she returned home widowed or divorced and had no children she could eat **'her father's food'** (22:13).

Anyone outside the family who ate the priest's food by mistake was commanded to replace the food and add an extra fifth of its value (22:14). Those who ate the forbidden food desecrated, de-sanctified ('profaned') what the people had given to the Lord. The priests had a duty to guard against any desecration of the holy food that they took home; otherwise it would have brought guilt and required compensation (22:15-16).

Preserving the perfection of the sacrifices (22:17-33)

The law now considers the topic of blemished and acceptable sacrifices. There is the familiar heading introducing this new section (22:17) and in addition to the priests, the people are also addressed (22:18). All are held responsible for detecting defects: the people when they choose their animal, and the priests when they receive the animal by the entrance to the tabernacle. What the regulation insists on is that sacrificial animals, like the priests who offer the sacrifices and the place of sacrifice, must reflect the holiness of God.

Defects that disqualify an animal (22:18-25)

The sacrifices considered are the vow and free-will gifts (see Lev. 27) that are presented as either a burnt offering (22:18-20) or a peace offering (22:21). Nothing was said about different types of burnt offering and peace offering when they were first introduced (Lev. 1; 3). Later the law did distinguish three separate occasions when a peace offering might be brought: a thanksgiving (7:12-15), a vow and a free-will offering (7:16-18). Here we are told that vow and free-will offerings, which were very similar, could, unlike the thank offering, be presented as a burnt offering as well as a peace offering. Because the sacrifice of thanksgiving is distinct from the other two it is not mentioned at this point but left until the next paragraph (22:29).

Interestingly, a difference is also made between the vow and free-will offerings (22:23). It is not immediately obvious why the law should be a little less stringent over the free-will offering. The most likely reason is that the latter arose out of a spontaneous situation requiring an immediate sacrifice whereas the offering in fulfilment of a vow gave ample time for the person to choose the best of the livestock for sacrifice.

1. Types of burnt offering (22:18-20)

In introducing the regulation it is made clear that an immigrant or foreign resident ('a stranger') who worshipped Israel's God could also come and offer sacrifice, as long as he kept the same rules as the Israelites (22:18). As these offerings are voluntary the rules are strict and make no concessions for the poor (cf. 1:14-17).

In order for vow or free-will burnt offerings to be accepted by God on their behalf,[2] the animal had to be **'a male'** from the flocks or the herd, complete, or flawless (**'without**

blemish', 22:19; cf. 1:3), with no obvious **'defect'** (22:20).[3]
The Hebrew term for **'without blemish'** is 'whole' or
'complete' and expresses the characteristic feature of holiness. Just as they were to find 'whole' stones, not ones
specially cut to size, for the stone altar that they were to erect
on Mount Ebal (Exod. 20:24-25; Deut. 27:5-7), so the
sacrifices that they offered there and at the tabernacle were to
be whole. Everything was to express symbolically the
completeness of their holy God.

2. Types of peace offering (22:21)

In the case of vow or free-will peace offerings they also had
to be whole, or **'perfect'** (the same word is translated 'without blemish' in verse 19). No reference is made to gender
because, with peace offerings generally, female as well as
male animals were allowed (see 3:1). If anyone assumed that
God might be more lenient just because he was not so
particular about the gender of the sacrifice, it is made clear
that he will not be fobbed off with some second-rate offering. The only concession made was for a free-will offering
(22:23).

3. A list of defects

There are twelve defects mentioned and they begin with
blindness (22:22) and end with damaged or removed testicles
(22:24).[4] All the defects are easily noticeable. Though the list
does not exactly match the defects which disqualify a man
from serving as priest, the arrangement of and parallels
between the two lists are significant and indicate the close
relationship between priest and sacrifice.[5] Instead of
'hunchback' and 'dwarf' (21:20) the corresponding defects
in an animal are limbs that are **'too long'** or **'too short'**
(22:23). It is because these are, relatively speaking, less

serious defects than the other items listed that such animals may be presented as free-will offerings. No excuses are allowed for presenting defective offerings, such as having bought from a foreigner an animal that subsequently proved to be flawed (22:25).

The prophet Malachi shows how the Jews in the period after the Babylonian exile were offering all kinds of sick, lame and blind animals, and he pronounces God's curse on those who had promised to sacrifice an animal as a vow offering and then substituted a damaged animal (Mal. 1:8-14). Ananias and Sapphira promised to give an amount and then substituted a lesser gift, for which they received judgement from God (Acts 5:1-11).

It is the apostle John who draws our attention to Jesus as the sacrificial Lamb who was brought before the high priests, Annas and Caiaphas. Caiaphas advised the Jews that one man should die on behalf of the people and he handed Jesus over to Pilate (John 18:13-14,24,28). After Pilate had interrogated Jesus he said, 'I find no fault [or "guilt"] in him.' Pilate was, in effect, as Matthew Henry aptly puts it, pronouncing the sacrifice without blemish. Peter draws our attention to Christ as the ultimate sacrifice to which these regulations point when he states that we are redeemed 'with the precious blood of Christ, as of a lamb without blemish and without spot' (1 Peter 1:19; see also Heb. 9:14).

Circumstances that disqualify an animal (22:26-30)

1. The seven-day rule (22:27)

Animals under eight days old were not allowed to be sacrificed (see Exod. 22:30). In many cases animals were required to be at least a year old before they could be offered in sacrifice (see 9:3; 12:6), but for these voluntary offerings those of any age were acceptable so long as they were not newly born. After the first seven days the animals would have grown a little, making it easier to assess whether they were healthy and flawless, and producing a slightly more substantial offering, especially if it was a sacrifice from which the priests and people were to have a share. But were these the chief concerns?

The eighth day is a significant number in the law of Moses and it presents a parallel with a male infant, who was required to be circumcised on the eighth day (see 12:2-3). The animal was not to be sacrificed before it had had time to be alive. The seven-day separation between the birth of the animal and its being offered up helped to keep that distinction between life and death that was so important in these Levitical laws, with their emphasis on life, wholeness and perfection.

Our Lord was not offered up as a sacrifice immediately he was born, even though Herod the Great made an attempt to kill him. His time to be lifted up as the sacrificial offering was not when he was a baby, but as a mature man whose obedience had been tested. He was approved by the Father at his baptism and transfiguration and he challenged his enemies: 'Which of you convicts me of sin?'

2. The same-day rule (22:28)

A mother and her young were not to be sacrificed on the same day (cf. Deut. 22:6). Again the reason for this ruling is not stated. Some have supposed it may be to counter some pagan rite intended to increase fertility, while others suggest it is to prevent overenthusiasm that might ruin a person with a small herd. 'Though God encourages generous giving, he does not encourage foolish giving.'[6]

It is often assumed that this regulation and the previous one display a compassionate, humanitarian concern. But we do not have to be animal-rights activists to find it difficult to

believe that it is more compassionate to take a young suck-
ling away from its mother on the eighth day than when it was
newly born. Again, is it really more compassionate to
slaughter a mother and its young on separate, successive
days than on the same day? However, 'conservation by
avoiding wanton destruction, rather than mere sentimental-
ity', as Wenham puts it, may be an added factor in these
laws. They are similar to those laws forbidding the Israelites
to cook a kid in its mother's milk (Exod. 23:19) and reck-
lessly to destroy trees (Deut. 20:19-20). In addition, anything
that appeared to be barbarous and cruel to animals was
certainly not in accordance with holiness.

This prohibition may in fact have more to do with theological concerns. There is so much symbolism, as we have
already witnessed, between the sacrifices on the one hand
and the priests and people on the other that it is not far-
fetched to suppose that this is where we should look for an
answer. Preventing a mother and her young from being
sacrificed on the same day — with the prospect of that
animal line being exterminated — spoke of the need for
family lines to be preserved in Israel. It reminded the people
of God's promises to Abraham that through his descendants
('seed') all the nations would find blessing (Gen. 12:3; Acts
3:25).

3. The morning-after rule (22:29-30)

The third type of peace offering is the **'sacrifice of thanksgiving'** (see 7:11-15). Unlike the other peace offerings,
where the people's share could be eaten over two days
(7:16-17), the meat had to be eaten on the same day that it
was sacrificed. If the meat was kept **'until morning'** the
whole offering was unacceptable.

The concluding demand (22:31-33)

The contents of chapters 21 and 22 are rounded off with inspiring words that urge the people to keep God's commandments. They include, for the sixth and final time, **'I am the LORD who sanctifies...'** (22:32). Why should God's people observe these laws and be careful to do his will?

Firstly, *because of who God is and what he has done for his people.* He is **'the LORD'** whose name is **'holy'**. He is their Saviour who has brought them **'out of the land of Egypt'** and has graciously and unashamedly associated himself with them as **'your God'**.

Secondly, *because this is the way God is sanctified among his people.* If they keep his commands God **'will be hallowed'**. Otherwise, they will desecrate, or **'profane'**, God's **'holy name'** by bringing shame upon it. Their violation of God's law will reflect badly on God in the eyes of the pagan nations.

Thirdly, *because this is the way God sanctifies his people.*

The principles laid down here are no different for God's people under the new covenant. The big contrast between the old covenant and the new is that all God's people under the new are born again, have a spiritual circumcision, worship by the Spirit of God and have the Spirit of God and of Christ dwelling within them, helping them to live in a way that pleases God (Heb. 8:10-11; Phil. 3:3; Rom. 8:1-14).

25.
Holy day: the Sabbath

Please read Leviticus 23:1-3

Towards the end of each year, among the Christmas cards and presents that arrive, there is often an assortment of calendars. There are some calendars that are in the form of wallcharts. Busy people can see at a glance where the annual holiday seasons fall. Leviticus 23 is like a yearly planner. It maps out the weeks and months, highlighting the special festivals and holy days.

Our calendars may show holidays that have no special significance other than that they are appropriate times to have a break. But most of our official holidays are either tied to religious events like Christmas and Easter, or to unique national occasions like Thanksgiving Day or Independence Day. Israel's calendar shows holidays that are of both religious and national significance.

Our calendars mark the passing of time. The beginning of each new year forces us to look back as well as forward to forthcoming events. Israel's calendar prevented them from thinking of life as going round in a never-ending circle. There was a beginning, a forward thrust and an end. It 'not only summarized what God had done for them in the past, but it also anticipated what God would do for them in the future'. [1]

While it does not matter too much if we forget the date of one of our public holidays, it was important that every Israelite remember all the special times in their calendar year. Their holidays were not optional. It was compulsory for all to observe them and they provided the whole community with an opportunity to express its identity in worship, celebration and remembrance.

Holy time (23:1-2)

The heading is repeated at various points to introduce new feasts (23:1-2,9-10,23-24,26,33-34) and, whereas the previous legislation was addressed to the priests (see 21:1; 22:1-2), this introduction informs us that the calendar is given specifically for the benefit of the people — **'the children of Israel'**.

We move from holy offerings and holy food, holy places, holy priests and holy people to holy time. The special occasions are referred to as the Lord's **'feasts'**, or better, 'appointed times' (see Gen. 1:14, where the word is translated 'seasons'). It is the same word that appears in the well-known phrase used to refer to the tabernacle — the tent of 'meeting'. Just as God had an appointed place to meet the people, so he had appointed, or fixed, times when the people would come to meet him. They are also called **'holy convocations'**. These special times and seasons were not so much for private meditation as occasions when the people were summoned to meet together in holy assembly (see Num. 10:2). Later in Israel's history, God condemned his people for their sin, despite their outward show of piety in 'the calling of assemblies' (Isa. 1:13-14). Yet when God speaks of a new beginning for his people, under the symbolism of

Zion, he promises to surround their 'assemblies' with the glory cloud that they experienced as they left Egypt (Isa. 4:5). The Lord's people are still encouraged not to neglect 'to meet together', remembering that by faith in Christ we have already come to Mount Zion, the heavenly Jerusalem, 'and to the assembly of the firstborn who are enrolled in heaven' (Heb. 10:25; 12:23, ESV).

Sabbath rest (23:3)

Before the annual festivals are introduced the people are reminded of the weekly set time for meeting — the **'Sabbath of solemn rest'**. This expression, which could be more literally translated 'the most restful rest',[2] is also used of the Day of Atonement and the sabbatical year. While in the latter case the land was to have a complete rest for one year (see 25:4) the rest of the weekly Sabbath and of the atonement day applied to people and animals.

A special holiday

Scholars are mystified because 'No other known culture has anything quite like the sabbath.'[3] There is a similar word to 'sabbath' in Akkadian, where it is used for 'a day of the resting of the heart'. However, this was fixed once a month on the day of the full moon, when special ceremonies were held 'to soothe the gods'. The other so-called Assyrian and Babylonian rest days have nothing in common with the biblical Sabbath and no reputable scholar will now suggest that the Jewish Sabbath derived from such days of the month, which were reckoned as times when it was unlucky to work.

The Sabbath is set apart from the other festivals that follow. Only after mentioning the Sabbath is it found necessary to repeat the words found in the introduction: **'These are the feasts of the LORD'** (23:4; cf. 23:2). The calendar of annual festivals is an entity on its own. This is confirmed by the summary statement towards the close of the chapter (23:37-38) where the Sabbath and its special offerings are distinguished from the festal occasions just mentioned. Within that list of festivals seven days are termed 'holy convocations': the first and seventh days of the Feast of Unleavened Bread (23:7-8), the Feast of Weeks (23:21), the first day of the seventh month (23:24), the Day of Atonement (23:27) and the first and eighth days of the Feast of Tabernacles (23:35-36). The inclusion of the Sabbath in the list would break the completeness of that sabbatical arrangement. It is placed at the beginning as a unique **'holy convocation'**, but it does provide the model for the other sabbatical days and seasons. The Sabbath is unlike the other holy occasions where Israel needed to work out the dates and proclaim when the holy days would occur each year. It is independent of the lunar calendar. God fixed the Sabbath as a weekly event irrespective of the moon's phases.

If the Sabbath is special, and not in the same category as the other holidays, why is it placed here? After all, the law has already insisted on the people keeping the Fourth Commandment (19:3,30). For one thing, it does follow the example of the earlier list, in which the Sabbath is mentioned before briefly setting out the three great pilgrim festivals (Exod. 23:12-17). Placing it at the head of all the holy convocations has the effect of emphasizing its distinctiveness, that it must not be forgotten or underrated in the excitement of keeping the other holy days. The reference to keeping the Sabbath on **'the seventh day'** also draws attention to the significance of the number seven in the sacred calendar. As we have already noted, there are seven holy convocation days during the festive seasons. We also find that the Feast of Weeks comes after an interval of seven weeks, the seventh month is marked out as special and, finally, the Feasts of Unleavened Bread and Tabernacles each last seven days.

The biblical Sabbath is the only holy day commanded in the Ten Commandments and the only one that is based on creation (Exod. 20:8-11). As the word 'Sabbath' suggests, the people are to rest and **'do no work'**. Not only when they are attending 'church' are they to cease from the work that has occupied them for **'six days'**; they are to rest when they are in their homes (**'in all your dwellings'**). It is **'the Sabbath of the LORD'**, for it belongs to him and should therefore be observed in honour of him.[4] He invented the idea of a day of rest, set it apart from the other days by his own example when he created the world ('he sanctified it') and — more remarkable still — he 'blessed' it (Gen. 2:1-3). This phrase, 'the Sabbath of the LORD', is most significant in the light of what Jesus had to say on the subject of the Sabbath. He made the divine claim that he was 'Lord of the Sabbath'.

In New Testament times many communities in the Greek-speaking world adopted the Jewish Sabbath as a day of rest and Josephus claims that 'There is not one city, Greek or barbarian, not a single nation to which our custom of abstaining from work on the seventh day has not spread.'[5] One can understand its attraction to thoughtful pagans, as they noticed so many Jews during the period between the Old and New Testaments keeping the Sabbath law so strictly. It was a very distinctive feature of their life and culture and proclaimed equal rights for all in that everyone, including slaves, and animals too, rested every week on this day.

The Christian Sabbath

For some Christians to assume that the Sabbath is simply another Jewish ritual requirement that no longer applies now that Christ has fulfilled the ceremonial law flies in the face of all the evidence. As this chapter indicates, the weekly Sabbath rest is distinct from the other sabbath days connected with the Jewish festivals. In addition, the phraseology — **'Six days ... but the seventh'** — echoes the familiar words of the Fourth Commandment (Exod. 20:9-10), which in turn reminds us that the Sabbath is a creation ordinance (Gen. 2:1-3). The weekly Sabbath rest cannot be dismissed as part of the ceremonial law that has ceased with the coming of Christ.

If the Sabbath-day principle is no longer binding, it is difficult to account for the numerous references in the Gospels to Jesus indicating by word and example how the Sabbath should be kept. At no time does Jesus say that the Sabbath principle no longer applies. As Lord of the Sabbath he rescues it from the tradition of the elders and strips it of its old-covenant significance. He directs his followers how to keep it and by his resurrection transforms it from being the sign of the old covenant to being the great day of the new covenant, anticipating the final day of consummation and triumph. Though, as Paul indicates, there are sabbaths connected with the ceremonial law that are no longer mandatory (Rom. 14:5; Col. 2:16-17), he nowhere suggests that the principle of God's rest day should be treated as something obsolete now that Christ has come. There is spiritual rest in Christ to which the Sabbath points, but the people of God still look for the eternal Sabbath rest, and the weekly day of rest reminds us of this.

The change of day from the seventh to the first day of the week should not come as a surprise for it is anticipated in the law. Attention has already been drawn to the eighth day in

connection with circumcision (Gen. 17:12), the commencement of the priestly activity on behalf of the people (see 9:1)
and the final restoration of healed lepers (see 14:10). This
particular chapter concerning holy time also emphasizes the
'eighth day' (23:36,39) and the 'day after the Sabbath'
(23:11,15-16). These passages concerning the first-fruit
offerings at Passover time (23:9-14) and Pentecost
(23:15-22) and the final great day of the Tabernacles festival
(23:33-43) look forward to their fulfilment in Christ's
resurrection, the era of the Holy Spirit and new covenant, as
well as the future glory when Christ returns. They are holy
days, days of sacred assembly, days like the Sabbath rest.
Jesus rose from the dead on the 'day after the Sabbath' and
encouraged his disciples to meet together on this first day of
the week, later called by John 'the Lord's Day' (Rev. 1:10).
Paul also draws the attention of Christians to this day by
meeting with believers on the first day of the week and
suggests that they should lay aside money on the first day of
the week towards the collection for the poor saints in Jerusalem (Acts 20:7; 1 Cor. 16:2).[6]

26.
Holy seasons: spring

Please read Leviticus 23:4-22

The festivals (23:4)

So important were the holy convocations to the life of Israel that they are mentioned five times in the law. The Book of the Covenant lists the three main pilgrim festivals (Exod. 23:14-19) and these are emphasized again when the covenant is being renewed (Exod. 34:18-26). In Numbers 28 – 29 the feasts are listed in order to indicate which offerings are to be presented on each occasion. They appear for the last time when Moses speaks to a new generation of people about to enter the promised land (Deut. 16:1-17).

Israel's calendar

God created the sun and the moon not only to be luminaries and to divide the day from the night, but to be 'for signs and seasons, and for days and years' (Gen. 1:14). It is from the sun and moon that human beings worked out the calendar. The ancient Sumerians, to whom we owe the calculation that sixty seconds equal one minute and sixty minutes one hour, were also responsible for the Mesopotamian calendar.

Unlike the Egyptians, who operated on a solar calendar, they preferred the lunar because they considered the moon superior to the sun; hence their worship of Sin, the moon god. This meant an eleven-day difference between the solar and lunar year, which was rectified by inserting an extra lunar month about every three years. It is this Mesopotamian calendar that is reflected in the Mosaic law.[1] The year began around the spring equinox (21-22 March — see 2 Sam. 11:1, which speaks of events happening, literally, 'at the return of the year') and introduced the first six months of the hot season. The second six months of the cold season began at the time of the autumn equinox (21-22 September — see Exod. 34:22, which speaks, literally, of 'the turn of the year').

The dates of the **'appointed times'** (23:4) were most probably in accordance with the lunar month, which the Jews still follow to this day, and which is the reason why the festivals fall on different days each year. In fact, the common word for 'month' in Hebrew is also the word for 'new moon', and the psalmist praises God for appointing 'the moon for seasons' (Ps. 104:19; cf. Gen. 1:14).[2] It is understandable, then, that the biblical calendar divides into two main parts: the spring festivals, which centre around the first month of the year (23:4-22) — the Feast of Weeks, by its very title, is tied closely to the first month — and the autumn festivals, which are all in the seventh month (23:23-43). As we have seen in other chapters, **'I am the LORD your God'** concludes each part (23:22,43). There is symmetry between the two parts, for each has seven-day festivals starting on the fifteenth of the month. In the spring there is the Festival of Unleavened Bread, with an extra day added at the beginning on the fourteenth for Passover (23:5). The closing festival in the autumn is Tabernacles, with an extra day tagged on at the end to form an eighth day (23:36).

The Lord's **'feasts'** (more accurately 'appointed times'), which the people are to **'proclaim at their appointed times'**, are not only associated with the agricultural year, but with Israel's redemption from Egypt. In this way the people were reminded that their Creator and Redeemer was also the one who provided for their daily needs. Observing these festive seasons also enabled Israel to preserve its national identity and encouraged each new generation to relive the experience of their ancestors who were redeemed from slavery and made that epic pilgrimage to Canaan.

Spring festivals (23:5-22)

The Passover (23:5)

'Passover' is only briefly mentioned here as full details have already been given in the account of the first Passover (Exod. 12:1-14,21-28,43-51). It is to be kept on the **'fourteenth day of the first month'**. The calendar name for this first month was Abib (Exod. 13:4; Deut. 16:1), but by New Testament times it was known as Nisan. If Israel's months always commenced with the new moon, then the **'fourteenth day'**, which is exactly halfway through a lunar month, would be the day of the first full moon after the spring equinox. Thus, like our Easter, it could be early or late — sometimes in March, sometimes in April. It was to begin **'at twilight'** (literally, 'between the two evenings'), when the evening sacrifices were offered (Exod. 29:39,41; Num. 28:4,8), around the time when the sun disappeared over the horizon (see Deut. 16:6).[3]

It is **'the LORD's Passover'** that they are to observe, commemorating the time when they were protected from the angel of death and escaped from Egyptian slavery.[4] The new meal that Jesus introduced during the course of celebrating 'the Lord's Passover' is described by Paul as 'the Lord's Supper' (1 Cor. 11:20), another indirect reference to our Lord's divinity (cf. 23:3). It is the meal which God's new-covenant people are to observe commemorating all that the old Passover foreshadowed.

John's Gospel draws our attention to the connection between Jesus and the Passover lambs. Right from the start we are told that Jesus is the Lamb of God who takes away the sin of the world (John 1:29,36), and in the account of the crucifixion we are informed that the death of Jesus took place at Passover time (John 19:14). In addition, John adds that the legs of Jesus were not broken (John 19:31-36). This fact not only fulfilled Psalm 34:20, but emphasized more strongly the connection with the Passover, for the Israelites were expressly told not to break the bones of any of the Passover lambs (Exod. 12:46). Jesus, as the true Passover Lamb, is the one whose life was substituted for people the world over and down the centuries to take away their sins. He did this so that all who trust him might be protected from the punishment of the second death and rescued from the older and far more sinister slavery to sin and Satan.

The Festival of Unleavened Bread (23:6-8)

The festival associated with the Passover, lasting **'seven days'** and beginning on the following day, **'the fifteenth'**, was the first of the three great occasions (the others being Pentecost and Tabernacles) when all adult males in Israel were to attend the central sanctuary (Exod. 23:14-19; see also Num. 28:16-25; Deut. 16:1-8). This is why it is called **'the Feast of Unleavened Bread'** (23:6). The word translated **'Feast'** is not the same as the earlier term in the expression 'feasts of the LORD' (23:4). Here the Hebrew word means 'pilgrimage festival' or 'festal gathering' and is related to the Arabic word '*hajj*'. A **'holy convocation'**, when no work was allowed, was to be held on the first and last days of this festival (23:7-8).[5] The festival is called *Matzoth* and takes its name from the command to eat bread with no yeast in it (**'unleavened'** 23:6 — see Exod. 12:15-19; 13:3-10). Besides eating unleavened bread during this week-long festival, they were also required to offer food gifts each day (23:8), the details of which are given in Numbers 28:19-23.

The Festival of Unleavened Bread is so closely associated with Passover that the latter name often does duty for both (see Deut. 16:1-7). Like the Passover, the festival reminded the people of the Exodus, when they were forced to bake bread quickly without the normal yeast to make it rise (Exod. 12:39; Deut. 16:3). After the initial historic Passover night, the people kept the first anniversary of the event before they began their journey from Mount Sinai (Num. 9:1-14). When the new generation of Israelites were about to take Jericho they were able to keep not only the Passover but the Feast of Unleavened Bread, using the produce of the land to make unleavened bread (Josh. 5:10-12). The Chronicler makes a point of emphasizing how the people overcame problems and kept the Passover and the Feast of Unleavened Bread with great joy during the reigns of Hezekiah and Josiah (2 Chr. 30:1-27; 35:1-19), and the book of Ezra also records how those who returned from captivity in Babylon kept the occasion with great joy (Ezra 6:19-22).

Leaven

Preparations for the first Passover began early on the tenth day of the month when the lambs were set aside ready for the day (Exod. 12:3,6). Succeeding generations also prepared for the festival by removing all leaven from their homes (Exod. 12:15). In many modern orthodox Jewish homes the mother will deliberately hide leavened bread in the house for the father and children to find prior to celebrating the paschal meal.

Leaven is often used in a figurative sense for corrupting influences (1 Cor. 5:6; Gal. 5:9). Jesus drew on this image when he warned his disciples of the leaven of the Pharisees and the Sadducees (Matt. 16:6,12). Paul also uses it in dealing with serious sin that is left unchecked. After viewing Christ's death as the culmination of the whole Passover tradition, the apostle continues the imagery by implying that, for Christians, keeping the Passover meal means that the whole of their lives should be lived in the light of Christ's death. This cannot be done if the leaven of their former sinful behaviour as pagans is allowed to creep back in. He writes, 'Christ, our Passover, was sacrificed for us. Therefore, let us keep the feast, not with old leaven, nor with the leaven of malice and wickedness, but with the unleavened bread of sincerity and truth' (1 Cor. 5:7-8).

The first-fruits offering (23:9-14)

'First fruits' is not another feast, or festival, as many insist on calling it. It is an important day within the Festival of Unleavened Bread, for it was the time when the first sheaf of the grain harvest was offered to the Lord. The first grain to ripen was barley, as we are told in Exodus 9:31-32. Ruth and Naomi came back to Bethlehem at the beginning of the barley harvest (Ruth 1:22; cf. 2:23). As there is only the vaguest hint of this first-fruits offering in Exodus 23:15 — 'None shall appear before me empty' — a full description of it is given here. It looked forward to the time when Israel would be settled in Canaan (23:10). As the name implied, the first **'sheaf'**, or bundle, of barley that they harvested sym- bolically represented their entire harvest.

While other parts of the law give regulations for individu- als presenting first-fruits offerings (see Num. 18:12-13;

Deut. 26:1-11), this requirement concerns a token communal offering that was brought to the priest for him to **'wave the sheaf before the LORD'**, in order for it to be accepted on behalf of the people (23:11). The act of waving, or elevating, the sheaf symbolized that this was a gift dedicated to God (see 7:30) as an expression of praise and thanksgiving. It also indicated that the whole crop belonged to him and expressed the hope that God would bless them with the new crop (see 19:25; Ezek. 44:30). No grain or bread was to be eaten until the first sheaf had been offered (23:14). Along with the bundle of barley they were to offer propitiatory sacrifices (**'for a sweet aroma'**): a burnt offering, a grain offering consisting of double the regular daily offering of flour (cf. Exod. 29:40-41) mixed with oil and a drink offering of wine (23:12-13).

The first-fruits idea is used figuratively in the New Testament on numerous occasions. Paul speaks of Christians having the first fruits of the Holy Spirit, of Israel being the first fruits of the nations and of Epaenetus as the first fruits of Achaia (Rom. 8:23; 11:16; 16:5). James describes those regenerated by God as 'a kind of first fruits of his creatures' (James 1:18) and John sees God's elect redeemed by the Lamb as 'first fruits to God and to the Lamb' (Rev. 14:4).

First fruits and firstborn

The symbol of the first fruits cannot be divorced from the use of the term 'firstborn'. Passover and the Feast of Unleavened Bread are associated with the time when all Egypt's firstborn were killed and God decreed that all Israel's firstborn were to be dedicated to God. The whole of Israel is also called God's firstborn son (Exod. 4:22). Walter Kaiser finds here a pattern for all God's saving activity spelled out in Paul's words, '... to the Jew first, and also to the Greek' (Rom. 1:16, AV): 'The nation, then, just as the harvest, symbolically signifies the consecration of all the nations in that a part of the nations is called to be God's firstborn.'[6]

Intelligent design

The offering during the Passover-Unleavened Bread festival is to be presented **'on the day after the Sabbath'** (23:11). Although various Jewish parties have made heavy weather of this, the most natural understanding of the Hebrew is that the Sabbath is the weekly Sabbath occurring during the festive period and that **'the day after'** is the eighth day, which is the first day of a new week.[7] In the year that Christ died, Passover fell on a Friday, so that the following day (Saturday) was not only the special Sabbath of the first day of Unleavened Bread but the ordinary weekly Sabbath. However one understands the phrase, 'the day after the Sabbath' in this momentous year was the first day of a new week (Sunday). It is of profound significance that the Lord Jesus Christ, who died at the time of the Passover, rose from the dead on 'the day after the Sabbath' to become the 'first fruits' of those who sleep in Jesus (1 Cor. 15:20). The resurrection of Christ is the guarantee that all who belong to him will be raised from the dead to be like him. This is a most wonderful demonstration of a divine design. Though lawless hands crucified him, Christ's death and resurrection took place 'by the carefully planned intention and foreknowledge of God' (Acts 2:23-24).

God first

The wisdom teacher uses the first-fruits offering to challenge God's people:

> Honour the LORD with your possessions,
> And with the first fruits of all your increase;

So your barns will be filled with plenty,
And your vats will overflow with new wine
(Prov. 3:9-10).

A good harvest is the great blessing God promises his old-covenant people if they are obedient to him (see 26:3-5,10) and it becomes the Old Testament's way of expressing all the riches that God has in store for those who love God and put him first. Jesus makes the same point in the Sermon on the Mount when he urges his disciples to 'seek first the kingdom of God and his righteousness, and all these things shall be added to you' (Matt. 6:33). Just as the people were not to partake of the harvest until God had been offered his share (23:14), so Christians, as Matthew Henry puts it, 'must always begin with God, begin our lives with him, begin every day with him, begin every meal with him, begin every affair and business with him; *seek first the kingdom of God'*.

But why is the first-fruits offering separated from the main festival by a fresh introduction (23:9-10) when it is clearly a part of it? The answer lies in its importance with regard to the timing of the following festival.

The Festival of Harvest, or Weeks (23:15-22)

The day on which this festival occurred is very dependent on the time when the first-fruits offering associated with the Festival of Unleavened Bread was made. This is why the Festival of Harvest is so closely attached to it. Israel is to **'count'** from **'the day after the Sabbath'** — that is, the day of the first-fruits offering — **'fifty days to the day after the seventh Sabbath'** in order to arrive at the exact time for holding 'the Feast of Harvest', the second of the three great pilgrimage festivals (Exod. 23:14-16). It was referred to as the 'Harvest' festival because it celebrated the completion of the grain harvest. Whereas the first-fruits offering during the

Festival of Unleavened Bread consisted of barley, this festival was referred to as 'the day of the first fruits' (Num. 28:26), for it was the time for gathering in the wheat. The festival was also called the 'Feast of Weeks' (Exod. 34:22; Deut. 16:10,16) because it took place after a week of weeks (after seven Sabbaths) and is the name by which the Jews call it — *Shavuot* (Weeks). In the New Testament it is called 'Pentecost' (Acts 2:1) from the Greek word for 'fiftieth' (the day after the week of weeks is the fiftieth day).[8]

This was a one-day festival and a day of **'holy convocation'** in which all work was to cease (23:21). Each adult male worshipper was to come to the sanctuary to present **'a new grain offering to the LORD'** (23:16). Whereas the earlier first-fruits barley offering consisted of a sheaf straight from the field, this later first-fruits offering of wheat grain to be waved, or elevated, by the priest was made into two loaves of leavened bread (23:17). This made it different from the regular grain offerings (see 2:4).

In addition to the bread, the worshipper was to present lavish sacrifices fitting for a harvest celebration. They included a burnt offering of seven first-year lambs, one young bull and two rams, together with a drink offering (23:18). A sin offering and a peace offering were also required (23:19; see Lev. 3; 4). Matthew Henry observes that this is the only occasion when peace offerings were required from the whole nation. This important day, with its special sacrifices, marks the climax of the festivals associated with the first half of the year. The law ends with the same reminder that closed the previous paragraph concerning the first-fruits offering, that this is a regulation **'for ever in all your dwellings throughout your generations'** (23:21; cf. 23:14).

Pentecost

The law finds its consummation in the events surrounding the coming of the Holy Spirit as a result of the death and resurrection of Christ. Luke draws our attention to this when he describes the promised Holy Spirit descending in power on Christ's disciples who had met together in Jerusalem. In the original Greek the opening clause, translated, 'When the day of Pentecost had fully come…', suggests that the Festival of Weeks was being fulfilled that day (Acts 2:1). This was 'the day of the first fruits' of the harvest when representatives from different parts of the Roman Empire heard the gospel and three thousand of them became believers and formed the New Testament church, the body of Christ. It was the beginning, a first-fruits presentation to the Lord, as Luke indicates in the book of Acts, of a worldwide harvest to be gathered in.

Pentecost is not only the first day of a new week, but the first day of a new week of weeks and, on the basis of the date in Exodus 19:1, it was regarded by the Jews as the day when the law was given at Mount Sinai. Instead of its being associated with the law, the old covenant and ethnic Israel, Pentecost is now associated with the new covenant, the gift of the Spirit and the Israel of God from all nations.

Poverty made history

The Harvest-festival regulations end by urging Israel to remember the poor and the immigrants by not reaping the corners of the field or gathering up the gleanings (23:22). This law is a quotation from an earlier section (see 19:9-10) and is appropriate at this point for, in their eagerness to celebrate the harvest and to rejoice in God's good gifts, Israel is called to show a generous spirit.[9] The law concerning the harvest assumes the blessings of the covenant that

will come when Israel obeys God's commands. When they
experience the blessing of good harvests the poor in society
are not left out. Everyone benefits when God is honoured
and obeyed. The evidence of a truly thankful spirit is shown
in an eagerness to be generous to those in need. The Christian, in offering praise and thanks to God, is urged not to
'forget to do good and to share, for with such sacrifices God
is well pleased' (Heb. 13:15-16).

27.
Holy seasons: autumn

Please read Leviticus 23:23-44

Autumn festivals

Before the third and final pilgrimage festival is mentioned two significant events intervene: the blowing ceremony and the Day of Atonement. Each special occasion is given the same introduction (23:23,26,33).

The day of trumpet-blowing (23:24-25)

This day of the new moon announces the beginning of the seventh month, called Ethanim but better known by its later name, Tishri. Daily work is to cease on this first day in order to have **'a sabbath rest'** (cf. 23:3)[1] and **'a holy convocation'** (23:2). The Israelites are to **'offer an offering made by fire to the LORD'**, the details of which are given later (see Num. 29:1-6). This offering was in addition to the regular sacrifices that were made on the first day of every month (Num. 28:11-15).

What is the significance of this **'first day of the month'**? We are told that it is **'a memorial of blowing of trumpets'**. The text does not actually mention the instrument used. It

literally says 'a memorial of blowing' (or, better, 'blasts'),
meaning that the day is a reminder by means of blasts from a
ram's horn or from a trumpet. It is later called 'a day of
blasts'. In the book of Numbers silver trumpets were blown
by the priests with different sounds for different types of
assemblies. Besides sounding the call to advance and an
alarm to warn, the trumpets were used 'in the day of your
gladness, in your appointed feasts, and at the beginning of
your months ... and they shall be a memorial for you before
your God' (Num. 10:10), thus encouraging some scholars to
think that the reference here is to trumpet blasts. Other
scholars assume that the instrument is the horn, on the basis
of what the psalmist says about blowing the ram's horn at the
time of the new moon (month) and the full moon on the feast
day (Ps. 81:3).

It would seem that, just as there were special offerings for
the first day of the seventh month in addition to the regular
new moon (month) offerings (Num. 28:11-15; 29:1-6), so, in
addition to the trumpet blasts made over their offerings at the
beginning of each new moon (month), there were special
blasts from the ram's horn to announce the commencement
of the seventh month. Since the time between the Old Testament period and the New the Jews have celebrated this day
as New Year's Day (Rosh Hashana), announcing it with
blasts from the ram's horn.

When the Jewish exiles returned home from Babylon, we
are told they made this first day of the seventh month a
notable occasion by coming together to hear Ezra read the
Law of Moses from a wooden pulpit, with the Levites
helping to explain the meaning. Hearing the Word of God
caused the people to weep, but Ezra, Nehemiah and the
Levites told them, 'This day is holy to the LORD your God;
do not mourn nor weep ... for the joy of the LORD is your
strength' (see Neh. 8:1-12).

The **'seventh month'** is set apart, just like the seventh day and the seventh year. In fact, the seventh month is to the other months of the year what the seventh day is to the other days of the week. The more haunting horn blasts, in contrast to the clear notes of the trumpets, proclaimed the first day of the holy month and summoned the people to make their special offerings and to prepare themselves for the solemn Day of Atonement and the final great festival of joy.

The blasts are also a reminder, or **'memorial'**, in that they call out to God on Israel's behalf that he would remember his covenant with them and continue to be favourable towards them. In the midst of their rejoicing at the end of the agricultural year the horn blasts drew attention to their need to implore God's mercy that he would be gracious as they looked towards a new season. At the same time the sound of the horns would have had the effect of reminding Israel of her responsibilities.

The holy month, with its accompanying sacrifices, has its consummation in Christ. As the horn blasts proclaimed the day, so preachers have the duty of announcing the reality to which all the events of the seventh month point. Like Isaiah, who was commissioned to blast out God's Word like the sound of the horn (Isa. 58:1), so the ministers of the new covenant are to preach the sufferings of Christ and his glory and to announce that 'Now is the day of salvation.' What the people of Ezra's day did should be an encouragement to Christians to meet together to hear God's Word read and expounded and for sorrow to be turned into joy.

Another lesson we learn from this passage is not to take God for granted, but to pray to him that he would have mercy and remember his covenant and bless his people and that he would use them, that many more might be saved from the nations and brought into the family of God.

We are also reminded by the psalmist of the use of the horn in praising God for his salvation and coming judgement

(Ps. 98:6). As the horn was used to arouse and warn the people, so it was also used to express joyful praise to God (Ps. 33:3; 47:5). In singing praises to God, David offers in God's tabernacle 'sacrifices of joy' (literally, 'sacrifices of [horn] blasts'). The Christian has every reason to joy in the God of his salvation, who has done marvellous things through Christ's victory on the cross, his resurrection and ascension, and who will finally make all things new when he returns in glory. 'Blessed are the people who know the joyful sound!' (literally, 'the [horn] blast'). 'They walk, O LORD, in the light of your countenance' (Ps. 89:15).

The Day of Atonement (23:27-32)

On the tenth day of this holy month the people were to keep the **'Day of Atonement'** (Yom Kippur). The day has been mentioned in Leviticus 16, where we are given details of the special rituals at the tabernacle and the important work of the high priest. Here we see the day in the context of the other calendar events and emphasis falls on the people's responsibilities. It is the only place in the calendar where the precise time is given for keeping the day — **'on the ninth day of the month at evening, from evening to evening'** (23:32). There are obvious practical reasons for giving this detail. It was important for the people to know exactly when the fast should begin and end, both for their own physical health and to save them from the disaster of being 'cut off' from their people (23:29).[2]

The very first word, **'Also'** — sometimes translated 'now' or 'indeed' — marks out the day as different, not like the joyous occasion on the first day of the month. This **'holy convocation'** day is like the weekly Sabbath. It is called **'your sabbath'** and a **'sabbath of solemn rest'** (23:32; cf. 23:3; 16:31). Three times it is stressed that no work was to be done, with the warning that God would destroy offenders

(23:28,30,31). As the earlier legislation laid down, the people are called to **'afflict'** themselves (23:27,29,32; see 16:29,31). As we see from Isaiah's prophecy against false fasting (Isa. 58:3-10), the affliction or deprivation involved going without food and expressing signs of mourning. The people's attitude was to coincide with what was taking place in the tabernacle when the high priest was making 'full atonement'.[3]

The Day of Atonement is wonderfully fulfilled in Christ's atoning work, as the letter to the Hebrews makes clear, but how should Christians view this special day that is termed 'the Fast' in Acts 27:9? Certainly it should sober us as we remember that it was on account of our sins that Jesus was crucified. It should subdue us to think that as believers we still sin in the light of all that Christ has done through his atoning death. But, 'Blessed are those who mourn, for they shall be comforted' (Matt. 5:4), both now and in the glory to come on account of the finished work of Christ. Those who would follow Jesus are called to a life of affliction in the sense that they are to say 'No' to self, take up the cross daily and follow Christ (Luke 9:23).

The Festival of Tabernacles (23:34-43)

During the time when the Jews were in Babylon it was impossible for them to keep any of the festivals in the way laid down in the law. There could be no attendance at the central sanctuary in Jerusalem for the three pilgrim festivals. But when they were allowed to return to their homeland seventy years later we are told that from the beginning of the seventh month they began to offer the regular sacrifices even though the temple was not yet rebuilt. They also remembered the special sacrifices for the first day of the new month and they kept the Feast of Tabernacles and the other festivals (Ezra 3:4-6; 6:19-22).

It was the prophets Haggai and Zechariah whom God used to urge the people to get on with building the sanctuary and to complete it (Ezra 5:1-2). Their very names must have been an encouragement to the people. Zechariah means 'The LORD has remembered,' for God had not forgotten the promises he had made and would see them through to their ultimate fulfilment. Haggai means 'my festivals' and indicated the importance of building the temple so that these pilgrim festivals could be strictly kept according to the law with a view to the coming of the Messiah.

The **'Feast of Tabernacles'**, or Booths (*Sukkoth*), is the third annual pilgrimage festival and brings to a grand finale all the other religious events of the year. For this reason it is often referred to simply as 'the feast' (1 Kings 8:2; 12:32; 2 Chr. 7:8).[4] The other name for this pilgrim festival is 'the Feast of Ingathering' (see Exod. 23:16; 34:22), for it was the time when the remainder of the harvest, such as the summer fruits, had all been gathered in. It was to last **'seven days'**, beginning at the time of the full moon on the **'fifteenth day'** with a **'holy convocation'** (23:35; cf. 23:2) on which no work was to be done. A large number of special sacrifices were to be offered to the Lord each day (23:36 — for details see Num. 29:12-34). An extra **'eighth day'** was added at the end of the festival for another **'holy convocation'**. The day is also described as a **'sacred assembly'**, when again work was to cease and more sacrifices were to be offered (23:36; see Num. 29:35-38). John refers to this day as 'that great day of the feast' (John 7:37; cf. 7:2,8,10-11,14).

By the time of Jesus it had become a spectacular celebration, with the lighting of lamps, dancing, processions, the priests pouring out water and wine in the temple, and the people marching around the bronze altar carrying fruit and waving palm branches. It had become a symbol of national hope as they looked forward to the coming of Messiah, who would finally liberate them from their enemies. In their prayers at that time they petitioned God for rain and for the resurrection of the dead. It was therefore a significant moment on that last great day of the feast to find Jesus standing in the temple and announcing, 'If anyone thirsts, let him come to me and drink. He who believes in me, as the Scripture has said, out of his heart will flow rivers of living water' (John 7:37-38).

The regular and the special (23:37-38)

Before the legislation is presented that gives meaning to the term 'tabernacles' or 'booths', there is a brief summary statement concerning all the feasts. It makes the point that the large number of offerings the people are to make during these special events is in addition to their spontaneous peace offerings and the weekly regular sacrifices. As one commentator puts it, 'This instruction particularly guards against any Israelite attempting to get double value from an offering, i.e., making a festive offering and claiming it as one of his other gifts or obligations.'[5] Matthew Henry draws from this a useful lesson by reminding us that 'Calls to extraordinary services will not excuse us from our constant stated performances.'

The meaning of the Feast of Tabernacles (23:39-43)

The festival was called 'tabernacles' or 'booths' because the native-born Israelites were directed to make temporary booths and to live in them throughout the festive week. Like the first pilgrimage festival, it was to remind the nation of its beginnings, when the first generation left Egypt and lived a nomadic life in booths (23:42-43). It does not say so here, but it is assumed that the makeshift shelters were made out of the large leafy branches they were instructed to cut from various magnificent trees (**'beautiful trees'**), such as the palm and the willow (23:40). This is what the exiles who returned from Babylon did when they kept the festival. They built booths in the temple area and by the city gates as well as in their own homes. We are told that there had not been such celebrations and obedience to the letter of the law since the days of Joshua (Neh. 8:14-17). We can also imagine them waving the large palm leaves in their joyful celebrations, as the pilgrims did when Jesus entered Jerusalem riding on a donkey (John 12:12-15).

Christians are to remember that the Christian life is a pilgrimage. Here we have no continuing city (Heb. 13:13-14). This old world is not our home and each of us lives in a body that Paul can only describe as 'a tent' (2 Cor. 5:1). Nevertheless, we are encouraged to praise God for all our spiritual blessings in Christ and we are urged to rejoice in the Lord always, knowing that our citizenship is in heaven from where our Saviour will appear who will transform our lowly bodies to be conformed to his glorious body.

Joy and thanksgiving

The Feast of Tabernacles was a great time for rejoicing. In fact, the people are commanded to rejoice (Deut. 16:14-15). It was, after all, the end of the harvest season, when they had **'gathered in the fruit of the land'**, which included the olives and the grapes (23:39). It is more like the harvest thanksgiving services that became so popular in Christian churches from Victorian times and still are in rural areas.

The future harvest home

While Passover and Unleavened Bread and the Feast of Weeks find their fulfilment with the coming of Christ and the Spirit, the festival of Ingathering awaits fulfilment. It looks forward to the grand climax of history when all the elect have been safely gathered in, to enjoy the eternal state of blessedness in the new creation. Jesus encouraged his followers to think in agricultural terms, of sowing and reaping, of fields white for harvest and of the end of the age as the time when the harvest is collected (Matt. 13:1-30,36-43; John 4:35-38). The apostle Paul also has the harvest scene in mind when he speaks of the 'fulness of the Gentiles' coming in and of 'all Israel' being saved (Rom. 11:25-26).

It is the prophet Zechariah who points God's people to the glorious end-time Feast of Tabernacles. He sees it fulfilled in the grand finale when the remnant from all nations will 'go up from year to year to worship the King, the LORD of hosts, and to keep the Feast of Tabernacles' (Zech. 14:16). Three times he mentions the feast by name in the closing words of his prophecy. Interestingly, before that final event, he seems to have the Day of Atonement in mind when he speaks of the sorrow felt by a remnant from Israel and of a fountain 'opened … for sin and for uncleanness' (Zech. 12:10 – 13:1). It is when the whole company of God's people have been gathered in that the Feast of Tabernacles will have been finally realized. It is the joy of an eternal 'Tabernacles' festival that is expressed in John's vision of the elect from every nation standing with God and the Lamb in the new creation 'with palm branches in their hands' (Rev. 7:9-17; 21:3-4; cf. Lev. 23:40). In the light of this section of Leviticus, with its emphasis on holiness, it is surely not without significance that Zechariah also views the final feast in terms of 'Holiness to the LORD' (Zech. 14:20-21).

Even so, Lord, quickly come
To Thy final harvest-home:
Gather Thou Thy people in,

Free from sorrow, free from sin;
There, for ever purified,
In Thy presence to abide:
Come, with all Thine angels come,
Raise the glorious harvest-home.[6]

28.
Pure oil and holy bread

Please read Leviticus 24:1-9

These regulations regarding the tabernacle lights and bread
and the case of blasphemy which follows are not as uncon-
nected with the calendar of religious events as it might at
first seem. As emphasis was placed on the nation's responsibility to make sure that the festivals were kept and the poor
remembered (23:2,10,22,24,34,44), so it was the people's
duty to see that the tabernacle was supplied with oil and
bread (24:2,8). In addition, before the text goes on to mention more long-term calendar events it is an appropriate
point at which to consider the oil and bread associated with
the grain and fruit harvests.

The chapter begins with the Lord telling Moses to **'Command the children of Israel'** (24:1-2) and ends with Israel
doing 'as the LORD commanded Moses' (24:23).

Oil for the lamps (24:2-4)

The regulations concerning the oil for the lampstand (the
Menorah) have been given earlier (Exod. 27:20-21). They
are repeated here to emphasize that, amid all the activities of

the special occasions, the people are not to forget the more mundane regular duties. While the initial supply of oil was brought by the rulers (Exod. 35:28), when Israel eventually reached Canaan the responsibility for maintaining the supply would fall on the people as a whole (24:2; Exod. 27:20). The promised land was full of olive groves (Deut. 6:11; Josh. 24:13) and excavations at Ekron and elsewhere have uncovered over a hundred oil presses, all of them inside ordinary houses. This indicates that in the seventh century B.C., 'The manufacture of olive oil was a cottage industry practised by families at their homes.'[1]

The olives were to be pounded, or **'pressed'**, in a mortar rather than crushed in a mill, and the pulp would have been passed through a strainer to produce **'pure'**, that is, 'clear', oil. While the clear oil would have resulted in less smoke and soot, the main reason for this process was to provide oil fit for the Holy Place. The same word **'pure'** is applied to the incense (24:7; Exod. 30:34). The first area inside the tabernacle, where only the priests were allowed, was the Holy Place, where the table for the bread, the lampstand and the incense altar were situated. Everything in this room needed to be of a higher standard than outside as a sign of the greater degree of holiness associated with the place. It was not the Holy of Holies, as the expression, **'outside the veil of the Testimony'**, makes clear (24:3; cf. Exod. 27:21; 30:6), but it was close enough to require the very best quality. The **'veil'**, of course, was the curtain that divided the holy from the most holy area and the **'Testimony'** refers to the Ten Commandments (Exod. 31:18; 32:15; 34:29) that were placed in the ark of the covenant (Exod. 25:16; 40:20).

While the people supplied the oil, Aaron, as high priest, assisted by his sons, the priests (see Exod. 27:21), was in charge of filling and tending the seven-branched lampstand of pure gold and making sure that the lights were lit and kept burning regularly all night **'from evening until morning'** (cf. Exod. 30:8; 1 Sam. 3:3). This was done **'before the LORD continually'** (24:3-4). The word **'continually'**, or 'regularly', is mentioned three times in this short paragraph to stress that the preparing and lighting of the lamps must never cease. It is **'a statute for ever'** (24:3) in the sense that it must be observed throughout Israel's history until the sanctuary and its furniture completed its symbolic usefulness. This happened with the coming of Jesus the Messiah. When he had offered himself as the perfect sacrifice on the cross and had cried out, 'It is finished!' the **'veil'** was split in two from top to bottom, thus indicating that the old shadowy worship had had its day.

A continual supply of oil was important so that the lamps in the Holy Place did not go out. The Holy Place needed light, and the lights spoke symbolically of the God who is light and in him there is no darkness at all (1 John 1:5; Ps. 27:1; Isa. 45:19). As the priests could not minister before God in the dark, so Christians cannot say they have fellowship with God and walk in the darkness (1 John 1:6-7).

Under the new covenant the people of God no longer need to supply oil for priests to keep lights flickering in a sanctuary, but certainly they need to support the ministry in their local churches. John views the glory of Jesus, the Head of the church, among seven golden lampstands that represented the seven churches in Asia Minor. The stars in his right hand are the messengers, or leaders, of the churches to whom the Lord sends messages. But the Lord's messages are for all the members who make up the churches and each is called to listen and to respond: 'If anyone hears my voice...' (Rev. 1:9 – 3:22). Each local church is to be a light 'before the Lord'. If God demanded of the people the purest oil for a worship that was only a shadow of the true, how much more should we who belong to the reality that is in Christ respond not with second-rate, half-hearted service, but give of our very best for the leaders of our churches to use to the glory of God! The offshoot of continued, ongoing service on our part in the churches will be that the light of God's knowledge and salvation will continue to shine, not in the darkness of a room with no windows, but in our spiritually dark world with no other light. 'You are the light of the world' (see Matt. 5:14-16).

Without pushing the image too far we could add, in view of the close association between oil and the Spirit (see Zech. 4:6), that our churches in these days need members and leaders who are full of the pure Spirit of God in the Lord's service in order to witness to our needy world.

Bread for the table (24:5-9)

The people were also responsible for supplying the bread each week for the **'pure'** gold table that stood in the Holy Place on the opposite side to the golden lampstand. The table's measurements have already been given (Exod. 25:23-30), but it is only here that details are given about the bread. It is named elsewhere as 'the bread of the Presence' (Exod. 35:13; 39:36, ESV). It was William Tyndale who invented the name 'shewbread' to translate the Hebrew phrase. The loaves are called 'the bread of the Presence' probably because they remained near the Holy of Holies, the area that symbolized God's presence with his people. The bread is also called 'the regular ... bread' (Num. 4:7, ESV) because there was to be a continual supply on the table (Exod. 25:30).

This 'holy bread' (1 Sam. 21:4) was to be made into twelve large **'cakes'**, or loaves (24:5), judging by the amount of flour that was used.[2] They were probably flat unleavened cakes to enable them to be eaten one week after being baked.[3] As the table was not very big (90 cm. by 45 cm. or 3 ft. by 1 ft. 6 ins.), it is possible that the two rows of bread, six to a row, meant that the loaves were piled on top of one another.[4]

In addition, **'pure frankincense'** was to be placed on the table with each row, **'for a memorial, an offering made by fire to the LORD'** (24:7). In other words, the incense, which was probably put in gold cups (see Exod. 37:16), was first placed with the bread and then subsequently burned. The bread with the incense was like the regular grain offering but in this case the frankincense on its own acted as the **'memorial'** portion that was burned as 'a sweet aroma to the LORD' (see 2:9). Because the bread and frankincense are in the Holy Place, the representative portion is burned on the incense altar that stood next to the 'veil' (see 24:3). The bread, though an offering to the Lord made by the people, became food that the priests could later eat in the Holy Place (24:9).

Unlike Israel's neighbours who had bread baked daily to put on tables for their gods to eat, there is no thought here of feeding God. God later says through the psalmist, 'If I were hungry, I would not tell you; for the world is mine, and all its fulness' (Ps. 50:12). This holy bread was a token offering changed regularly every Sabbath as **'an everlasting covenant'** (24:8). The same is said of the Sabbath itself (see Exod. 31:16). Both were to act as signs of the Sinai covenant. As the high priest symbolically bore the names of the twelve tribes on his holy garments before the Lord (Exod. 28:12,21,29), so the twelve loaves spread **'before the LORD'** each Sabbath day served as a reminder of God's covenant with Israel. The loaves came **'from the children of Israel'** so that this special grain offering served as a weekly renewal of the covenant.

It was this **'most holy'** bread, which only the priests could eat in the Holy Place (24:9), that the high priest Ahimelech gave to David and his men when they were desperately hungry (1 Sam. 21:1-6). David was not yet the acknowledged King of Israel, even though he had been anointed, whereas Saul, the present ruler, had become David's enemy and wanted to kill him. It is therefore very significant that Jesus should draw attention to this incident in his discussion with the Pharisees concerning the keeping of the Sabbath (Matt. 12:1-8). Far from suggesting that God had changed his mind about observing the Sabbath, Jesus was attacking the way the Pharisees were interpreting it and he used the story of David to show that 'Common sense and compassion for human need far outweigh a stringent inter-pretation of the law.'[5] But there is more to Jesus' use of this Old Testament incident than that.

Jesus continues by mentioning the fact that the priests in the temple 'profane the Sabbath' and are blameless (Matt. 12:5). What he had in mind was the work of the priests, which did not stop on the Sabbath. It included not only offering more sacrifices on that day but changing the 'shew-bread'.[6] Astonishingly, Jesus states that 'In this place there is one greater than the temple' (Matt. 12:6). Not only is Jesus saying, as Lord of the Sabbath, that human need overrides strict observance of the law, but that he is greater than the temple itself. This is another indication that the old taber-nacle laws have their ultimate realization in Jesus, our great High Priest, and his atoning sacrifice. Furthermore, he was also teaching that he is a second David, the ultimate King of his people, anointed by God at the time of his baptism but not yet enthroned, while the Jewish leaders had become his enemies and were acting like Saul to get rid of him.

Jesus is the representative of his people before the Lord and, as we humble ourselves and receive him as our repre-sentative and substitute offering, God remembers his coven-ant and we are accepted.

The two regulations concerning the preparation of oil and fine flour by the people have the effect of emphasizing the importance of the end products, 'the light' and 'the bread' that are **'before the LORD'** (24:2-3,7-8). The bread, as we have seen, clearly represented Israel, and it is interesting that the seven-branched lampstand that gave the light has become the symbol of Judaism now that it is without a sanctuary. But Jesus is the fulfilment of Israel's destiny. He is now 'before the Lord' in the true tabernacle on behalf of all his new-covenant people. He is the real bread of life (John 6:35,48), the real light of life that the darkness cannot extinguish (John 1:5; 8:12). In John's vision of the new creation, the New Jerusalem, which is a picture of God's people from all nations, is also the true temple where God lives among his people (Rev. 21:1-3), where there is no need of light because 'the Lamb is its light' and where they shall be hungry no more (Rev. 21:23; 7:15-17).

29.
Holy name

Please read Leviticus 24:10-23

Blasphemy has come to be associated in many people's minds with the Moslem world. It was the Salman Rushdie affair in the UK that brought home to British people the Islamic ruling (the *fatwa*) that he should be killed for what he had written in his novel, *The Satanic Verses*. There is a blasphemy law on the British statute books that relates to the Christian faith, but it is rarely used.

In these holiness laws priests and people have been urged not to profane God's holy name by immoral behaviour or by activity in the tabernacle that is contrary to God's commandments (18:21; 22:2,32). A case is now presented where instead of sanctifying God's holy name, someone does the very opposite.

There are only two narrative sections in Leviticus and both relate very solemn incidents. The first occurs in the middle of regulations for the priesthood and concerns Nadab and Abihu, who offered unauthorized fire (10:1-7). The second concerns a blasphemer and it provides the context for laws that affect the whole community. Both involve disrespect of God's holy name (10:3; 24:11), the first in the setting of the holy sanctuary and the other within the holy camp. They impress upon us again the need for everyone, whether specially privileged or not, to treat God with the respect that is due to him. Such episodes also remind us that these laws are set in the context of a journey from Egypt via Sinai to the land of promise.

The situation related (24:10-12)

The incident of a man caught in the act of committing blasphemy reminds us that we are in a living historical situation with people going about their daily lives in an immense camp in the middle of a desert where arguments could easily flare up and turn nasty.

This particular man had an Israelite mother and an Egyptian father. His mother's pedigree cannot be faulted (24:11), even if **'the tribe of Dan'** turned out later to be wayward and idolatrous. We do not know whether the father remained in Egypt at the time of the Exodus or was a member of the 'mixed multitude', or riff-raff, that accompanied Israel when they left (Exod. 12:38; Num. 11:4). What is clear is that this man of mixed blood got into a fight with an Israelite and in the course of the exchange blasphemed God's holy name. What the man actually said and did we are not told but he used God's personal **'name'**, Yahweh or Jehovah, in a blasphemous curse (24:11,16). The 'glorious and awesome name, THE LORD YOUR GOD', which Israel was encouraged to revere (Deut. 28:58) was brought into dishonour by this man of mixed race.

The incident is one illustration of what it meant to break the Third Commandment: 'You shall not take the name of the LORD your God in vain, for the LORD will not hold him guiltless who takes his name in vain' (Exod. 20:7). In a similar law which states, 'You shall not revile God' (Exod. 22:28), the word 'revile' is the same as that translated

'**cursed**' here (24:11). To curse God is to belittle him, while
the word for blaspheme suggests 'wounding with the
tongue'. Both words together point to a blasphemous attack
on God's person and character.

The issue that needed to be clarified was whether this
grave offence applied to those who were not full-blooded
Israelites and what the penalty should be. Until Moses knew
the mind of the Lord on the matter, the blasphemer was held
in custody. In Israel, as generally in the ancient Near East,
custodial sentences were not usually handed out. A convicted
person was either put to death for a capital crime or required
to pay out various forms of compensation. This was the first
of a number of recorded cases where Moses needed special
guidance and it is very reminiscent of the incident where a
man was caught violating the Sabbath. He too was placed in
custody until a divine ruling was received (Num. 15:32-34;
cf. 9:6-14; 27:1-11). Though Moses was in a powerful
position he did nothing on the basis of his own whim, but
asked the Lord for guidance. In this, as with his meekness, he
prefigured the sinless Saviour who said, 'I have not spoken
on my own authority; but the Father who sent me gave me a
command, what I should say and what I should speak' (John
12:49).

The sentence revealed (24:13-14)

God instructed Moses that the blasphemer, even though he
was of mixed blood, should be taken outside the camp and
there be stoned to death. Death sentences and burials were to
take place outside the holy camp settlements (Num. 15:35;
cf. Lev. 13:46), to prevent any pollution caused by the death
penalty from affecting the whole community. Jesus was
crucified outside the camp gate and, paradoxically, that was
in order that 'he might sanctify the people with his own

blood'. Those who belong to him are urged to go outside to him, 'bearing his reproach' (see Heb. 13:11-13). It is part and parcel of what it means to take up the cross daily and follow him.

The people who had heard the man blaspheme were to **'lay their hands on his head'** (24:14; cf. 1:4; 16:21). In this symbolic act the responsibility for the sin was seen to rest with the blasphemer alone. It indicated that, though the witnesses had heard the polluting language, no guilt accrued to them, and so the ritual contamination rested entirely on the head of the guilty man. The offender carried all the blame and punishment.

It was not left to a black-hooded executioner to carry out the death penalty; rather, the entire covenant community had a hand in stoning him, with the witnesses throwing the first stones (Deut. 17:7). This is what happened to Naboth the Jezreelite when he was falsely accused of blaspheming God and the king (1 Kings 21:13). The same happened to Stephen, the first Christian martyr. He too was falsely accused of speaking blasphemous words against Moses and God. They threw him 'out of the city and stoned him' (Acts 6:11; 7:58).

Specific laws recited (24:15-22)

Cursing God (24:15)

Anyone who showed disrespect for God, even though in his cursing he did not use God's special name, was still to be held responsible and to suffer the due penalty.

Blaspheming the Name (24:16)

This reminds us of the actual case. A name was much more than a label for distinguishing one person from another. It stood for the very being of the person. So when the psalmist prays that the name of the God of Jacob would defend his people it is a blessing carrying the powerful assurance that the God who had revealed so many amazing things about himself would defend them (Ps. 20:1). To blaspheme God's name is to undermine all that God is and all that he stands for.

Whereas in the narrative, in the Hebrew it simply mentions 'the name' (24:11 — some translations add 'of the LORD'), in stating the rule it is spelled out in full: **'the name of the LORD'**. The law did not say that the people could never use God's special name that had become so precious to the Israelites at the time of the Exodus, but they were not to use this name in a disrespectful way. However, it is on the basis of this verse that the Jews to this day follow a long-established tradition of not using or pronouncing the four-letter Hebrew name, *YHWH*, not even when reading Scripture. They substitute the word *Adonai*, which means 'Lord'. As a result scholars are not absolutely sure how God's personal name should be pronounced although there is good reason to believe it is 'Yahweh'. English translations use the word 'LORD' for Yahweh (following the Jewish tradition), using capital letters to distinguish it from the normal word for 'Lord'.

Sadly, Jesus had to expose the hypocrisy of those who piously or superstitiously avoided using God or Yahweh when swearing oaths but swore by things associated with God, such as heaven or Jerusalem. It is the same today when cursing occurs in casual speech. The name of God is usually drawn in somewhere, even if not openly, then by the use of such expressions as 'by heaven'. In our daily conversations with people, Christians are to witness to a different way, to a whole new dimension of living, where our speech does not need swear words to substantiate what we say (Matt. 5:33-37). On occasions when there is need to formally swear an oath, as in a court of law, the mention of God's name becomes a reminder not to be economical with the truth or to bear false witness.

When we pray, 'Hallowed be your name', we are showing concern for God's holy name in a world which blasphemes God every day (see Matt. 6:9-10). We look forward to the day when God's character and reputation will be held in honour everywhere and by everyone.

Principles of justice (24:17-22)

Before reference is made to the actual execution of the blasphemer, we are introduced to principles of divine justice. The way these regulations are set out would have made them easy to remember, for the final verses are a mirror image of the first: the law concerning killing humans occurs twice (24:17,21) and likewise concerning animals (24:18,21). This arrangement also adds force to the central statement, the fundamental principle that the punishment must fit the crime, the so-called *lex talionis* (24:19-20). Surrounding the whole is one of the main points of the passage — that the same law applies equally to foreign residents and native-born Israelites (24:16,22).[1]

A number of items arising from these laws call for attention.

Firstly, while a distinction is made between murder and manslaughter (see Exod. 21:12-14), the deliberate, premeditated killing of a fellow human being is viewed as a capital crime worthy of the death penalty. This law is based on the principle that all human beings, of whatever class, caste, creed or colour, are made in God's image (see Gen. 9:6).

Murder is another form of blasphemy, for the person is destroying the bearer of God's image, however distorted that image might be through sin. It is a stark reminder of human rebellion against God seen first in what Cain did to Abel his brother (Gen. 4:3-15).

Secondly, in contrast to pagan codes of law at the time that took into account the social standing of those accused of crimes worthy of death, the reference to murder is spelled out here to indicate that the ruling covered anyone within the Israelite community, whatever his or her background and standing in society might be (24:16,22). The same law applied to the native-born as to immigrants and half-castes.

Thirdly, contrary to the views of so many in the modern animal-rights movement, where humans are considered to be merely higher life forms on the evolutionary ladder, a distinction is made between an animal and a human. There is a proper respect for all life in the Mosaic law and it may be because of the special way in which the sacrificial animals were slaughtered that a ruling concerning them occurs at this point. The law stipulates that if someone deliberately killed an animal belonging to someone else — for example, out of spite or hatred of the owner — the death penalty was not operative, but the guilty person was required to pay appropriate compensation, **'animal for animal'** (24:18,21). The 'life for life' principle means one animal to replace the animal that had been killed. This gives the lead for introducing the so-called tit-for-tat rule (24:19-20; Exod. 21:23-25; Deut. 19:21).

Fourthly, the **'eye for eye, tooth for tooth'** expression (24:20) has often been thought of as a clear indication of the barbaric, bloodthirsty nature of the Mosaic law. Nothing could be further from the truth, for it demonstrates a humane standard of fair justice in a godless world where there are people like Lamech, who killed a man for hurting him (Gen. 4:23). The law sets the maximum punishment and maintains that the sentence must fit the crime. This is a principle acknowledged in ancient Near-Eastern cultures, as in the Code of Hammurabi, but in practice they only applied it to the better-off in society. Not so in Israel, where it is emphasized that there is one rule for all. This is how God, the Judge of the earth, operates: 'As you have done, it shall be done to you' (Obad. 15).

As in the case of 'animal for animal' (24:18), the law was not meant to be taken literally except in the case of premeditated murder (Num. 35:16-21). The fact that no compensation was allowed in the case of murder (Num. 35:31-32) implies that reimbursing for loss was how the law was normally understood. Jewish history records no cases where the principle was applied literally. Nothing, however, could compensate for the deliberate taking of another person's life (see Ps. 49:7-8).

Fifthly, it is because of what Jesus taught in the Sermon on the Mount on the subject that it has been assumed that he was attacking the law of Moses as 'primitive' and harsh. Jesus, however, was not criticizing the Mosaic law, but indicating that what is just and necessary in the public courtroom is not the way his disciples should behave among themselves. In this he was being entirely consistent with what the Mosaic law had already indicated when it insisted that members of the covenant community should not seek personal vengeance and bear grudges (19:18). Jesus was not sweeping away the need in human sinful society for rules to prevent people from taking the law into their own hands. He actually upheld the authority of the state and Paul and Peter both acknowledged the place of civil authority in punishing those who commit crimes (Matt. 22:21; Rom. 13:4; 1 Peter 2:14).

Sixthly, when Jesus quoted the 'eye for eye' rule it was in the context of presenting a new society where a higher kind of justice operated. His authoritative word was spoken against those who used the Mosaic law to get even with people. Vengeance and retaliation have no part in the rule that Jesus came to establish, and so Christians are not to be governed by a tit-for-tat spirit. It also means that if the state does not deal with the criminal who has wronged us, or a grievance arises where the state cannot intervene, the Christian must still not resort to private revenge. We must leave it to God to punish the wrongdoer, for in the final analysis vengeance belongs to him and he will hand out justice fairly and impartially with no mistakes (Rom. 2:6,11). This kind of situation will reveal whether we do trust God and the promises and warnings he makes concerning the Day of Judgement. Christians are urged to 'repay no one evil for evil' and if it is possible and it depends on us, we are to live peaceably with everyone (Rom. 12:17-21). Why is it that there are too many obnoxious people who call themselves Christians going about picking fights and undermining the work of other believers? If you are a culprit, repent and receive the Word with a meek spirit!

Finally, our Saviour himself practised what he preached and he is the one who is able to help his followers to act in the same way. When he was reviled he did not retaliate; when he was slapped in the face he took it; when people put him on the cross he prayed for them. He did not threaten them, but committed himself to him who judges righteously. Jesus did this to save us from our sins and to open this new way of life for all who trust and follow him. This is the good news (1 Peter 2:23).

Sentence executed (24:23)

The sentence is carried out, not in a fit of pique by an enraged mob bent on ridding the camp of a misfit and undesirable character, as happened in the case of Stephen (Acts 7;54,57). The blasphemer was not 'thrown out', but taken '**outside the camp**' and executed. It was a judicial action carried out by the people in response to the ruling received from God through Moses.

Sir John Salmond, a leading jurist, once said, 'We have too much forgotten that the mental attitude which best becomes us, when fitting justice is done upon the evildoer, is not pity, but solemn exultation.' It is this solemn exultation that is seen in the fall of the anti-God, anti-Christian society whose members continually blasphemed the name of God and did not repent and give him glory (Rev. 16:9,11,21). Heaven and all God's servants are encouraged to 'rejoice' in the fall because God has punished its citizens for the way they have treated God's servants, and the hallelujah chorus arises out of this just punishment on the enemies of God and his people (Rev. 18:20; 19:1-3).

The Mosaic law concerning the death penalty for blasphemy and other such crimes was formulated for the old-covenant society. By word and example Jesus taught the end of the old-covenant theocratic society, with its special regulations for worship, legal practice and forms of execution. Obvious instances are his teaching that instead of the death penalty for adultery divorce was allowed, and his remarks in the case of the hypocrites who presented him with the woman caught in an adulterous act (Matt. 5:27-32; 19:1-10; John 8:1-11).

The new society that Jesus established through his death, while taking the abiding lessons and principles of the old, leaves criminals to be dealt with by the civil authorities (Acts 25:11; Rom. 13:4; 1 Peter 2:14,20). It is not that blasphemy is no longer the crime it was considered to be. Like the other sins of the old covenant that deserved the death sentence, blasphemy is still a dreadful offence and members who claim to belong to the new covenant are warned of its seriousness. James does so as he speaks of the power of the tongue (James 3:5-10). Church discipline demands that blatant unrepentant blasphemers be put out of fellowship, which seems to be what Paul means when he speaks of Hymenaeus and Alexander being handed over to Satan 'that they may learn not to blaspheme' (1 Tim. 1:20).

Human justice at its best is only a very imperfect and fallible shadow of divine justice. Jesus was sentenced to death on trumped-up charges that included blasphemy. Pilate, the representative of Roman justice, knew that Jesus was inno-cent of the sedition charge that was brought (Matt. 27:24) and yet he washed his hands of the case and handed him over to be executed. It was the greatest miscarriage of justice of all time by the acknowledged experts in jurisprudence.

Of course, in reality Jesus was equal with the Father and is the anointed King. The true blasphemers were his accusers for rejecting him and handing him over to be crucified, for in treating the Son of God in the way they did they were showing contempt for the Father. The Roman soldiers too joined the blasphemy by mocking him (Mark 15:17-20; Luke 22:63-65). One of the crucified criminals also blasphemed and others who passed by joined in (Luke 23:39; Matt. 27:39). It is also true of all those from that day to this 'who oppose the gospel (1 Tim. 1:13; cf. Acts 26:11) and bring discredit to Christianity (Rom. 2:24; 1 Tim. 6:1; Titus 2:5; James 2:7; 2 Peter 2:2)' that they are blaspheming God by their actions.[2]

Yet, beyond the human miscarriage of justice and blas-phemy, the deep mystery of the Christian message is that Jesus was on the cross because God planned it that way in order that sin in all its blasphemous ugliness might be exposed and dealt with justly and adequately. The cross is good news, for it means that blasphemers like Saul of Tarsus who repent and trust the Saviour can know the forgiveness of all their sins and be saved from the coming wrath of God.

But make no mistake, God has not gone soft on blas-phemers and punishment is certain for the unrepentant. To those who blasphemed and said that Jesus was in league with the devil, Jesus warned that though there is forgiveness for every sin and blasphemy, blasphemy against the Holy Spirit would not be forgiven. The people who should worry about this statement are not those who are concerned whether they have committed it or not, but those who could not care less and deliberately and knowingly treat with contempt the only way to forgiveness (Matt. 12:22-32; Heb. 6:4-8; 10:26-31).

30.
Holy years

Please read Leviticus 25:1-22

At the opening of this remarkable piece of legislation we are
informed again that God revealed it to Moses and that he did
so from Mount Sinai (25:1; cf. 7:38). We are encouraged to
understand that all these laws are an expression of God's will
for Israel, his covenant people.

Two important years are brought to our attention: the
sabbatical year, which means every **'seventh year'** (25:1-7);
and the jubilee year, that is, every fiftieth year (25:8-17). As
these special years are discussed three subjects are addressed: the need for the land to have a sabbath rest
(25:2-22), the redemption of property (25:23-38) and the
redemption of people (25:39-55). The familiar formula, **'I
am the LORD your God,'** marks the conclusion of each
subject (25:17,38,55), with 25:18-22 providing supplemen-
tary teaching to answer a natural objection to the sabbatical
years. Clearly the instruction looks to the time when the
people will be settled in the land of promise. The first part of
the chapter deals with these special years in which the land is
allowed to rest.

The sabbath year (25:1-7)

This commentary is being brought to completion during a sabbatical period. The idea of theological teachers and gospel ministers taking a sabbatical is based on this Levitical law. It is an extension of the weekly sabbath rest (see Exod. 23:10-13). Every seventh year the land of Canaan, the land that God had promised to give his people, was to be given rest. This did not prevent people from doing other forms of work, but it did mean that all agricultural labour was to cease. The land was to lie fallow. No seed was to be sown in their fields; their vine and olive trees were not to be pruned, and there was to be no reaping or harvesting. Anything that the ground did produce of itself during the sabbatical year (literally, 'the sabbath of the land', 25:6), whether of grain or fruit, was not to be harvested by the landowner for his personal benefit. On the contrary, the farmer was to open his fields so that the servants, the hired labourers, the temporary residents and the domestic and wild animals might freely eat (25:6-7), in addition to the poor people mentioned in Exodus 23:10-11.

This was an amazing provision for an agricultural community — a complete rest from working the land, beginning at the end of the harvest in the sixth year (September/October) until the same time the following year. Farmers today would throw up their hands in dismay if they were obliged by the state to carry out such a requirement. A weekly sabbath rest is often seen as too restrictive and unworkable, never mind a whole year. But organic farmers will readily appreciate the need for land to lie fallow. It has also been shown that high quantities of alkaline substances in the soil, such as sodium and calcium, due to water irrigation, brought about crop failure and economic ruin in ancient Mesopotamian lands. Allowing the land to rest had the benefit of reducing the sodium in the soil.[1]

As with so many of the laws, Israel failed to observe this command. The eventual removal of God's people from Canaan is seen as the final and severest punishment for their disobedience in general, and specifically as a result of their neglect of this requirement. For seventy years the land lay desolate, thus allowing it to enjoy the rest it had been denied (see 26:34-35; 2 Chr. 36:21; Jer. 29:10; Dan. 9:2).

Other laws relating to this special sabbatical year are mentioned later. During the Feast of Tabernacles, at the close of the sabbatical year the law was to be read to all the people, men, women and children (Deut. 31:10-13), which one commentator describes as 'the most remarkable Sunday School that the earth ever knew'.[2] There was also to be a general release from debt (see Deut. 15:1-2; Jer. 34:12-17).

Why did God require his people to keep this sabbatical year?

• It indicated, as Matthew Henry aptly puts it, that God 'was their landlord, and that they were tenants at will under him'. The people were not allowed to forget that the land belonged to God and it was he who was giving it to Israel for an inheritance — **'the land which I give you'** (25:2).
• Keeping this law would clearly demonstrate dependence on the Lord their God for their daily food. Every good gift came from God. He blessed them with fruitful seasons. Rather than thinking always in terms of their own activity in ploughing, sowing, reaping, pruning and harvesting to feed themselves and gain wealth by selling their produce to others, they were taught that God supplied their needs (see further on 25:21).
• This year of rest is described as **'a sabbath to the LORD'** (25:4). By observing it the Israelites would be indicating their commitment to God. They would be

honouring the God who had brought them into the land of promise.

- It reminded each new generation that they were not to use the land in a selfish way and helped to curtail human greed. Allowing the land to lie fallow enabled it to recuperate so as to be of value to the next generation.
- During this year all were reduced to the same level. The rich resorted to the fields like the poor. Employers and native-born had no advantage over employees and foreigners.
- It encouraged a generous spirit and helped to alleviate poverty.
- It reminded them of the paradise they had lost, when man ate of every good thing not in the curse of hard labour, but under the blessing of God.
- It typifies the rest that the people of God enjoy in Christ.

What does it mean for us today?

- The early church practised a kind of sabbatical year during which they had all things in common. Ananias and Sapphira's action broke the spirit of this brotherly trust.
- Paul's concern for the poor Jewish Christians in Jerusalem and his efforts in encouraging the Gentile believers to contribute towards their support draw upon the principles of this passage. Love for members of the covenant community in Christ includes concern for those in financial difficulties.
- Besides the Christian's duty to be specially concerned for those of the household of faith, we are called to do good to all.

- It teaches us that all that we have is on trust from God. We are stewards. The earth is the Lord's and all its fulness.
- It reminds us of what Jesus taught his disciples — namely, that, as God provides for the birds, so he cares and provides for his people.
- It underlines the truth that human beings are not to live by bread alone.
- Though this law was given to God's chosen people in the context of his special agreement with them, it does provide societies with a blueprint of what is fair and equitable. Ultimately, the land belongs to God and governments and societies would do well to act responsibly with regard to ecological issues and concern for the poor and needy among their own people and those of other nations.

The jubilee year (25:8-22)

The pope declared a jubilee year for the new millennium in 2000. It was used to support the unbiblical belief in plenary indulgences whereby the pope pronounced freedom from the fires of purgatory to faithful Roman Catholics who made a pilgrimage to Rome or engaged in other forms of religious devotion. We are more likely to hear of jubilees in the context of anniversaries such as the jubilee celebrations for Queen Elizabeth II.

On my sabbatical my wife and I had the privilege of visiting the United States for the first time. In Philadelphia, Pennsylvania, we were taken to see Independence Hall, made famous as the building in which independence from British rule was declared and where the United States constitution was written. On display nearby is Liberty Bell, which once hung in the tower. On the bell are the words announcing the jubilee year from Leviticus 25:10: **'Pro-claim liberty throughout all the land to all its inhabit-ants.'** That same bell was used as a symbol of freedom by those wishing to see the end of African slavery in the States and, more recently, by those involved in the Civil Rights movement.

What is the jubilee year really about?

We get our English word **'jubilee'** from the Hebrew term for this special year, *yobel* (see 25:9-11).[3] It probably took its name from the horn blasts (not 'trumpets' as in so many translations) that announced its commencement.

Repentance and reconciliation

The jubilee year forms the climax to the calendar of special holy occasions. The year was proclaimed on the Day of Atonement (25:9), the most solemn day of the year, when the people were reminded of their sins, commanded to humble themselves (see 16:29,31; 23:29,32) and when provision was made for them to be purified from all their sins.

Rest

The jubilee year is structured on the same principle as the religious calendar and makes use of the sacred number, seven. Just as there are forty-nine days (7 x 7 weeks) plus one from Easter to Pentecost, so there are forty-nine years (7 x 7 years) plus one to the jubilee.[4] Further, as there are seven festivals in the annual religious calendar, so there are seven sabbatical years between one jubilee and the next. Exodus 12:2 specifies that Passover time, which is in the spring, around March/April, was to be the first month of Israel's religious year, but the jubilee year was to begin in the autumn, around September/October, during the holiest month of the year and on the holiest day of the year, the Day of Atonement (25:9).[5]

Although the jubilee is not called a sabbath, Israel is directed to **'consecrate'** it (25:10) by not working the land. In this it is like the seventh year that has just been mentioned, which is called a 'sabbath' (25:4). It is to be regarded as a sacred year — **'it shall be holy to you'** (25:12), and specially set apart by the blowing of the ram's horn.

Release

This **'Year of Jubilee'** (25:13) proclaims release or freedom (see Ezek. 46:17, which speaks of the 'year of liberty', or 'year of release') because all land returned to its original owners and all slaves were set free. The ancient Babylonian rulers would sometimes issue edicts declaring the cancellation of all debts and freedom from slavery. This proclamation in the Mosaic legislation is not left to the whim of an earthly ruler. It is ordained by God as a once-in-a-lifetime experience.

Restoration

Proclaiming the jubilee was truly a happy occasion, for it decreed that Israelites who had become dispossessed of their land inheritance were allowed to return to their family possessions and debtor-slaves became free persons again. For such people and their families it would have been a truly happy new year, bringing about a new beginning, an opportunity for the poor to make a fresh start in life.

Redemption

Land and people could be redeemed at any time (see 25:23-55) but for people and property that were still tied the jubilee proclaimed the immediate release of debt-slaves and the return of land to its original owners (25:10,13). Though God is never referred to in this section as a redeemer, the implication of the jubilee legislation is that if no human redeemer intervenes, then the Lord acts in the fiftieth year to release land and slaves. He is the supreme Redeemer. It speaks to us of the ultimate divine intervention and redemption through Christ that includes redemption from sin and Satan, the redemption of our physical bodies and of the whole created order (see Rom. 8:18-25).

Honesty and fairness (25:13-17)

The jubilee law meant restrictions on the way land was bought and sold. Selling land amounted to leasing it until the year of jubilee, when property reverted to the original owner. The price was therefore governed by the number of years to the next jubilee. It should also be remembered that the one selling or renting had the right to redeem the land at any time. The people of Israel are therefore warned not to cheat or **'oppress one another'** (25:14,17). Prophets like Amos, Hosea, Micah and Isaiah show how the unprotected and underprivileged in both the northern and southern kingdoms were exploited by the rich and powerful. Lack of reverence for God leads to disrespect of people (see 19:14). The fear of God, which is the beginning of wisdom, is basic to all ethical practice (see 25:36,43). Our attitude towards God will ultimately determine the way we regard fellow Christians and all humanity.

Obedience and security (25:18-22)

As in earlier sections, Israel is urged to obey God's laws
(25:18; see 18:4-5,26; 19:19,37; 20:8,22). With the exhortation comes a gracious promise and incentive: they will live
safely in the land, and the land will be productive, providing
plenty to eat (25:18-19). God also takes account of their
natural and genuine concerns. As he assured them earlier that
he would protect their land when, in obedience to his command, every male journeyed to the central sanctuary for the
three pilgrim festivals (see Exod. 34:24), so the Lord promises to provide for them during the sabbatical and jubilee
years. There would be no sowing or harvesting during these
years and what grew of itself would be insufficient to feed
everyone. A sabbatical year would be difficult enough, but in
a jubilee year the land would be lying fallow for two con-
secutive years. But God promised such blessing in the sixth
year that the harvest would produce enough to supply their
needs not only for the sabbatical year but also for the jubilee:
'it will bring forth produce enough for three years'
(25:21).[6] This assurance would not be too difficult to accept
for they were already experiencing in the gift of manna a
double amount on the sixth day to carry them over the
weekly Sabbath (see Exod. 16:22-23).

The continuing significance of these laws

This revolutionary view of the land has inspired social
reformers and fed utopian dreams of a classless society
where the rich are not allowed to amass large areas of land at
the expense of the poor. The debt-release provision encouraged many Christians to support the Jubilee 2000 campaign
in persuading governments and banks to wipe out the debts
crippling the world's poorest countries. The pop slogan,

'Make poverty history,' is a wonderful idealistic sentiment, but the law of Moses itself teaches that 'The poor will never cease to be in the land' (Deut. 15:11), a point made by Jesus when his disciples criticized the woman who showed her devotion to the Saviour by pouring costly oil on his head (Matt. 26:11). Many people who make gestures of goodwill towards the poor want nothing to do with the living God revealed in his Son, Jesus Christ, yet it is precisely this rebellion against God that lies at the heart of the social and economic problems of the world. It is because human beings have rejected God's authority that the whole creation, humans included, is under a divine curse in which natural disasters, physical disabilities and diseases and the results of human greed bring many to starvation and death.

The prophets used the jubilee manifesto in their vision of the future. Unlike the utopian dreams that end in frustration and failure, the end-time picture that they present of God's glorious rule is realistic and destined to be realized. Isaiah 61:1-3 announces a new era in which God's special Servant, the anointed King, will preach good news to the poor and 'proclaim liberty to the captives, and the opening of the prison to those who are bound'. The word 'liberty' is the same term that is used here in describing the year of jubilee (**'proclaim liberty'**, 25:10). Ezekiel 46:17 also introduces the jubilee 'year of liberty' in his colourful description of the future inheritance of the prince and his people. Daniel 9:24-27 uses the jubilee idea in the symbolic numbering of the weeks of years — 'seventy weeks' (70 x 7 = 490 years) and includes Atonement-Day activity, with which the jubilee is associated (see 25:9). This great occasion involving the Messiah will make atonement for iniquity, bring sin to an end and introduce everlasting righteousness.

Jesus uses the words of Isaiah 61:1-2 to announce the commencement of this new age of Messiah (Luke 4:17-21). He came to deal with the deep underlying causes of all the troubles and struggles of society. Jesus did not read the part of the paragraph from Isaiah that spoke of vengeance, for he had come not to judge the world but to save it. The jubilee age that began with Christ's first coming will find its grand consummation at his second coming with the resurrection of the body and the 'restoration of all things' (Acts 3:21). Then the Lord's rule will be seen in all its fulness and glory and the old curse will finally be removed. This hope is not a pipe dream, but is based solidly on what happened to Jesus himself, who died to bear the curse and rose to be the guarantee and living proof of all that the prophets and apostles have promised.

The church of Jesus Christ therefore has something very wonderful and exciting to announce to a sad world enslaved by the dark powers of the Evil One. Individual Christians can also be involved in relieving poverty and exercising their democratic rights in bringing pressure to bear on governments and commercial organizations to show more understanding and to act in a just and honourable way towards peoples and nations in dire distress. They should be in the forefront in their concern for social justice, as they have been, and still are, in bringing relief and showing compassion to those with physical and mental ailments and disabilities. But the Christian's greatest service to a needy world, and certainly the primary task of the church of Jesus Christ, is to proclaim the good news of a Redeemer who delivers from sin and Satan and who sets us on the road to a glorious future beyond this present world order.

How my raptured soul rejoices
That the jubilee is near…![7]

31.
Redemption

Please read Leviticus 25:23-55

We often use the word 'redeem' in the context of exchanging coupons for goods, converting shares into cash or paying off a loan or debt. Nearer to the biblical idea is what happens at the pawnshop, where an article of value is deposited as security for money borrowed. The article is redeemed when the money is paid back.

Redemption in Israel

In Israelite society redemption was practised in a variety of situations. In general, it brought about a return to a previously existing situation. The cases dealt with here involved the buying back of inherited property or purchasing the freedom of people reduced to debt-slavery. If the persons themselves could not raise the money to redeem themselves or their property, the responsibility then rested with the next of kin, who was called **'the kinsman-redeemer'** (25:25).

The responsibilities of the kinsman-redeemer were quite onerous. Besides being under obligation to buy back family property sold by a poor relative (25:25-28) and to purchase the freedom of a family member reduced to being a 'slave' (25:47-55), the redeemer was also responsible for seeing that the unlawful killer of a family member was brought to justice (Num. 35:9-34) and for providing, where possible, children for a deceased relative who had died childless by marrying his widow (Deut. 25:5-10: Ruth 3:13). The redeemer also received restitution money due to a deceased relative (Num. 5:8).

In cases where, for some reason, the redemption ruling did not function, the jubilee year gave people hope of a day of restitution. The jubilee implied that God himself was the ultimate Kinsman-Redeemer who, when no human family member intervened, acted to release his people from debt-slavery and give them back their inherited lands. At the time of the exodus from Egypt, God spoke of Israel as his 'son' (Exod. 4:22-23). The Israelites were his special possession (Exod. 6:7), as Pharaoh was constantly reminded by Moses in those famous words: 'Let my people go!' (Exod. 5:1; 7:16; 8:1,20; 9:1,13; 10:3). He was their next of kin and it was this Lord, who had redeemed them from Egyptian slavery by his mighty power (Exod. 6:6; 15:13), who provided for the redemption of debtors and their lands.

Through these divine rules and actions the Old Testament community were taught gospel truths. Isaiah uses the redemption theme to speak of the Lord as Israel's Redeemer from Babylonian exile, which in turn served as a pointer and preparation for the greater redemption accomplished by the Servant of the Lord through his sacrificial atoning death on behalf of his people (Isa. 43:1-21; 48:17-21; 49:25-26; 52:7 – 54:8). Jesus the Messiah is our hope. He is the ultimate Redeemer. We are redeemed not with silver and gold, 'but with the precious blood of Christ, as of a lamb without blemish and without spot' (1 Peter 1:18-19). The Lord's redeemed people can sing to Jesus:

> For you were slain,
> And have redeemed us to God by your blood
> Out of every tribe and tongue and people and nation
> (Rev. 5:9).

Fundamental principles (25:23)

At various points in the text God presents the people with teaching that undergirds the practice he requires (25:23,38,42,55). This verse gives the theological reason both for the jubilee laws concerning reclaiming land in the previous section (25:13-17) and for the following legislation concerning the redemption of land (25:24-34).

The reason why 'the land of Canaan' (25:38) cannot be sold permanently, but must return to the original owner and his family, is that the land belongs in a special way to God: **'The land is mine.'** Though the people of Israel have been given the land by God (25:2) as their 'possession' (25:10,25,41), in fulfilment of God's promise to Abraham (Gen. 12:1,5-7), they cannot do with it as they like. The Lord remains the supreme Landowner and the Israelite people are in effect God's tenants: **'... you are strangers and sojourners with me.'**[1] Just as the resident alien came under the authority and protection of an Israelite, so each family in Israel was like a foreign resident under God's authority and protection ('with me' can mean 'under my protection' or 'under my authority').[2] We are later shown how each tribe and family received their portion of land by lot (Num. 33:54; Josh. 14 –19).

When Abraham negotiated with the Hittites over buying land in Canaan to bury his wife Sarah, he described himself as 'a foreigner [literally, "a stranger"] and sojourner' (Gen. 23:4). The people of God continued to think in this way about their earthly existence. David acknowledged that he was a resident alien, having a temporary status in this world, a pilgrim like all his ancestors (Ps. 39:12; 1 Chr. 29:15; cf. Heb. 11:9,13). This terminology is used of Christians (1 Peter 2:11). The present world order is not our permanent residence. We look with anticipation for that enduring city to come, the home of righteousness (2 Peter 3:13; Heb. 13:14).

In what way is Canaan different from the whole earth? Earlier God had said, 'All the earth is mine' (Exod. 19:5). Canaan is similar to the Garden of Eden. The God who created the whole world by his word, and was ruler over all, produced a garden in Eden, full of life and plenty, as a special area where the first created and married couple were to live and communicate with God. As the garden was set apart from the rest of creation to fulfil God's purposes, so Canaan was set apart to be a reminder of that lost paradise and to point towards, and prepare for, the garden city of the future in the new creation, when God brings about the grand jubilee in the restitution of all things (Rev. 21:1-3,22-23; 22:1-5). Then the glory of God will fill the whole earth, which is what all God's people have been given to inherit. Like the Garden of Eden, Canaan was to be a kind of sanctuary where God would live on earth among his people and where his rule could be seen in operation and his will done on earth as in heaven (Exod. 19:5-6; Lev. 26:11-12; Num. 35:34). The theology of the 'land' is further developed in God's final word through Moses to a people about to take possession of Canaan (see Deut. 8:7-10).

The law against permanent alienation of ancestral land played a crucial part in preparing for the coming of the Messiah. It kept intact, first the family, then the tribe and ultimately the nation. Many centuries later, Luke records how Joseph took his pregnant wife from Nazareth in Galilee to his own city of Bethlehem in Judea for taxation purposes, 'because he was of the house and lineage of David'. Unlike today, every member of God's ancient people knew their tribal and family line and land. It was there, in David's city, that the Messiah, our Lord and Saviour, was born (Luke 2:1-11).

Redeeming property (25:24-34)

The redemption of land (25:24-28)

Imagine an Israelite who found himself in financial difficulties and was forced to sell part of the family land. Three avenues were open to him by which he could regain the original parcel of ground. A close family member could come to the rescue and redeem it (25:25), or the person himself, presumably due to an upturn in fortune, could redeem, or buy back, the land (25:26), the price being determined by the number of harvests since it was sold (25:27). Those options failing, the land would eventually be returned to the family in the jubilee year (25:28). In each case it is clear that the land 'sold' could more accurately be described as 'leased' subject to the redemption clauses.

The sale of houses (25:29-31)

If an Israelite sold **'a house in a walled city'** (25:29) it could be redeemed for up to a year after the sale, but after that it became the permanent possession of the purchaser (25:29-30). This is similar to the period of grace given in modern business and purchase transactions. On the other hand, houses in unwalled villages could be redeemed at any time and reverted to the original family in the jubilee year (25:31). This distinction looks forward to a time when homes within town walls would generally not be associated with the

land, while homes in unwalled villages would belong to
farmers and be attached to the land they worked.

Levite homes (25:32-34)

In the case of Levites an exception is made to the rule about
houses in walled cities. Unlike the other tribes, the tribe of
Levi was allotted no land in Canaan. Instead, they were
given special cities, with their surrounding pastureland,
within the boundaries of the other tribes (see Num. 35:1-8;
Josh. 21). Because of their unique position, a house within
the forty-eight Levitical walled cities that a Levite sold could
be redeemed at any time and was to revert to the family in
the jubilee year. The pastureland surrounding the Levitical
cities could not be sold, **'for it is their perpetual possession'** (25:34).

Land not redeemed (25:35-38)

The way in which the legislation is presented in the second
half of this chapter expresses a situation where members of
the covenant community become increasingly poor and
desperate. First, the law considers an Israelite who becomes
poor and sells some of his land (25:25), and then goes on to
mention one whose poverty continues so that he is unable to
redeem that land (25:28). In this section it repeats the words,
'if one of your brethren becomes poor' (25:35; cf. 25:25),
but the context suggests that the man is in a worse situation
than in the earlier passage. The Israelite has been forced to
sell not some but all of his land, so that his position is similar
to that of a foreign resident or tenant (25:35). However, his
state is not as desperate as that depicted in the final scenario
(see 25:39).

The poor person in this section has probably become a tenant farmer, renting his former farmland from the creditor and therefore continuing to make a living under the creditor's authority and protection (25:35; cf. 25:23).[3] In this case, where the creditor has the upper hand, he must remember that, though the Israelite may be in the same kind of state as a resident alien and foreign tenant, he not only deserves the sort of courtesies shown to them but he is actually **'your brother'** (25:36), a member of God's holy nation, **'one of your brethren'** (25:35; cf. 25:25). Therefore the creditor must not charge him interest on debts owed, or sell food to him for a profit, as was allowed in the case of foreigners (Deut. 23:19-20). In other words, the whole covenant community was to consider itself a family, caring for each other as brothers and sisters, with no one taking advantage of a fellow Israelite's calamity in order to make a quick gain. Loaning money for business enterprises is quite a different situation from the one envisaged here. The poor are not to be exploited.

They are also to remember that they live under the all-seeing eye of God. Any unbrotherly action, even if it lies outside the jurisdiction of the courts, will not go unpunished by God. They are called to fear God. Devotion to God is an important motive in showing compassion towards fellow countrymen in distress. It is an expression of loving one's neighbour as oneself (see 19:18). To further impress upon the people the importance of these laws, God identifies himself as the one who revealed himself in all his glorious majesty at the time of the Exodus, who acted graciously towards them by redeeming them from Egyptian slavery to bring them into the land of promise and who entered into a special relationship with them to be their God (25:38; cf. 19:36; Gen. 17:8; Ezek. 36:28). In a similar way, new-covenant people are to behave generously towards all, and especially to believers. The early Christians were quick to take up the principle of helping poor widows and the needy saints in Jerusalem (Acts 2:42-47; 4:34 – 5:1; 6:1-7; Rom. 15:25-27).

Redeeming people (25:39-55)

Three situations associated with slavery are brought to our attention.

An Israelite in the service of a fellow Israelite

First, the law addresses the case of an Israelite who sells himself to a fellow Israelite (25:39-43). The introductory words are repeated again (see 25:25,35) but this time the **'poor'** person who has already sold the family land and has become a tenant under the creditor's authority and protection[4] now finds, perhaps through personal illness, crop failure or enemy action, that he can no longer support himself and his family. He has become so poor that he is forced to sell himself to the creditor or some wealthy Israelite (25:39). Debt-slavery was certainly better than starvation. The Israelite master, however, was not allowed to take advantage of his sad situation, but was to remember once again that the poor man was a brother and to treat him with respect.

Such a brother Israelite was not to be treated **'as a slave'**, but considered to be like a hired worker and tenant **'until the Year of Jubilee'**, when he could return with his children to his ancestral home and land (25:40-41). Further, the Israelite master was to bear in mind that every Israelite belonged to the Lord. Their redeemer God brought them out of Egyptian slavery to be his slaves (25:42; cf. 25:55). No member of the covenant community was to be sold as a slave or ruled over ruthlessly (25:42-43,46). Respect for God (**'You shall fear**

your God') naturally led to respect for all those who were in a special relationship with him (25:43).

All this reminds Christians of what is taught in the New Testament — that the same Lord, through the death of his Son Jesus Christ, has brought us from slavery to sin and Satan and has set us free to be 'slaves of God', and that we should use our bodies 'as slaves of righteousness' for holiness (Rom. 6:6-7,18,22). Paul also urges slaves and masters who have become Christians to act in a Christ-honouring way (Eph. 6:5-9; Col. 3:22 – 4:1). In addition, a Christian slave should regard himself or herself as the Lord's free person, and Christians who are not slaves should regard themselves as slaves of Christ. As in the Mosaic law, Paul's appeal is made on the basis of God's redeeming grace: 'You were bought at a price' (1 Cor. 7:22-23).

Foreign slaves

Secondly, the law addresses foreign slaves (25:44-46). Israelites were permitted to own male and female slaves that had been purchased from the surrounding nations, from resident foreigners or from foreigners born in Israel (25:45). Later legislation allowed Israel to make slaves of those taken as prisoners in time of war (see Deut. 20:10-15). These slaves were considered among their permanent possessions that could be handed down as part of the family inheritance (25:45-46).

Allowing the Israelites to purchase and own foreign slaves in perpetuity, while forbidding them to make slaves of their own people, was all part of God's provision under the old-covenant legislation to keep this chosen nation in existence, and quite distinct and separate from the rest of the world until the coming of the Messiah. It was God's intention all along to bring blessing to all the nations through this special nation. He had given promises to that effect to

Israel's ancestors, to Abraham, Isaac and Jacob. Under the new covenant there are to be no distinctions based on race, sex or colour. In Christ all are one in God's new society. The old wall set up under the Mosaic legislation to keep Jew and Gentile separate has been torn down as a result of Christ's sacrificial death on the cross (Gal. 3:26-29; Eph. 2:11-22).

In addition, this legislation taught the people that when God redeems his people from foreign slavery they are not meant to become slaves again. They belong to God, and to God alone. It provides the background for the New Testament teaching that when we are redeemed by the blood of Christ we are no longer slaves to the gods of this world, as we once were, but serve the Lord's Christ. How can we then think of turning again to be under such bondage? (See Gal. 4:8-9).

An Israelite in slavery to a foreigner

Finally, the case is presented of an Israelite who has sold himself to a prosperous foreigner (25:47-55). Here is a situation where a non-Israelite, resident in Canaan on either a permanent or temporary basis, but under the authority and care of an Israelite,[5] has become wealthy, and an Israelite has sold himself to this affluent man or to a member of his family. The poor man's position is similar to that of an Israelite who has sold some of his ancestral land (see 25:25-28). He is protected by the redemption laws in that a relative may redeem him, or if he himself has an upturn in fortune he may redeem himself. The redemption price is calculated according to the years remaining until the jubilee. Failing these options, he must be freed in the year of jubilee along with any children born before or during his time of service. Again, the Israelite is not to be treated by the resident alien as a slave but as a hired worker (25:53; cf. 25:40).

The significance of the redemption laws

This piece of legislation emphasizes that both the people of Israel and the land of Canaan belong solely to the Lord. Neither the one nor the other can be sold permanently. Individual Israelites and portions of land may be leased for a certain period of time under special conditions, but neither can be sold. The people and the land belong together in the purposes of God. In the next chapter we see how the final covenant curse affects this union and the future realization of God's promises.

This is a most amazing piece of legislation to safeguard against abject poverty. Scholars of various backgrounds are agreed that these laws were the most humane and socially advanced in the ancient Near East. Indeed, we could add that they are the most enlightened laws in any society, past or present. They were intended to prevent the wealth of the nation from accumulating in the hands of a few. In a world full of natural disasters and human weaknesses due to ill-health and varying physical and mental abilities, here is a blueprint for the establishment of a more egalitarian society. We might wistfully think, 'If only such laws were put into operation today, what a difference it would make in helping to maintain that fine balance between the ugly face of capitalism and the kind of communism that blighted so many countries in the twentieth century!'

The sad fact is that it did not work, not because the laws were unsound, but because of Israel's failure to obey. Despite God's goodness towards them and the motives for obedience that are spelled out in the legislation, the Israelites failed to honour their obligations. These laws remained an unfulfilled ideal. The prophets warn those who 'join house to house, who add field to field, till there is no place where they may dwell alone in the midst of the land' (Isa. 5:8), or who 'sell the righteous for silver, and the poor for a pair of sandals' (Amos 2:6).

Having said that, this is no reason for people to give up and do nothing. Christians must play their part in society so that laws might be passed for the general good of humanity, as was the case particularly in nineteenth-century Britain. But no political party and no national leader can bring utopia.

32.
Covenant commitment

Please read Leviticus 26:1-46

The remarkable feature of this chapter is not the blessings promised Israel for their obedience or the curses for their disobedience, but God's commitment to Israel's ancestors (26:42). Because of the promises that God made to Abraham, Isaac and Jacob, even the final curse of removal from the promised land is meant to bring the Israelites to repentance and to seek their God. As if to underline God's complete faithfulness to the promises he has made, the term **'covenant'** is found seven times in this chapter. The apostle Paul writes that

> If we are faithless,
>   he remains faithful;
>   he cannot deny himself
>
> (2 Tim. 2:13).

The chapter is in three main parts.

Commitment to the Lord (26:1-2)

The repeated statement that **'I am the LORD your God ... I am the LORD'** directs the people's thoughts to the God of the covenant. This double reference to God also occurs at the end of the section (26:44,45; cf. 19:2,3,36,37).

While Israel is called to obey all the ritual and ethical commands of Leviticus (26:14-15,43,46), the chapter begins by focusing on two of the Ten Commandments that encapsulate the entire law — the prohibition of idolatry and Sabbath observance. These became two of the main pillars of later Judaism.

The reference to idolatry (26:1; cf. Exod. 20:4) is no surprise, for Israel had only recently broken the covenant at Sinai through the golden-calf incident (see Exod. 32 – 34). God, who is spirit (John 4:24), deliberately revealed himself to the people by word rather than in visible form (see Deut. 4:12), and when he did condescend to show himself, the few representatives who 'saw God' could get no further than describing what was under his feet whereas, for the rest of Israel, the sight of the glory of the Lord was like a consuming fire (Exod. 24:9-11,17). To make a physical representation of God for the people to look at and worship would have meant reducing and confining him to some object of their own devising, and bowing before that, rather than the invisible, limitless and almighty Being that he is. For worship to be true there must be a right perception of who God is. The book of Exodus emphasizes the importance of knowing God as he really is and Leviticus builds on this by stressing the holiness of God, who cannot be compared to anything or anyone. He stands alone in awesome splendour. We are called to worship this God and to keep ourselves from idols of every sort (1 John 5:21; 1 Cor. 10:14; Rev. 19:10; 22:9).

Observance of the Sabbath laws and reverence for God's sanctuary follow in this summary call to obedience (26:2). The laws outlined in the last chapter concerning social justice depended on the sabbath principle. No wonder the weekly Sabbath was regarded as the sign of Israel's special relationship with God (Exod. 31:12-17). Further, as Matthew Henry comments, 'As nothing tends more to corrupt religion than the use of images in devotion, so nothing contributes more to the support of it than *keeping the sabbaths* and *reverencing the sanctuary.*' Building on this, Andrew Bonar writes that 'All declension and decay may be said to be begun wherever we see these two ordinances despised — the *sabbath* and the *sanctuary*. They are the *outward* fence around the *inward love* commanded by v.1.'[1]

The sanctuary was to be respected, for it represented God's visible presence among his people. The Lord has promised to be present with his new-covenant people as they fellowship together for worship. Christians gather for communal worship particularly on the first day of the week. Ironically most calendars and diaries now depict Sunday as the seventh day!

Covenant blessings and curses (26:3-39)

This section is very similar to the blessings and curses found in Deuteronomy 28 – 30. The Lord presents the material in a way that would be familiar to people living in the ancient Near East. A superpower would impose a treaty on a lesser nation in which both sides would agree to certain obligations. The lesser power would agree to the stipulations laid down as conditions of submission, and in turn the great superstate would promise protection and defence. These international treaties would often include a historical introduction, recounting past relationships, and a closing list of benefits that would be the reward of compliance and curses that would be incurred by rebellion. The book of Leviticus does not parallel the ancient treaties as Deuteronomy does, but it nevertheless draws attention to the history of God's dealings with Israel, particularly in rescuing them from Egyptian slavery (19:36; 25:38; 26:13,45), setting out laws for Israel to keep and concluding with blessings and curses.

Covenant blessings (26:3-13)

If Israel as a nation obeys God's directives then the Lord promises to be faithful to his special agreement with them. God is the source of all blessing, as emphasized by the repeated use of 'I will …' (26:4,6,9,11,12). The blessings can be summarized under the following headings:

Productivity and plenty (26:4-5)

The blessings of the land yielding its fruit and the people eating their fill and living in safety are what God promised Israel if they kept the sabbath and jubilee years (25:18-19). Important to the fulfilling of this promise is **'rain in its season'**. If we bear in mind that the new year began with the seventh month of the religious calendar, the early rain came during October-November to enable the ground to be ploughed and sowed. The latter rains came in April to swell the fruit and ears of grain. While lack of rain brought famine and was seen as a divine curse (see Amos 4:7), unseasonable rain could rot the harvest. As a sign of God's displeasure with Israel in the days of Samuel, rain fell during the wheat harvest, accompanied by thunder, causing the people to fear (1 Sam. 12:15-19). In the present context living **'safely'** in the land refers to economic stability and security.

Peace in the land (26:6)

Economic stability naturally leads to political stability. There will be no civil unrest or war, and the wild animals that roamed the land, such as the lion and the bear (see Judg. 14:5; 2 Kings 2:24; 17:24-28), will be driven out.

Power over enemies (26:7-8)

They are also promised success against enemy attack. Acting as a united body with the Lord's help, they would be victorious against overwhelming odds. Joshua encouraged the people by elaborating on this promise: 'One man of you shall chase a thousand, for the LORD your God is he who fights for you, as he has promised you' (Josh. 23:10). Gideon found God faithful to his word when his band of 300 was victorious over a Midianite army of 135,000 (Judg. 7:1 – 8:4).

Prosperity and population growth (26:9-10)

Another way of expressing divine blessing is by portraying God as 'looking upon' someone in a favourable way. We have the same idea in the high-priestly blessing that called on God to 'lift up' his face upon them (Num. 6:26). The blessing promised is growth in their numbers and good harvests to sustain the increase. The words **'fruitful'** and **'multiply'** remind us of the creation blessing that was repeated after the Flood (Gen. 1:28; 9:1,7). More particularly, they call to mind God's covenant with Abraham, which produced such results that the Egyptians felt threatened (Gen. 17:6; Exod. 1:7). God records that he will maintain that same covenant promise when Israel is in the land.

The presence of God (26:11-12)

The greatest blessing of all is to experience the presence of God. This supreme gift is conveyed by the pictures of the tabernacle and the Garden of Eden.[2] The glory cloud of fire and smoke that had accompanied Israel thus far and that had recently rested on the newly constructed tabernacle was symbolic of his special presence (Exod. 40). Instead of God being so sickened by them that he would want to abandon them (see 26:15,30,43-44), they are assured of this presence when they enter the land and erect the tabernacle. The reference to God walking about among his people is a reminder of the fundamental loss that our first parents experienced when they were removed from the earthly paradise (Gen. 3:8). Israel in the land of Canaan under the Lord's blessing would reflect the conditions that existed in the Garden of Eden before the Fall.

In this final part of the blessing God's response mirrors Israel's obligation: **'If you walk ... I will walk'** (26:3,12). Israel's walk means a way of life that is committed to doing God's will, whereas God's walk involves his active, watchful care over them.[3] Echoes of God's covenant with Abraham are picked up in the formula which declares that the Lord will **'be your God, and you shall be my people'** (26:12; cf. Gen. 17:7-8). This personal relationship between God and Israel lies at the very heart of the divine covenant. In this the agreement is unlike the ancient political treaties but more akin to a marriage, a theme that is later used by the prophet Hosea.

The items of blessing are brought to a close with another reminder of their deliverance from Egyptian slavery (26:13). God had freed them from foreign domination so that they might serve him freely with confidence. **'I have broken the bands of your yoke'** (26:13) is a graphic way of portraying Israel's freedom. The yoke was the wooden pole that often rested on the necks of a pair of oxen and was fixed on each side with bands to keep the animals together as they pulled a plough or heavy load. The Israelites are not only free, but they can stand erect with their heads held high. They have been given back their dignity. Jesus used this illustration when calling those burdened and weighed down to come to him for rest, 'For my yoke is easy and my burden is light' (see Matt. 11:28-30).

The so-called 'prosperity gospel' uses passages like this to encourage people to believe that if they follow the Lord wholeheartedly and keep his commandments they will be blessed with plenty of money, good health and long life. Neither Jesus nor his apostles encourage such a belief and the history of the Christian church down the centuries shows true followers of Christ suffering poverty, ill health and early death, as well as experiencing severe physical persecution for their faith. God does bless believers with all spiritual blessings in heavenly places in Christ Jesus (Eph. 1:3) and Jesus promises to make up for family losses that come through commitment to Christ with a new spiritual family. We are also taught that the present sufferings of the people of God cannot be compared to the glory that is to come.

The promises presented in this passage were only experienced by Israel for short periods of their history and then not in all their fulness. This is because they were so disloyal to the covenant. The later prophets, particularly Ezekiel, take up the words of these blessings and apply them to an end-time period when they will be realized in their widest and fullest sense. In the future golden age, there will be 'showers of blessing' at the right time and fruitful seasons with harvesting lasting until sowing (Ezek. 34:26-27; Amos 9:13). The prophets also depict the idyllic scene on a renewed earth as a land free from wild beasts and enemy attack (see Ezek. 34:25,28; Isa. 11:6-9; 65:25; Hosea 2:18). God will be their God and there will be an end to all famine (Ezek. 34:24-31).

The last book of the Bible uses the language of Moses and the prophets to show that the prophetic hope refers to the new creation, where there will be an abundance of life and produce, with healing for the nations and the presence of God among his people for evermore (Rev. 21 – 22).

Covenant curses (26:14-39)

The curses involve the withdrawal of all the blessings previously outlined. As in international treaties, the curses are much longer and more detailed than the blessings. They point out the dire consequences that will result if the agreements are broken. But in the biblical case the lengthy curse section also has a positive function in teaching the people a fundamental lesson. As Gordon Wenham comments, 'It is very easy to take the blessings of rain, peace, and even God's presence for granted. It is salutary to be reminded in detail of what life is like when his providential gifts are removed.'[4]

The introduction to the curses is twice as long as the one to the blessings (26:14-15; cf. 26:3). Failure to listen to God and keep his commands involves an attitude of mind that despises his statutes and that finds his laws repulsive. Wilful sinful acts express a mind that is at war with God. Violating the terms of the covenant, however, does not mean Israel has broken free. Far from it! The people's rebellious actions result in their experiencing the Lord's disciplining activity, which is part of God's agreement with them. They cannot get away from the covenant they have entered into.

Again, God is seen as directly involved in the curses, as he was in the blessings: **'I also will do this to you'** (26:16). The number 'seven' that has such symbolic significance in Leviticus is used here to indicate repeated punishments and also their completeness (see 26:18,21,24,28). It is used also by John as he describes the sevenfold judgements on a rebellious world (Rev. 16). The curses can be summarized as follows:

Disease and defeat (26:16-17)

Instead of peace and security (26:6), God will **'appoint terror'**. As I was writing this book, terrorists suddenly struck the London Underground causing confusion, panic, injury and death. Furthermore, sickness and enemy occupation will occur. They will be so nervous that they will want to seek shelter when there is nothing to fear. All this will be an indication that they are experiencing God's face being set against them, the opposite of God's favour and blessing (26:17; cf. 26:9).

Drought (26:18-20)

In contrast to the blessing of fruitful seasons (26:4-5), the description of the **'heavens like iron'** and the **'earth like bronze'** would mean no rain, resulting in dry, hard ground that could produce no harvests. The curses are not only to punish Israel for their sins, but to discipline and break their stubborn, proud hearts.

Destruction and desolation (26:21-22)

The people have already been encouraged to 'walk with God' through the examples of Enoch and Noah. Here there is a repeated warning that if they **'walk contrary'** to God and disobey him, then he will turn against them in an ever-increasing series of troubles. Instead of savage beasts being removed (26:6), they will attack people, and roads once crowded with people will become desolate.

Devastation (26:23-26)

They will experience 'covenant vengeance' in the form of war, pestilence and famine. Bread will be so scarce during enemy hostilities that it will not satisfy them. God's justice will be executed for violating the covenant.[5]

Deportation (26:27-39)

In a complete reversal of the final blessing (26:11), the Lord warns that he will **'abhor'** them (26:30). The word conveys the idea of making someone sick. If God's laws nauseated Israel (26:15), then the Lord would loathe them. A similar graphic way of conveying God's attitude to his people's sinful state is used by Jesus as he warns the church of Laodicea: 'I will spew you out of my mouth' (Rev. 3:16).

The ultimate curse is to be removed from the land altogether, with all the horrors of siege and enemy action. It will include people being forced into cannibalism, with parents killing their own children for food (26:29). The false places of worship would also be destroyed. These were often natural high points where altars were erected and were associated with an amalgamation of the worship of Yahweh and Canaanite fertility rites. Such activity is roundly condemned later by the prophets (see Amos 7:9; Hosea 10:8; Jer. 19:3-5). The language used to describe what the Lord will do to Israel and their idols is graphic and highly derogatory. What could be more insulting than to speak of **'idols'** using a word similar to 'dung' and to describe them as 'corpses'? The sentence literally reads: 'I will ... cast your corpses on the corpses of your dung-like objects' (26:30). What could be more sacrilegious than to dump dead bodies on top of sacred objects? The picture of God not being willing to **'smell the fragrance of your sweet aromas'**

(26:31) is used by the prophets in their condemnation of the people's worship (see Amos 5:21-22).

When the people have been removed, then the land will **'enjoy its sabbaths'** (26:34-35,43). The land at rest will compensate for all the lost weekly Sabbaths and sabbatical years which the people had not kept (cf. 2 Chr. 36:21). The exiles, on the other hand, will be far from restful. They will be so 'shell-shocked' that they will be startled at the slightest sound (26:36). As they scatter in fright they will fall over one another. Their numbers will decrease, and for those who are left it will be a miserable existence (26:37-38). The punishment will be due not only for their own sins, but also for the sins of their forefathers. Continual rebellion over many generations will result in expulsion from the land (26:39).

The two ways

Throughout the Bible the same two ways or lifestyles are presented. There is a lifestyle that honours God and seeks to do his will and that experiences the blessing of God. On the other hand, there is a lifestyle that disobeys God and that leads to God's wrath. Jesus indicated that there is a road to life and to destruction. Those who obeyed his word were like the wise man who built his house on rock, and that stood firm when the storms and floods came. On the other hand, those who disobeyed were like the foolish man who built on sand, and all was destroyed (Matt. 7:24-29).

Commitment by the Lord (26:40-46)

The prophets were not only biblical in presenting the curses to the people, they were also biblical in presenting a message of hope to a humbled and subdued people. A future is held out to them after the final curse of total defeat and exile. Just as the Lord remembered his covenant with Abraham, Isaac and Jacob and acted to deliver Israel from the Egyptian bondage, so he promises to act again (26:42,45). As there are conditions that relate to the series of blessings and curses (see 26:3,14-15,18,21,23,27), so a condition is set at the commencement of this passage of hope. They are urged to confess the sinfulness of their own treacherous disloyalty and that of their ancestors in living so contrary to God's standards, to acknowledge that God has rightly punished them by removing them to the land of their enemies and to turn to God in humbleness of heart. If they show these marks of repentance then God will act in accordance with his covenant promises to Abraham, promises that include **'the land'** (26:42).

The land has a very important place in the divine purposes. God is giving these covenant stipulations to a people whom he has redeemed from Egypt and who are about to move forward to enter the land promised to Abraham. Like the original human couple who were exiled from the Garden of Eden, Israel will be exiled from the land for their disobedience. Implied in the reference to the promised land is the encouragement that Israel will return there, and this is what the prophets later promise. But the land to which Israel returns is still not the ideal place that Moses and the prophets depict and for which the people longed. As with so many other parts of God's promises to Abraham, they look to the great consummation when in the new creation the whole earth will be a sanctuary and paradise, with every effect of sin removed — a place of perfect peace and tranquillity with no prospect of exile ever again.

While the emphasis at the beginning of the paragraph is on Israel's responsibility to show true-hearted repentance in order for God to keep the promises made to Abraham and his descendants (26:40-42), God's promise not **'to utterly destroy them and break my covenant with them'** (26:44) implies a gracious commitment that is not dependent on anything that Israel is called to do. How can these two be reconciled? The answer lies in the fact that the change in the nation's heart will also be the work of God. Later, towards the end of his life, Moses urges the people to have their hearts circumcised (Deut. 10:16) and declares that God himself will operate on their hearts to enable them to love the Lord with all their beings (Deut. 30:6). God's promise to uphold the covenant with Abraham is unilateral and it is for this reason that he acted at the time of the Exodus and that he will act again after the exile. He is true to his word: '**... for I am the LORD their God**' (26:44-45).

The new beginning for Israel is used by the prophets to speak of a new covenant, a transformation of the heart and a resurrection from the dead. The nation is to be raised from their death in exile and a return to the land is emphasized, all in preparation for the coming of the Messiah. He is the 'real' Israel who is faithful to God's law and carries out God's purposes for the salvation of humanity. God works with repentant, humble, obedient believers and God is the one who makes them willing in the day of his power. The same heart religion that was seen in Daniel, Ezra and Nehemiah was later expressed in the attitude of Zechariah and Elizabeth, Joseph and Mary. They were used to bring God's purposes to fruition. Mary portrays that spirit of humble devotion when she describes herself as a servant of the Lord and submits to the angel's words concerning her favoured position saying, 'Let it be to me according to your word' (Luke 1:38).

Implied in the references to God's covenant with Abraham and his descendants is the ultimate aim to bless the whole world (Gen. 12:3). As Christopher Wright comments, God's 'commitment to Israel was because of his commitment to all nations'.[6]

33.
Promises, promises, promises!

Please read Leviticus 27:1-34

People are quick to denounce politicians who make promises in their party manifestos and then fail to deliver when they are elected, but what about ourselves? Did we make vows at the time of our conversion or baptism, or when we became members of our local church? Have we kept them? And what about our marriage vows? Maybe we have made commitments that we now regret and we seek ways of backing out of them. This chapter makes it clear that when you make a commitment to God, it is a serious undertaking and must not be entered into lightly.

Why end with this subject?

It is often debated why the content of this final chapter is placed at this point. Is it tagged on at the end like an appendix, unrelated to the previous part? This is most unlikely. The subject matter is not unrelated to what has gone immediately before. For instance, we move from promises and warnings made by God, which he always keeps, to a chapter largely about promises or vows that people often do not keep. But the connection may have more to do with the way the final chapters are structured.

With the references to valuation, redemption and the jubilee (27:17-21,23-24,27-29,31,33) it might have seemed logical to us to place the whole immediately after chapter 25. But we must not be governed by our own cultural way of thinking. The three chapters are a unit. What is happening is that the two outer chapters (25 and 27), which focus mainly on the land and related issues, envelop the crucially important chapter 26, which also stresses the importance of the land. The covenant blessings, curses and future hope concerning the promised land form the climax of the book and bring to a dramatic end the stipulations that 'the LORD made between himself and the children of Israel on Mount Sinai by the hand of Moses' (26:46).

Vows, dedications and tithes

There is no instruction on when and how to make a vow. Apart from the regular tithe offerings and the consecration of the firstborn, there is no command in the law of Moses for making special religious promises. Vows are voluntary and the law reminds people that they do not sin if they refuse to make a vow. What is sinful is making a vow and not keeping it (see Deut. 23:21-23). The procedure set out in this chapter for retracting religious vows emphasizes the seriousness of making rash vows. While some consecrated offerings vowed to God are redeemable at great cost, others could not be bought back.

Throughout history it has been a common practice for human beings to make vows to God, particularly when they are in difficult circumstances. They promise to do something for God if only he would rescue them from their predicament. Have you made vows like that? Jacob offered vows to

God at Bethel when he was fleeing from his brother (Gen. 28:20-22). The Israelites made a vow when the Canaanite King Arad took some of their people as prisoners (Num. 21:1-2). Later, we read of vows made by Jephthah (Judg. 11:30-31), Hannah (1 Sam. 1:11), Absalom (2 Sam. 15:8), sailors on board their ship and Jonah while he was in the fish (Jonah 1:16; 2:9).

There are ten laws grouped into three main blocks.

Vows concerning people and animals (27:1-13)

The valuation of people vowed to God (27:1-8)

'**When a man...**' (NKJV) would be better translated, 'If anyone...'[1] Women had the same right as men under the law of Moses to make vows (see Num. 6:2; 30:3-16). The vow is described as 'extraordinary' or 'special' (ESV)[2] because it concerns the dedication to the Lord of a person. When someone made a vow to dedicate a person to the Lord, instead of human sacrifice (Exod. 13:13) or lifelong service at the sanctuary (something that was not needed in Israel as the Levites were set apart for this purpose), provision was made for an 'equivalent value' in money to be donated to the sanctuary. This **'valuation'**, or 'assessment money', in-cluded all the silver collected by the priests and was used for the repairs to the temple in the time of King Jehoash (2 Kings 12:4-5). It indicated that the people of Judah did in fact convert a person's dedicated service to the temple into silver. There are two special cases in the Bible involving the dedication of humans to the Lord. If Jephthah did actually sacrifice his daughter (see Judg. 11:30-39) he was acting like a pagan. Although Samuel's parents were of Levitical stock Hannah's vow involved the boy residing continually at the tabernacle rather than merely working the regular periods of service and within the fixed age limits.

It is not the actual vowing of persons that concerns these regulations, but the equivalent value in money that is to be paid in substitution. In order for people to free themselves or their family from a vow of service to God they were required to give to the sanctuary what amounts to a redemption price based on a person's gender and age. The value is not based on sex or age discrimination, as is sometimes thought, but on a person's physical strength. In other words, the valuation is not tied to a person's dignity or worth. The highest value is on a male aged between twenty and sixty. A female in the same bracket is judged to be of less value in terms of the work she could do, such as lifting the heavy carcasses of animals slain in sacrifice and disposing of their remains. It is a factor recognized in the athletic and sporting world that a man is, generally speaking, stronger than a woman. For this reason men and women do not compete against each other, otherwise the men would have an unfair advantage. People over sixty and children under five are also valued at a lower rate and males and females between the ages of five and twenty are also considered separately. The Factory Acts that came about in Britain in the wake of the Evangelical Revival of the eighteenth century sought in some way to recognize the different strengths and powers of the sexes, as well as of old people and children. For instance, they legislated against women and children labouring in the coalmines and other such places of work.

Buying oneself out of the commitment was a costly business, for it is estimated that on average a person only earned about one shekel a month. It would therefore cost nearly a whole year's wages to redeem a male in the prime of life. For those who were too poor to pay such a valuation, the priest was given the power to set a value according to the person's ability to pay. It is assumed that the valuations were deliberately set high to discourage rash vows involving people.

The valuation of animals vowed to God (27:9-13)

Animals could be dedicated to God through a vow. It depended on the status of the animal whether or not it could be redeemed. If the animal that was the subject of the vow was one that could be offered in sacrifice, it could not be redeemed or substituted, for it was **'holy'** and remained in that state. Imagine a farmer vowing to offer at a later date a newly born calf. When the time came to fulfil his vow the farmer had second thoughts. He could perhaps see that the animal would grow into a fine cow that would produce good milk and so he did not wish to part with it. The law states that such a person can neither offer money in exchange for it nor substitute another animal. If he did try to substitute another animal for the one vowed then both were pronounced holy. In other words, both the original animal vowed and the substitute animal were considered as set apart for God and were to be sacrificed on the altar (27:10). In the period after the Babylonian exile when the people had returned to the land, there were attempts at substituting inferior animals for fine-looking ones when paying their vows (Mal. 1:14).

In the case of unclean, non-sacrificial animals, the priest named a price for the animal and it was then probably sold at the market and the proceeds of the sale put to sanctuary use (27:11-12). On the other hand, if this person wished to reclaim the unclean animal that he had vowed to give to God he had to pay a surcharge of a fifth, or 20%, of its value before it could be retrieved (27:13). This surcharge was again to deter people from making rash vows.

Consecrated houses and lands (27:14-25)

Houses set apart for God (27:14-15)

Houses could be sanctified, or consecrated to God, by being donated to the sanctuary. Probably field houses as well as town houses are to be included (see 25:29-31).[3] The priest assessed the value of such **'holy'** houses. If the original owner who sanctified his house to be **'holy to the LORD'** wished to **'redeem'** it he could do so by paying the valuation price plus an additional one-fifth penalty charge. In this it was similar to redeeming unclean animals that had been offered to God (see 27:13).

Inherited land set apart for God (27:16-21)

Land too could be sanctified, or set apart to the Lord, by offering it as a gift to the sanctuary. In order for the priests, the sanctuary officials, to assess the value they took into account the quantity of seed required to sow the land and the number of years to the next jubilee. The jubilee law required all land to be returned to the original family owners (see 25:10,13-17). Thus, a **'homer'**, or 'donkey load', of barley seed over a period of forty-nine years sets the maximum price at **'fifty shekels of silver'**. If the land was offered to the sanctuary in the year of jubilee, then the value of fifty shekels **'shall stand'** (27:17). But if the ground was given later then its value would be reduced in proportion to the number of years left to run to the next jubilee (27:18). Fixing a price was necessary from the start so that if the priests ever sold the land all would know what the land was worth at a given time.

This would be the case if the original owner wished to redeem the land. He could redeem it by paying its value plus 20% (**'one-fifth'**, 27:19). However, if he did not redeem it by the time the next jubilee came round he could not buy it back later. If he was continuing to work the consecrated land on behalf of the priests and he dealt deceitfully by selling it to someone else, then again he had forfeited his redemption rights (27:20). When the land was due to be released in the jubilee year it would become **'holy to the LORD … a devoted field'**, which in this case meant that it passed permanently to the priests (27:21). In this way priests, who were not allotted any land by God, did gain various plots throughout the country.

Purchased land set apart for God (27:22-25)

Whereas in the previous case the law dealt with the consecration of part of the family land, the situation addressed here is where a person wished to consecrate land that he had purchased, or to be more precise, in view of the redemption laws, leased (see Lev. 25). The priest assessed its value in relation to the jubilee year, when the land would automatically revert to the original owner (27:24). In this case the person presenting the land had to redeem it immediately by paying the full amount to the priest (see 25:23-28). Thus the money paid on the day the land was consecrated became a **'holy'** donation to the Lord (27:23). All assessments were to be made **'according to the shekel of the sanctuary'** (27:25; cf. 5:15). At a time when there was no minted currency, the sanctuary shekel or weight was the natural standard for weighing silver and gold, especially when the money was due to the tabernacle and its priests. In Abraham's day the merchants set the shekel standard (see Gen. 23:16). The **'gerah'** (the name suggests a seed of grain) was the smallest of weights.

Exceptions to consecrated items (27:26-33)

Firstborn animals (27:26-27)

As the firstborn of all human and animal life automatically belonged to the Lord,[4] firstborn animals could not be consecrated. They were already consecrated to the Lord and if they were clean, sacrificial animals then they were sacrificed on the altar (see Num. 18:17). This law stopped a person from seeking to present a firstborn animal as a vow offering to impress his neighbours with his religious devotion when in fact the animal was not his in the first place. It was already the Lord's. You cannot present to someone what that person already owns! But the firstborn of unclean animals, even though they also belonged to the Lord, because they could not be slaughtered for sacrifice or given to the priests, could be redeemed by their owners (see Exod. 13:13). The redemption price was the assessed value plus 20%.

The law concerning the firstborn in Israel finds its fulfilment in Jesus, who is described as the firstborn among many brothers (Rom. 8:29; cf. Heb. 2:10-13).

Totally 'devoted' items (27:28)

No **'devoted'** offering could be consecrated. This concerns a special vow in which an owner of property had voluntarily put a special restriction on an item that he had given to the Lord. The restriction meant that it was not just 'holy' (27:9,14,21,23) but **'most holy to the LORD'**. The object that had been 'devoted' could never be redeemed by the owner or sold by the priest, because of its special status. It was banned from ever again being used for common purposes and was therefore set apart permanently for sanctuary use.[5]

Persons 'under the ban' (27:29)

Again the term 'devoted' is used, but this time of people who are to be **'put to death'**. Instead of being 'devoted' permanently for God's service in the sanctuary, as in the previous case, the person was to be set apart for destruction. The word used for 'devoted' can also be translated 'banned', 'proscribed' or 'cursed'. In the days of Joshua the city of Jericho was put 'under the ban'. The whole city was to be dedicated to the Lord for destruction, with the precious metals being saved for the sanctuary treasury (Josh. 6:17-19). Achan, however, kept some items he fancied for himself despite the warnings that had been given. This was sacrilegious, for it all belonged to God and so he, his family and his possessions all came under the ban (Josh. 7:10-26). Those whom God decrees to place **'under the ban'** cannot be redeemed. It would appear that an Israelite court could also brand a person or group 'devoted', or 'banned', which meant they were condemned to death and no money could buy them out. Examples are given of a person who sacrificed to a pagan god (Exod. 22:20) or of a rebellious group who would lead Israel into idolatry (Deut. 13:12-18). In both cases they are 'doomed to destruction'. The ban is irrevocable and such people could not be 'redeemed'.

These are very solemn passages and remind us that all of us deserve to be doomed to everlasting destruction. But the grace of God is such that he devised a way for guilty idolatrous rebels to be redeemed through the precious atoning death of the Messiah. Our Lord suffered the curse in order to redeem his people from 'under the ban'. This is the only sacrifice allowed to release us from our debt and condemnation. Those who look to Jesus for salvation from the curse we deserve will not perish but have everlasting life.

Tithes from the harvest (27:30-31)

When God made himself known to Jacob at Bethel, Jacob made a vow. He promised that if God would be with him and bring him back to his father's home in peace then he would start tithing (Gen. 28:20-22). It was his grandfather, Abraham, who led the way in giving tithes to King Melchizedek, priest of the Most High (Gen. 14:20). It is because tithes originally involved a commitment that they are included in this section. The tithe became part of the law of Moses for the support of the ministry in the tabernacle.

A tithe, or tenth, of the produce of the land — whether of grain or fruit — belonged to the Lord (Deut. 14:22-26).[6] It was therefore **'holy to the LORD'** (27:30). Such tithes could be redeemed or repurchased in the usual way, the owner paying a price to the sanctuary of one-fifth, or 20%, over and above its value.

Tithes from the livestock (27:32-33)

A tenth from the flocks and herds was also to be given to the Lord, but no provision was made for redeeming them. Whatever **'passes under the rod'** refers to the farmer counting the animals with his club in order to set aside every tenth one, **'whether it is good or bad'**. This provided a more objective method for selecting the tithe to prevent anyone picking out the weakest animals every time to give to God. This **'rod'** or club that a shepherd used to ward off wild animals was also a help in holding back the flock from the sheepfold while he examined each one that passed through, to inspect for damage or illness or, as here, to count them (see Jer. 33:13; Ps. 23:4; Ezek. 20:37; Micah 7:14). If anyone tried to exchange an animal that had been set aside, **'then both it and the one exchanged for it'** became holy, which

meant that they were for sanctuary use by the priests and
Levites.

Before the Babylonian exile, during Hezekiah's good
reign, we read of the people bringing their tithes and laying
them in heaps so that the temple staff had more than enough
to eat. The Lord certainly blessed his people during that
period (2 Chr. 31:4-10). After the exile, however, when the
people had returned to the land, the prophet Malachi warns
against those who would try to deceive by paying their vows
with blemished sacrifices and robbing God by failing to
present their tithes and offerings. He urges the people to
bring 'all the tithes into the storehouse, that there may be
food in my house', promising that the Lord would give such
blessing that there would not be enough room to receive it
(Mal. 1:12-14; 3:8-10). This is in line with the covenant
blessings of Leviticus 26.

A tenth of all produce already belonged to the Lord, but
could be redeemed at a price. If it became necessary to
redeem a person's tithe, a 20% penalty was again paid to the
priests. But tithes of flocks and herds could not be redeemed
(see 2 Chr. 31:6).

A parallel exists between those who ministered full-time
in the tabernacle and those who are occupied fully in gospel
ministry under the new covenant. Paul emphasizes the
command of Jesus that 'those who preach the gospel should
live from the gospel' (1 Cor. 9:1-14; cf. Luke 10:7). Just as
the priests and Levites were dependent on the people's tithes,
so those who are called and set apart by the church to be
preachers and teachers of the gospel are dependent on the
financial support of Christians. The tithing principle is most
appropriate in this context.

Neither the Old nor the New Testament forces God's
people into making vows, but if they do make such special
promises then these should be kept. The Preacher calls out:

> When you make a vow to God, do not delay to pay it;
> For he has no pleasure in fools.
> Pay what you have vowed.
> It is better not to vow than to vow and not pay
>
> (Eccles. 5:4-5).

What happened to Ananias and Sapphira when they made promises and then tried to cheat God and the Christian community should make us think twice before we make such commitments. Making vows to God does not make a person any holier, but if we do make them we should do so seriously and reverently, remembering who God is and what he expects from his people. God's people should be honest and truthful and keep the promises they make. In the context of the new covenant, vows should be seen as part of a Christian's total commitment to the Lord. Leviticus began with the whole burnt offering and it is appropriate that we end with a reminder that we are to present our whole bodies as living sacrifices. This is the kind of holiness that is impressed upon us throughout Leviticus.

The concluding verse again reminds us that Leviticus is not a collection of human laws but God's revealed will for his people, given at an important moment in their history (27:34). The psalmist delighted in these commandments (Ps. 119:47) and so should we who live in the era of the Spirit when our Saviour has fulfilled all the types and shadows of the Sinai covenant. The principles of God's law still apply, as the New Testament indicates, so that Christians may live their daily lives to the glory of this same God who has redeemed us to himself through the death of his Son.

Notes

The following commentaries have been of particular help:

Andrew Bonar, *A Commentary on Leviticus,* Banner of Truth edition, 1966

John Calvin, *Commentaries on the Four Last Books of Moses arranged in the form of a Harmony,* Baker reprint, 1979

John E. Hartley, Word Bible Commentary, *Leviticus,* Word, 1992

Matthew Henry's *Commentary on the Whole Bible* (various editions available)

Walter C. Kaiser, 'The Book of Leviticus' in *The New Interpreter's Bible,* vol. I, Abingdon Press, 1994

Samuel H. Kellogg, *The Book of Leviticus,* Klock & Klock reprint, 1978

Jacob Milgrom, Anchor Bible, *Leviticus 1-16,* Doubleday, 1991; *Leviticus 17-22,* Doubleday, 2000; *Leviticus 23-27,* Doubleday, 2001

Mark F. Rooker, The New American Commentary, *Leviticus,* Broadman & Holman, 2000

Gordon J. Wenham, The New International Commentary on the Old Testament, *The Book of Leviticus,* Eerdmans, 1979

Unless otherwise stated, all references to Bonar, Calvin, Hartley, Henry, Kaiser, Kellogg, Milgrom, Rooker and Wenham are from these volumes.

Chapter 1 — God and his spokesman
1. In Hebrew Leviticus begins with 'and', which suggests a continuation of the narrative from Exodus. This is not an absolute rule, for Ruth and Jonah also begin with 'and'. However, the fact that the word

The beauty of holiness

'LORD' does not appear in the original as the subject of the first verb suggests that Leviticus is to be seen as continuing at the point where Exodus finished. The Hebrew reads, literally: 'And he called to Moses and the LORD said...'

2. The term is only found four times in Leviticus, but many times in Exodus and Numbers.

3. Vernon Higham, *Christian Hymns,* Evangelical Movement of Wales, 1977, no. 473.

4. This particular formula, 'when a human being ...', only occurs elsewhere in 13:2 and Numbers 19:14.

5 Because the noun and the verb are related, the phrase could be translated literally: 'When a human being among you offers [brings near] an offering [something brought near] to the Lord, you shall offer your offering...'

Chapter 2 — The burnt offering

1. The noun is related to the verb 'to go up'; the whole offering ascended in smoke.

2. No demand is indicated in verse 2. This applies whether or not 'of his own free will' is the right translation.

3. *Mishnah* tractate Menahoth 110a.

4. Isaac Watts, 'Not all the blood of beasts', *Christian Hymns,* no. 556.

5. The word for 'kill' (1:5,11) is a special term for the slaughter of sacrificial animals.

6. Many of these preliminary duties were taken over by the Levites after the temple was built (2 Chr. 35:11).

7. This is the meaning of the Hebrew noun in all the other occurrences in Leviticus and the corresponding verb is used in the next verse.

8. The idea of using blood for ritual cleansing appears to be unique in the ancient Near-Eastern world (see Lev. 17 for more details).

9. Ray Palmer, *Christian Hymns,* no. 516.

Chapter 3 — The grain offering

1. The poorer classes who could not afford an oven tended to eat only parched grain (see Kaiser, p.1017).

2. The oil is that used in the home, not the special anointing oil kept in the sanctuary.

3. It is the same Hebrew word that is used for the first month, 'Abib', the month of the Exodus and Passover.

4. The Hebrew word is *'carmel'*, which is also the name of the mountain by the Mediterranean.

Chapter 4 — The peace offering

1. The plural form found here is probably an abstract noun. For a fuller treatment of the meaning of the term, see Wenham, pp.76-7 and Hartley, pp.37-8.
2. Tremper Longman, *Immanuel in our Place,* P&R, 2001, p.90.
3. Rooker, p.103. Rooker adds that this may shed some light on Paul's warning about idols. Partaking of pagan sacrificial meals lays oneself open to having fellowship with demons.

Chapter 5 — The sin offering

1. They follow a different pattern and both are introduced with the words: 'Now the LORD spoke to Moses, saying...' (4:1; 5:14; cf. 1:1).
2. The examples form a chiastic construction where the latter two cases mirror the former (ABBA) and the 'oath' situations encompass the unclean cases.
3. Kaiser, p.1036.
4. See Roger T. Beckwith and Martin J. Selman, *Sacrifice in the Bible,* Paternoster/Baker, 1995, p.29.
5. Frank H. Gorman, *Divine Presence and Community, A Commentary on the Book of Leviticus,* Eerdmans, 1997, p.38.
6. Milgrom, vol. 1, p.306; Kaiser, p.1036.
7. Augustus Toplady, *Christian Hymns,* no. 558.

Chapter 6 — The trespass offering

1. 'Debt' is the regular Aramaic word for sin.
2. John Stott, *The Cross of Christ,* IVP, p.88.
3. This is due to the presence of the Hebrew word that is sometimes translated as 'trespass or guilt offering' in the same sentence as a reference to the sin offering (see 5:5-7).
4. It is not the same word that is translated 'trespass offering' or 'guilt'. The verb means 'to act unfaithfully' (see Num. 5:27); and the noun that goes with it means 'an unfaithful act'. The Hebrew phrase is used elsewhere for serious offences like apostasy and Achan's sin (Josh. 7:1; 22:20). But in the present context it is not dealing with treasonable acts of defiance.
5. In Hebrew the whole section is in chapter 5, which means that 6:7 in the English versions is 5:26 in the Hebrew Bible.
6. 'Shekel of the sanctuary' is, literally, 'in holy shekels'.
7. See Eifion Evans, *When He is Come,* Evangelical Movement of Wales, 1959, p.57.
8. Instead of 120% restitution as here, the figure for those convicted in Exodus 22:1-15 varies from 200% to 500% depending on the situation.

9. The law in Numbers 5 also mentions what is to be done in such cases when the victim has died in the meantime. It directs that the compensation is to go to the priest.
10. Philipp Paul Bliss, *Christian Hymns,* no. 131.
11. Charitie Lees De Chenez, *Christian Hymns,* no. 258.

Chapter 7 — The offerings and the priests

1. Calvin, vol. II, p.364.
2. Milgrom, vol. 1, p.389.
3. A special ash dump existed outside the walls of Jerusalem to the north. Milgrom mentions that it has been chemically analysed and found 'to consist exclusively of the remains of animal flesh, bones and teeth' (vol. 1, p.240). See also Jeremiah 31:40; Ezekiel 43:21.
4. Note that it should be translated 'must be holy', not as in the New International Version (NIV). It is possible to translate this as: 'Whatever touches them shall be holy.' While persons cannot become ritually holy through contact, objects can.
5. One tenth of an ephah (an omer) is equivalent to a day's supply of bread for one. It was mixed with oil and baked on a griddle before being offered. The translations 'baked pieces' and 'broken in pieces' (NIV) are guesses at an unknown Hebrew word.
6. The Hebrew word for 'wholly' means 'entire' or 'whole' and is found on its own in 6:23 as a synonym for 'holocaust', or 'burnt offering', the sacrifice wholly consumed by fire on the altar (see also Deut. 33:10). In Psalm 51:19 (51:21 in Hebrew) the two sacrifices wholly consumed by fire are found together.
7. Suggested by Derek Kidner, *Tyndale Bulletin* 1982, no. 33, p.135.
8. The word translated 'sprinkle' in 4:6,17 is not used here, hence the word 'dashed', which is also used in 1:5 and 3:2.
9. Bonar, pp.128-9.
10. Only in the case of the sin offering was the skin to be burned outside the camp (see 4:11-12,21).
11. Later, the priests were divided up into groups to facilitate the better running of the work and distribution of benefits (see 1 Chr. 24; Luke 1:8-9).

Chapter 8 — Peace-offering meals

1. The Hebrew word usually translated 'thanksgiving' can mean 'confession' of sin in the context of glorifying God (see Josh. 7:19; Ezra 10:11).
2. The traditional translation, 'heave offering', is based on the Hebrew noun's relation to the verb 'to be high'. From its usage it is generally

understood by scholars to mean 'something set apart' — in this case, a sacred gift, an offering for sacred use. To show that it was dedicated to the Lord for the priest, it may well have been lifted up for people to see.

3. It is not the person but the meat that is an abomination. The Hebrew word only occurs elsewhere in 19:7; Isaiah 65:4 and Ezekiel 4:14. It is quite different from the other terms translated in the older English versions as 'abomination'.

4. The phrase suggests that the person has no posterity (see Ps. 109:13; Mal. 2:12). 'Cut off' may also suggest the opposite of being 'gathered to' one's people in the afterlife. Milgrom believes the two meanings are not mutually exclusive in that the person has 'no descendants in this world and no life in the next' (vol. 1, p.460). See Leviticus 20 for further discussion.

5. A different Hebrew word is used in Isaiah 53:8 from that in Leviticus 7:20-21, but 2 Chronicles 26:21 employs the same Hebrew verb as Isaiah 53:8 to describe King Uzziah being 'cut off' from the temple.

Chapter 9 — The investiture of the priests
1. Vern S. Poythress, *The Shadow of Christ in the Law of Moses,* P&R, 1991, p.54.
2. Wenham shows that both the Lord and Moses are acting jointly in Aaron's ordination (*Leviticus,* p.142).
3. The text does not always tell us every detail. Having given the ruling in Exodus 29:20 and indicated how Aaron's extremities were smeared with blood, it leaves us to assume that the same happened to his sons.
4. Bonar, p.171; see also Kellogg, p.208; Wenham, p.143 and Hartley, p.116.
5. Wenham, p.144. We shall see this emphasized later in the rituals required after healing from unusual skin diseases and bodily discharges.

Chapter 10 — Ministering for the first time
1. The Hebrew word for 'bull' is not the same as in 4:3, but it is the same as in Exodus 32:4 in the golden-calf incident. Jewish interpreters have drawn the conclusion that by this offering the guilt of that incident is finally removed.
2. We find it explicitly stated in 16:6 that it is 'for himself and for his house'. The fact that the text here does not mention this need not imply that the offerings were for Aaron alone. The accounts do not tell us everything and we pick up further information in other parts of Leviticus. For instance, we would assume from chapter 1 that in the

burnt offering the whole animal was consumed by fire. But that was not the case, for we learn later that the priests were allowed to keep the skin of the burnt offering (7:8).

3. 'Come near' is often used for coming near to God.

4. The word in this context means to 'remove sin', as it does in 8:15.

5. The Hebrew verbal form suggests that the Lord's appearance had already occurred, in which case it can be compared to the so-called prophetic perfect, where the event foretold is so certain that it is depicted as having already happened.

6. The phrase introduced by 'and' is a purpose clause and should be translated 'in order that the glory of the LORD may appear to you'.

7. Warren Wiersbe, *Be Holy — An Old Testament Study — Leviticus,* Chariot Victor Publishing, 1994, p.36.

Chapter 11 — Judgement and mercy

1. In the Law of Moses 'strange' refers to people who are not priests, who do not belong to the sanctuary. They are outsiders who have no authority to be in the Holy Place.

2. Kellogg, p.239.

3. At other times his name is coupled with that of Moses.

4. 'Common' is only used here in Leviticus and is the opposite of 'holy', but it is not necessarily unclean. It is found in Ezekiel 22:26; 42:20; 44:23 (see also Acts 10:14).

5. Kaiser, p.1072.

Chapter 12 — Uncleanness from creatures

1. See Hartley, p.158 and R. K. Harrison, *Leviticus* (Tyndale Old Testament Commentaries), pp.120-21 for the camel, and Kaiser, p.1080 for the hare.

2. Not literally having four legs, of course, but creatures that can creep and crawl around as well as fly.

3. The Hebrew word for 'belly' is only found here and in Genesis 3:14. Interestingly, the scribes who painstakingly copied the manuscripts calculated that the third letter of the Hebrew word for belly was the middle letter of the Pentateuch!

4. Rooker, p.174.

5. Wenham, p.21.

Chapter 13 — Uncleanness from giving birth

1. Mary Ann Sanderson Deck, *Christian Hymns,* no. 875.

2. See W. H. Bellinger, *Leviticus, Numbers* (New International Biblical Commentary), p.78, and Mike Butterworth, *Leviticus and Numbers* (The People's Bible Commentary), p.62.
3. Wenham, p.188.

Chapter 14 — Uncleanness from leprosy

1. The term is a broad one and includes scaly, disfiguring skin conditions as well as disfigurements either due to mildew or fungus in linen, wool and leather clothing, or household articles made from animal skins, or due to mould or dry rot in walls. Wenham uses the evidence of S. G. Browne, *Leprosy in the Bible* (Christian Medical Fellowship, 1970) to show that Hansen's disease is not being described here or elsewhere in Scripture (p.1950), while Kaiser argues strongly that Hansen's disease is included (p.1095).
2. Various forms of the word 'clean' appear thirty-six times and of 'unclean' thirty times — which emphasizes that ritual, not medical, questions are being addressed (see Milgrom, vol. 1, p.817).
3. The verb for 'struck' has the same root letters as the noun for 'plague'.
4. Milgrom, vol.1, p.782.
5. The Hebrew reads: 'It is an attack' (13:22). This is the only place in this chapter where the word 'attack' (or 'plague', 'disease', 'mark') is found alone without 'leprous' (see 13:2).
6. Literally, 'cover the moustache', but clearly they are to cover the lower part of the face from the upper lip.
7. Thomas Binney, *Christian Hymns,* no. 5.

Chapter 15 — Restoring the outcasts

1. D. A. Carson, *The Gospel According to John,* IVP, p.624.
2. Calvin, vol. II, p.26.
3. The full list of references is: 13:2,3,9,12,13,17,20,22,25,27,30,31,32, 44,46,47,49,50,51,53,54,55,56,57,58,59.

Chapter 16 — Uncleanness from genital discharges

1. The Nazirite (literally, 'separated one', or 'one consecrated', from the same word group as the verb translated 'separate' in 15:31) expressed in an even more obvious way the negative and positive aspects of separation. He was to be 'holy to the LORD' by separating himself to the Lord — symbolized in letting his hair grow long. On the other hand, he was to separate himself from anything produced by the vine (see Num. 6:2-6).

2. The literary structure of the passage is called a chiasmus after the Greek letter Chi, which is our X, in which there is a crosswise arrangement. The order in the second half of the passage is the exact opposite of that in the first — abnormal, normal, normal, abnormal.

3. See Wenham, p.219, note 6, for the suggestion that Numbers 5:2-4 only applied during the desert wanderings.

4. Josephus, *The Wars of the Jews,* 3.227; *The Antiquities of the Jews,* 3.261.

5. Literally 'living water' — that is, water that is not stagnant (see 14:5-6).

6. The nocturnal happenings of Deuteronomy 23:10 could either be referring to these involuntary emissions of semen or to urinating within the camp instead of going outside.

7. See note 2 above.

8. Milgrom, vol. 1, p.931.

9. Sexual intercourse during a woman's period was forbidden (see 18:19; 20:18).

10. The word that Zechariah uses for 'uncleanness' is the same as the one translated 'impurity', or 'menstruation' (ESV) in Leviticus 12:2; 15:19-20,24-26 (see also its figurative use in 2 Chr. 29:5; Ezra 9:11).

Chapter 17 — The Day of Atonement

1. The Greek translators of the Septuagint render the term 'propitiation'.

2. Christopher J. H. Wright, 'Leviticus' in *New Bible Commentary, 21ˢᵗ century edition*, edited by Carson, France, Motyer and Wenham, IVP, p.143.

3. The Septuagint adds 'with strange fire', which the New King James Version adds to the text without marginal comment. Many scholars spend considerable time seeking to date the origins of this unique day. Because there is no direct reference to the day in the rest of the Old Testament, liberal scholars have often considered it to be of late origin, dating it after the period of Ezra and Nehemiah. The clear evidence of this chapter is that God revealed it to Moses soon after the erection of the tabernacle and the ordination of the priests. Some scholars suggest that the chapter is misplaced and should come immediately after chapter 10, but the need for the Day of Atonement becomes even more necessary in the light of the uncleanness described in Leviticus 11-15 that disqualified a person from coming near before the Lord.

4. It may be that the high priest cast lots through the use of the Urim and Thummim.

5. The old versions took it as a compound word meaning 'a goat for sending away'. Some Jewish authorities suggested that it was the name

for a rocky precipice from which the goat was thrown down. Another idea is that it is the name of a demon.

6. In Hebrew the definite article followed by an adjective can often stand for a superlative. Thus, 'the holy' means 'the most holy' or 'the holiest', which in the present context stands for the inner sanctum, 'the Holy of Holies' (see 16:2,17,20,23).

7. Horatio Gates Spafford, *Christian Hymns,* no. 766.

8. Perhaps the high priest was to remove his clothes and wash, as one commentator puts it, 'in a screened area near the Tent'.

Chapter 18 — The sanctity of life

1. The Hebrew word used here for 'life' is *nephesh*, translated 'soul' later in this same verse. It is used for both humans and animals.

2. Milgrom boldly declares that 'The substitutionary theory of sacrifice, based largely on this verse and championed by so many in the scholarly world, must once and for all be rejected' (vol. 2, p.1477). It is, of course, not based merely on this verse but is implied throughout Scripture.

3. Kaiser, p.1119.

4. Alan M. Stibbs, *Meaning of the Word 'Blood' in Scripture,* Tyndale Press, 1948, p.30.

Chapter 19 — The sanctity of sex

1. See Allen P. Ross, *Holiness to the LORD, A Guide to the Exposition of the Book of Leviticus,* Baker Academic, 2002, p.339.

2. Wenham, p.252.

3. *The Oxford Dictionary of Current English, 1992.*

4. 'Levirate' is from the Latin *levir,* meaning 'husband's brother'.

5. To indicate a new section there is a change in the way each prohibition is introduced. The previous section commenced each decree with the word 'nakedness', but from verse 18 onwards each new law begins with the Hebrew letter *'w'*, often translated 'and' or 'also'.

6. The AV translates it as 'vex', for the word is from the root 'vex, show hostility'. It is similar to the word translated 'rival' in 1 Samuel 1:6.

7. Rooker, p.245.

8. Wenham notes that the Old Testament definition of adultery is narrower than that in the New Testament. It did not include a married man having intercourse with an unattached woman (*Leviticus,* p.258).

9. Hartley, p.297.

10. The Jewish commentator Milgrom argues this.

11. Milgrom, vol. 2, p.1570.

12. Wenham, p.260.

13. See Leviticus 20:3.

Chapter 20 — Living the godly life: an introduction

1. This introduction, using the term 'congregation' or 'community', is unique in Leviticus and indicates how important the contents of this chapter are for the whole Israelite community — men, women and children.

2. See Milgrom, vol. 2, p.1606.

3. Wenham, p.264.

4. Kaiser, p.1136.

5. As above.

Chapter 21 — Living the godly life: the challenge

1. The same word, 'revere', is used in reference to God in 19:14,32.

2. Though in the plural, it does not refer to all the festivals in the Jewish calendar, but to the weekly day of rest (see 23:3 for more information).

3. Hartley, p.323.

4. The use of 'abomination' here is unfortunate because it is not the same Hebrew word as in 18:22,26,29-30.

5. The word only occurs here in the Old Testament and is associated with the verb 'to seek'. Kaiser suggests it means 'indemnity', based on an Akkadian verb, but this is unlikely.

6. It is reminiscent of the very first divine prohibition (Gen. 2:17).

7. See Milgrom, vol. 2, p.1679.

8. See Hartley, who presents the view that in pagan rites animal blood was drained into a deep trench to draw the spirits to help in fortune-telling, and then the meat of the sacrifice was eaten (pp.319-20). See 1 Samuel 14:31-35.

9. Prostitutes were often engaged at temple sites to boost income and were known as 'holy women' (see Gen. 38:20-23; Deut. 23:17-18; 2 Kings 23:7). According to recent research, while prostitutes were sometimes employed by pagan temple authorities for financial purposes, there is no evidence in the ancient Near East that they were actually engaged in cultic prostitution associated with fertility rites (see Milgrom, vol. 2, pp.1695-6). For a brief statement supporting the traditional view see John D. Currid, *Ancient Egypt and the Old Testament,* Baker, 1997, p.42.

10. See Milgrom, vol. 2, pp.1704-5.

11. See 25:14,17, where the word 'oppress' is used in business transactions. The following prohibition (19:35-36) actually deals with business deception.

Chapter 22 — Death: the punishment for disobedience
1. Kaiser, p.1142.
2. Kellogg, p. 431.
3. The construction is a chiasmus (see chapter 16, note 2).
4. See Hartley, p.338.
5. Milgrom, vol. 2, p.1755.
6. The verb is literally 'take', which is the usual Hebrew word for 'marry' (see Hosea 1:2).
7. According to Hittite law bestiality with a horse or mule was permitted.
8. The actual word used (*hesed*) is usually translated 'lovingkindness', 'mercy' or steadfast love'. It has this opposite meaning also in Proverbs 14:34 ('... but sin is a reproach to any people') and Proverbs 25:10 (in the phrase translated 'expose your shame'). Another case where a word has an opposite meaning to its normal usage is 'bless' (*barah*), which means 'curse' in Job 1:5,11; 2:5,9.
9. Hartley, p.340.
10. Used in 12:2 for a woman's menstrual impurity but used here for what is foul or unclean.

Chapter 23 — Holy priests
1. Wenham, supported by Milgrom, argues that the Hebrew word *bethulah* does not necessarily mean 'virgin', otherwise the following clause becomes redundant (see also Gen. 24:16). It refers to a girl of marriageable age. The word for 'virgin' ('*almah*) occurs in Isaiah 7:14.
2. The word for 'relative' is a word used for flesh with its blood, as distinct from the normal word for flesh. Both terms for flesh are used in 18:6, where it says literally, 'any flesh of his flesh'.
3. The word for 'chief' is '*baal*', which is often used as the name of the Canaanite god, 'Baal', but more generally it means 'owner', 'lord' and 'husband' (see Hosea 2:16 [2:18 in Hebrew]).
4. Milgrom, vol. 2, p.1802.
5. This is not likely to be another word for prostitute in view of its use in 21:14.
6. It literally reads: 'the priest who is greater than his brothers'.
7. Wenham, p.291.
8. Hartley, p.349.
9. Milgrom, vol. 2, p.1821.
10. See 21:6 for 'bread of his God'.
11. The meaning of the Hebrew word is not known, but there is a similar word in Arabic used for a slit lip or nose.
12. The Hebrew meaning is uncertain. It may point to one limb being longer than the other.

13. The meaning is uncertain, but it is certainly not a reference to the skin diseases mentioned in Leviticus 13 – 14.

14. Milgrom is of the opinion that verse 23 is directed to the high priest and prohibits him from officiating either inside or outside the Holy Place (vol. 2, pp.1830-31).

15. Derek Tidball, *Discovering Leviticus,* Crossway Books, 1996, pp.171-2.

Chapter 24 — Holy sacrifices

1. The verb is from the same word group as Nazirite (see 21:12).

2. The AV and NKJV rendering 'of your own free will' is not helpful. It should read 'for you to be accepted'. So also at 19:5.

3. The Hebrew terms 'perfect/complete' and 'blemish/defect' present the same point in positive and negative language.

4. It is universally accepted that the four defects refer to the testicles and are listed in order of increased severity, ending with castration ('cut').

5. The number of defects listed in both catalogues is twelve and both lists begin with blindness and end with the male genitals. The priestly list is structured in the pattern: four (21:18), two (21:19), six (21:20) while the animal list has the pattern: six (22:22), two (22:23), four (22:24). This makes a chiastic construction, showing that the lists are to be taken together and that the priestly defects were chosen to match the animal ones. This is the reason why deaf or mute priests are not mentioned but why a priest's genitals are.

6. See Hartley, p.362.

Chapter 25 — Holy day: the sabbath

1. Wiersbe, *Be Holy,* p.102.

2. The phrase expresses the superlative, like 'holy of holies'. The verb associated with the noun 'Sabbath' means 'to cease', as in Genesis 8:22: 'Seed time and harvest ... shall not cease.'

3. Milgrom, vol. 3, p.1960.

4. Hartley, p.376.

5. Quoted by Milgrom, vol. 3, p.1962.

6. See further P. H. Eveson, *The Book of Origins,* Evangelical Press, 2001, pp.48-56.

Chapter 26 — Holy seasons: spring

1. The Mesopotamian calendar is believed to have been only introduced into the Sinai area around the time of the Exodus.

2. Whatever the people were used to Egypt, the Israelites were told to begin their religious year in the spring.

3. There is disagreement among the Jews as to whether it means between sunset and darkness, or between the sun declining and sunset, between 3 p.m. and 5 p.m. Orthodox Judaism takes the latter view.

4. 'Passover' is said to be an erroneous translation of Exodus 12:23, based on the Septuagint. The verb 'pass through' is translated 'protect' by the Septuagint in Exodus 12:13 and it is the general consensus of the experts that the Hebrew word for 'Passover' conveys the idea of protection. The paschal blood protected the people from the angel of death.

5. The Hebrew phrase for 'no customary work' includes both the words 'labour' and 'work' that appear in the Fourth Commandment (Exod. 20:9).

6. Kaiser, p.1158.

7. The other view is that the Sabbath refers to the first day of Unleavened Bread, which was a day of rest.

8. It is to the Septuagint that we owe the name Pentecost.

9. It omits the reference to grapes, for that is not appropriate at this point.

Chapter 27 — Holy seasons: autumn

1. The word is similar to, but not the same as, the word for 'sabbath'. In 23:3 both 'Sabbath' and 'sabbath rest appear together as a superlative expression.

2. There is great debate as to whether, in ancient Israel, the other special occasions began in the evening of the previous day and whether, in fact, each day was calculated from the evening (see Gen. 1:5). Drawing attention to the evening for the Day of Atonement would suggest that this is an exception to the norm. It was only in later times that the rabbis directed that all days should begin in the evening.

3. The word for 'atonement' is found in the plural both here and in 25:9. It expresses the superlative.

4. There are two other festivals that the Jews now keep over the remaining five months of the religious year that are not in the law of Moses. One is Purim, or 'Lots', commemorating the defeat of those who plotted to exterminate the Jews (Esther 9:18-32). The other is Hanukkah, the festival of lights, commemorating the purification of the temple in 165 B.C.

5. Hartley, p.389.

6. Henry Alford, 'Come, ye thankful people, come', *Christian Hymns*, no. 826.

Chapter 28 — Pure oil and holy bread
1. Milgrom, vol. 3, p.2083, quoting Mazar, 1990.
2. See Wenham, p.310. One fifth of an ephah of flour went into each loaf, which it is estimated amounts to three and a half pounds of flour per loaf, or about eight cupfuls.
3. Certainly unleavened bread was used by New Testament times, as we know from Josephus.
4. This is suggested by the Chronicler's use of the phrase 'pile', or 'layer bread' (still translated 'shewbread' in 1 Chr. 9:32; 2 Chr. 13:11; Neh. 10:33).
5. Hartley, p.402.
6. It witnesses to the fact that in God's special service in the holy place certain requirements are suspended, such as the Sabbath and the rule about mixing linen and wool in the priest's garments and for the inner curtains of the sanctuary (Exod. 28:6,37,39; 26:1).

Chapter 29 — Holy name
1. The construction is a chiasmus — ABCCBA (see chapter 16, note 2).
2. See S. J. de Vries, 'Blasphemy' in the *Interpreter's Dictionary of the Bible*, ed. G. A. Buttrick and others, vol. 1, p.445.

Chapter 30 — Holy years
1. B. A. Levine, *Leviticus,* The Jewish Publication Society Torah Commentary, 1989, p.170.
2. B. H. Carroll, *An Interpretation of the English Bible,* 'Exodus, Leviticus', ed. J. B. Cranfill, Baker, 1973, p.377.
3. *Yobel* probably took its name from an ancient word of the same root meaning 'ram', or 'ram's horn'. When the book of Joshua was written the term needed explaining by the addition of the more common term for ram's horn (*shophar*), which is the word used in Leviticus 25:9 and translated 'trumpet' (see Josh. 6:6,8, where it says literally, 'seven horns [the *shophar* horn] of ram's horns [from *yobel*]'.
4. There is a difference of opinion among scholars concerning the jubilee year, whether it overlapped with the seventh sabbatical year or was an additional sabbatical year. Kaiser, for instance, argues that the jubilee year coincided with the seventh sabbatical year. It is thought that two fallow years in a row would be impractical. Other scholars, such as Rooker, consider that 'fiftieth year' should be taken to mean the year following the seventh sabbatical year.
5. For the Jews the first day of the seventh month has become New Year's Day in their civil calendar (see Lev. 23).

6. We must assume that the sabbatical year began during the autumn of the sixth year and the jubilee year in the autumn of the seventh year on the basis that the Day of Atonement began on the evening of the ninth day.

7. William Williams (Pantycelyn), 'Onward march, all-conquering Jesus', *Christian Hymns,* no. 465.

Chapter 31 — Redemption

1. The two words connected by 'and' may be taken together to express the one idea of 'resident alien' (a hendiadys), although many scholars still treat the phrase as expressing two thoughts, that of the 'resident alien' and 'tenant'. Psalm 39:12 would suggest that we treat them as separate ideas.

2. A similar expression is found in Genesis 23:4 — 'a stranger and sojourner with you'.

3. The phrase to 'live with you' does not mean in this context residing in the same house as the creditor, but surviving under the authority and protection of the creditor.

4. Understanding again the prepositional phrase 'by you' (literally, 'with you') to mean 'under your authority or protection' (see 25:23,35,40).

5. Again the phrase translated 'close to you', or 'among you', is literally 'with you' (see 25:23,35,39,40).

Chapter 32 — Covenant commitment

1. Bonar, p.473.

2. The garden suggested a sanctuary. See Eveson, *The Book of Origins,* pp.59-71.

3. The form of the verb, in 26:12 and Genesis 3:8, is the same. It suggests 'walking up and down' (see Deut. 23:14). The more usual form is used in 26:3 and means 'walking on to a destination'.

4. Wenham, p.330.

5. 26:25 literally speaks of 'the vengeance of the covenant'.

6. Wright, 'Leviticus', p.156 in *New Bible Commentary,* 21st edition.

Chapter 33 — Promises, promises, promises!

1. The Hebrew word for 'man' or 'husband' used here can also mean 'someone', 'anyone' or 'each one' in contexts like this.

2. The NKJV fails to translate what the old AV renders as 'singular'. See Milgrom for the translation 'extraordinary' (*Lev. 23-37,* p.2369).

3. Wenham suggests that this ruling only affects town houses (p.339), but Milgrom states, 'There is no indication that the word "house", being unqualified, is limited to town houses' (vol. 3, p.2381).

4. The law of the firstborn was a reminder of the tenth plague that struck Egypt and of Israel's position as the Lord's redeemed people. This was why all Israel belonged to God; they were God's firstborn son (Exod. 4:22; 13:2; 34:19-20).

5. When the verse speaks of 'man', as well as beast and field, we must suppose it is referring to foreign slaves owned by the person.

6. In Hebrew 'tithe' is associated with the word for 'ten'.